THE MACDONALD
ENCYCLOPEDIA OF
TREES

THE MACDONALD ENCYCLOPEDIA OF
TREES

MACDONALD & CO
LONDON & SYDNEY

This edition first published in Great
Britain in 1982 by
Macdonald & Co (Publishers) Ltd
London & Sydney

Holywell House
Worship Street, London EC2A 2EN

ISBN 0 356 08574 0

Printed and Bound by Officine
Grafiche di Arnoldo Mondadori,
Verona Italy

CONTENTS

Trees in this book not identified by a color bar are not grown outdoors in the mainland United States and Canada, but may be grown under glass.

Text for the Italian edition by Paola Lanzara and Mariella Pizzetti.
Drawings by Francesco De Marco.
English translation by Hugh Young.
American edition edited by Stanley Schuler.

INTRODUCTION

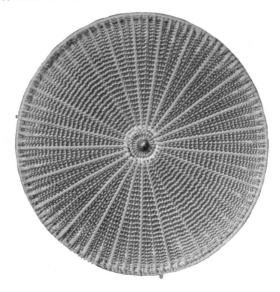

History of the Trees

We do not always use the scientific classifications to distinguish plants within the vegetable kingdom; for practical purposes, at least, we often distinguish them according to their height and their substance. Leaving aside of course the most primitive forms—algae, mosses, fungi etc.—this gives us four great subdivisions: *herbaceous plants*, which, as their name implies, are composed throughout of herbaceous material; *subshrubs*, plants whose composition is woody at the base only and herbaceous in all the upper part; *shrubs* (more often called *bushes*), a term applied to all woody plants that have branches growing from the base up, densely grown and generally not more than 5 m (16 ft) high; and finally *trees*, or *arboreal perennials*, taking in all species which have a columnar, woody stem with branches growing from it, and whose height varies according to species, environment and various other factors. Although the term "tree" is normally applied to those which reach a height of 6 m (20 ft) or more, the shape and general manner of development are so decisive that species of lesser size are also included in this category, though they may be specifically described as "dwarf" trees. Since the distinctions we are speaking of are not strictly scientific, however long established, we are perfectly justified in interpreting them in a fairly elastic way.

The history of plants is identified with the history of our planet, on which man, three million years ago as nearly as we can tell, was the last living creature to make his appearance. Biologists and geologists

are pretty well agreed in dating the appearance of the blue-green algae, the first forms of life that contained chlorophyll, between two and three billion years before the present age; they agree too that algae were undisputedly dominant for about two billion years until the first plants with a vascular system began to appear. It is not really surprising that the earth's colonization by plants should have proceeded so slowly when we consider that the plants had not only to acquire the ability to build up tissues capable of producing thick cellular walls that could resist the air and wind (walls which later were to reach the climax of their development in the wood of trees) but also to evolve those complex physiological adaptations which made nutrition, metabolism and reproduction possible through the root system and the aerial structure. Reproductive means in particular changed strikingly in the new environment, for the plants could no longer rely on water as a vehicle for the mobile male gametes to reach the stationary female gametes.

Once these transformations were completed, arboreal plants became possible, but they still had to pass through a phase in which reproduction depended on spores, and flowers did not exist. The immense forests that existed in the Carboniferous period (so called because the deposits that form the fossil coal—carbon—were laid down at this time by great arborescent plants) consisted of equisetums and arboreal ferns. Those giants, now extinct except insofar as they still exist in the tropics in certain types of arboreal ferns, acted for tens of millions of years as highly effective purifying

9

agents for the air, which until then had contained much more carbon
dioxide than it does now. By fixing carbon and giving off oxygen they
permitted evolution toward vegetable and animal forms which
needed great quantities of that element, and of the solar energy
which could now reach the earth's surface in increased quantities
through the clearer, purer air. That is how the large group which we
call Gymnosperms appeared, which include among others a number
of the still extant conifers together with some other plant families like
Gingko and *Cycas*, which are still found growing today but are
regarded as living fossils. The advent of the more recent geological
eras finally brought the appearance of the Angiosperms, the plants
with true flowers and seeds enclosed in fruits, and it was during the
comparatively recent Tertiary period that trees began to appear
resembling the trees of our own time, many of which still survive.
However, in the last period, that in which man, last of the mammals, is
thought to have appeared, the surface of the earth was swept by at
least four glaciations, which have been given the names of Gunz,
Mindel, Riss and Würm. Of these, the second was the most severe,
and although it was separated from the first by a relatively temperate
period of some 50,000 years (probably very much like that in which
we are living today) the fact that during the Gunz the poles had been
covered with what was by now a permanent icecap had caused the
less hardy plants to disappear from the cooler zones. When the cold
drove southward again, it was climatic conditions that determined
whether the various species should disappear or survive; and those

When the atmosphere cleared and the sun's rays were able to enrich the earth with their energy, the Angiosperms, or flowering plants, appeared.

that survived had to overcome tremendous difficulties, including competition with species already firmly established. Particularly influential were the high mountain ranges, which checked the migrations and gave some protection to the flora which already enjoyed a more favorable environment.

The evolutionary process was extraordinarily accelerated by the diffusion of different families of plants in different continents and different climatic zones, which led to mutations with quite astonishing adaptations. Plants became more and more specialized to meet changing demands of these new conditions. Indeed, this evolutionary process is not finished, even though plants appear to us to be at a standstill. If, as is probable, the period in which we are living now is another interglacial era, plants must meet this new environmental challenge.

Climate and Ecosystems

Amid the cataclysms that changed the surface of our planet so profoundly during past geological eras, both land movements and climatic changes, the plant world went on gradually adapting itself to the new systems, dividing and subdividing itself over millions and millions of years, adapting to the new conditions and creating systems of mutual adjustment which we call *ecosystems*.

Ecosystems (a word coined by Tansley in 1923) are biological communities of species which are found together in more than one

Chart showing the zones of natural forest vegetation worldwide.

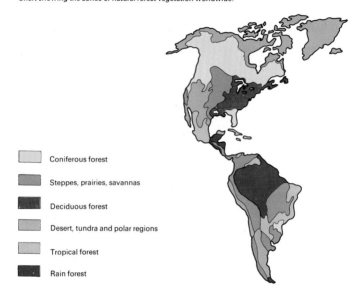

☐ Coniferous forest

■ Steppes, prairies, savannas

■ Deciduous forest

☐ Desert, tundra and polar regions

☐ Tropical forest

■ Rain forest

place, dependent on the physical environment of which they form part and often forming an indivisible whole with that environment. Every ecosystem is strictly bound up, not only with the climate and other environmental factors, but with every form of life that develops within it, animal as well as vegetable, in an interdependence which cannot be changed without completely upsetting the whole equilibrium.

The withdrawal, adaptation or disappearance of many species of plants during the glaciations and the stabilizations that followed in the intervals of relatively mild weather cannot in any way account for the survival or existence of individual species from the same family, even the same genus, in habitats often quite different and a great distance apart from one another. One hypothesis attributes this to "continental drift," which assumes the splitting up of an original land mass into several great continents; but geologists think that any such phenomenon would have taken place too long ago to affect present-day plants. We find such remarkable distributions—especially of species descended from other species most remote from them—that they cannot simply be explained by differences of climate, which today form endemisms well worth examination. Let us look at three very striking examples: the genera descended from the very old family Cycadaceae, the species belonging to the genus *Araucaria* and those of the genus *Ravenala*. In the first instance, a genus left over from those living fossils is found on every continent, always in tropical or subtropical zones: *Cycas* mostly in Asia, *Encephalartos* in

Africa, *Zamia* and *Dioon* in America. Despite slight morphological differences, their shared ancestry they can be seen at once, and since their fossil remains have been found from the Mesozoic Era, their survival in places so far apart can actually be attributed to continental drift. *Araucaria*, a very old genus, is quite remarkably distributed today, and climate must undoubtedly have played a part; the most delicate species must have retreated before the glaciations or at least partially adapted to them. But even so it is hard to explain the presence of *A. araucana* at considerable heights in the Andes, *A. angustifolia* in Brazil and the species *excelsa*, *columnaris* and *bidwillii* in Norfolk Island, New Caledonia and Australia respectively. Even more striking is the case of *Ravenala*, a genus comprising only two species; one, the principal one, is the famous Traveller's Tree of Madagascar, and the other, *R. guianensis*, not actually big enough to be called a tree, is native to the northern part of South America.

These few examples show how, in the classification of plant communities, it will be necessary to leave all systematic reference aside and concentrate exclusively on the general picture of today's climate and environment, within which every ecosystem is formed of a great number of coexistent plant species which exhibit uniformity in certain characteristics. It is obvious that in such complexes it is not simply latitude that favors one type of development over another, but also height above sea level and whether we are considering a continental or island situation; indeed, island flora will differ according to whether we are dealing with continental islands which

have retained the features of the mainland from which they were detached, or oceanic islands.

Phytogeography distinguishes a certain number of floral kingdoms and subdivides them in turn into regions, provinces etc.; and in each of them the trees, wherever they are able to exist, are plainly dominant. Where forests (i.e. the community of tall-trunked woody plants) are specifically concerned, their general conformation, like that of all living creatures, is subject to the environment. A great many factors go to making up of the environment: atmospheric factors like light, temperature, air humidity, precipitation, wind, carbon dioxide content; edaphic factors such as the physical and chemical properties of the soil and its water content; biotic factors such as the living organisms present, both vegetable and animal. The action of the plant world on the ecosystem is always complex and affects the various components of the whole system.

The final outcome of the reciprocal action of the environmental factors is governed by certain laws:

1. Law of the minimum (Liebig's law). The action of the various factors which combine to bring about any phenomenon is limited by the action of the factor which is present in the least quantity. As first formulated, this law was applied only to nutritive elements, but later it was extended to all the elements that make up the environment. Allen expresses the same concept when he states that maximum action is exhibited by the factor furthest from its optimum (the law of the most significant factor).

2. Law of compensation. The action of one factor can be compensated by that of another acting at the same time — light and temperature, for example.

3. Law of physiological limits. There is a maximum, a minimum and an optimum for every factor in the environment as it affects the possibilities of plant life and of each individual function.

Although in practice a rather oversimplified subdivision has been adopted which divides forests into only a few principal types, several other classifications have been tried. In general the main classes are:

a. The conifer or narrowleaved forest, which extends over the entire southern part of the Euro-Siberian region and of North America as well as considerable areas in the higher mountain ranges.

b. The temperate broadleaved forest, which occupies the temperate zones of America, Europe and Asia except where prairies, steppes or savannas predominate as a result of rainfall either insufficient or too greatly concentrated in particular periods.

c. The tropical forests, either deciduous or evergreen, where a rest period is caused by a dry season.

d. The rain forest, found only in the equatorial zone, where heat and humidity are as high and as constant as possible.

As has been said, there have been other elaborate classifications which take a greater number of factors into account. Among them it is worth mentioning parts of that of E. Rübel and H. Brockmann-Jerosch, insofar as they refer to forest formation:

a. Pluvisilvae, tropical forests found in oceanic climates. Characterized by evergreen trees with unprotected vegetative summits and containing a great number of species, they have numerous levels of vegetation and permit the growth of lianas and ephiphytes.

b. Laurisilvae, evergreen forests found in oceanic climates. These have temperatures as their minimum factor and so spread toward the cold regions, and are restricted to coastal areas; the trees of which they are composed have protected vegetative tips. In some cases the transition to the coniferous forest is hardly perceptible, since their borders are made up of trees with scalelike leaves (*Taxus, Thuja* etc.).

c. Hiemisilvae, deciduous forests in continental tropical climates, growing during the rainy season and resting in the dry season. The trees mostly have small leaves, often protected by tomentum in the juvenile stage.

d. Durisilvae, also called xerophilous-sclerophyllic evergreen forests because the trees that compose them have great resistance to dry climates. Their leaves are almost always covered with some means of protection such as waxy substances that give a characteristic shiny look or a general covering of hairs, giving them a whitish appearance; in some genera the leaves are greatly reduced in size. In subtropical climates they replace the laurisilvae where the oceanic climate passes into the continental; they are typically found in warm temperate climates (*Casuarina, Eucalyptus*).

e. Aestatisilvae, formed mainly of deciduous trees which drop their

leaves in winter, typical of the temperate-warm and temperate-cold climates (oaks, beeches).

f. Aciculisilvae, or coniferous forests, with needlelike leaves, consisting of trees with persistent foliage, with some exceptions (e.g. *Larix*). They are found in cold or temperate-cold climates and are the last forest formations met before reaching the poles or the extremes of temperature in alpine climates.

Of course, whatever classifications we may adopt, we do not see a sudden change from one community to the next; there are countless transitional forms, including of course those environments where trees do not grow, or at any rate do not predominate.

The equilibrium achieved within an ecosystem is generally advantageous to all the elements that compose it; there will therefore be found in all of them specific animal forms, ranging from insects to mammals, which not only obtain their nourishment from the forest but in their turn assist its growth, for instance by help in pollination or dissemination.

Human intervention, unless it is very careful, can alter this equilibrium to the point of destroying it, demolishing with thoughtless superficiality something that nature has taken millions of years to build up.

Wood: Essence of the Tree

The upward thrust, the quest for air to breathe and light for

photosynthesis are features common to all the most highly developed plants; but while in herbaceous plants there is only a fragile stem rising out of the soil, the tree is characterized by a woody structure that rises high above the ground—the trunk. This structure grows larger every year as it carries out its function of sustaining the leaves, flowers and fruit.

The trunk of a tree is a part of a living creature, and as such is made up of cells; these, since we are considering a vegetable organism, are furnished with membranes formed from material produced by the cell itself. Such membranes actually surround every plant cell throughout the whole course of its life, from the most primitive organisms to the most evolved, until finally, when it is necessary for the economy and the purpose of the organ, they become so thick that they constitute the principal part of the cell and preserve the shape and size of it even after it is dead. The membranes can also act as a receptacle for the deposit of substances, and this is extremely important not only in the formation of the various tissues but also in applications which they may have in industry; the different, complex substances deposited can give rise to cellulose membranes, pectic membranes, celluloso-pectic and mucilaginous membranes, ligniferous or suberiferous or cutinized membranes, membranes impregnated with mineral salts, even membranes that produce wax; each in accordance with the function that the particular group of cells is required to perform.

Besides the chemical composition of a membrane it is important to know its thickness, because the more it is infiltrated by other

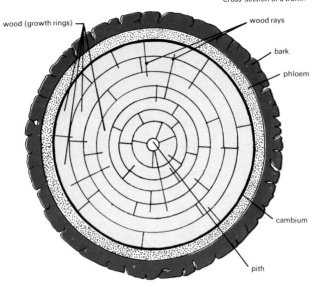

wood (growth rings)

wood rays

bark

phloem

cambium

pith

substances the less permeable it is to the passage of sap, which is of course a fundamental function performed by a tree trunk; however, some cells have thickened walls of lignin which still retain their permeability, since the thickening is not uniform but is broken at points, often circular or lenticular. What we commonly call wood is actually made up of a number of tissues each differently adapted to perform particular functions: support, transport, deposit and secretion.

If we cut a section through a tree we shall see, going from the outside to the inside.

1. The *bark* or *cortex*, which may look rough or smooth, in a range of striking colors which have led to its being described as the plant's ID card. This part of the trunk protects it from sudden changes of atmospheric temperature and humidity and also, as far as possible, from the damage that may be caused by animals and man; it is a means of recognizing a tree when there are no leaves to help us.

2. Immediately beneath the bark is a layer (pinkish or reddish, more rarely white) which is—wrongly—called the inner bark; this is the *liber* or *bast*, the tissue through which the sap descends and is redistributed after it has been "elaborated" by photosynthesis in the leaves. This tissue, generally extremely thin compared with the wood, is so called because the growth circles it gives rise to each year are compressed until they become as thin as the pages of a book (Latin, *liber*).

3. The *cambium*, not easy to see with the naked eye, is none the less

Chart illustrating the different phases of the activity of the cambium. It produces wood toward the inside of the plant and bast toward the outside, the bark.

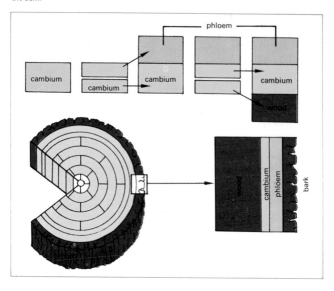

the tissue responsible for the whole growth of the trunk in diameter. Lying between the wood proper and the liber, separating them with a single layer of thin, transparent-walled cells, it produces new woody elements on the inside and new elements of liber on the outside, toward the bark.

4. Inside the cambium is the *wood* itself, and on it we can observe a number of concentric rings, one for every year that the trunk has lived. The wood is composed of fibers and vessels; these last have the function of transporting the raw sap (an aqueous solution of the mineral salts contained in the soil) from the roots to the leaves, where the process of photosynthesis takes place which transforms this inorganic solution into a solution of organic compounds.

5. The *pith* or *medulla* is the central part of a trunk or a root in its first year, round which there is a single circle of cribriform woody bundles; in the adult plant it may be reduced, or may even be destroyed when the plant reaches a certain age, leaving an empty medullary cylinder, as in *Pawlonia*. In the cypress, juniper, alder and apple, for example, the pith is some 1–2 mm (a little over 0.2 in) thick; it is thicker, 2.5 mm–8 mm (0.1–0.33 in) in the pine, Red Fir, poplar or fig, and thicker still, over 8 mm (0.33 in) in the *Ailanthus* or the elder. Also to be observed in the cross section of the trunk are the *medullary rays*, which, as their name suggests, are fine lines of cells that run radially from the pith to the bark and distribute nutrients to all parts of the plant.

In some trees, such as oaks, elms and larches, we can see a

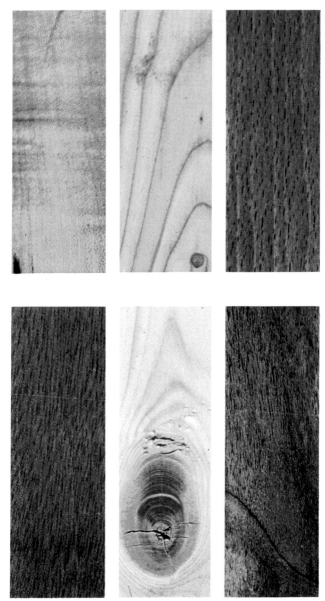

21

difference in color between the outer part of the wood, the *sapwood* or alburnum, and the inner part, the *heartwood* or duramen; in other trees, the birch for example, this difference does not appear and the woods are called undifferentiated or concolor. The sapwood, the light part of the wood as seen in cross section, is the most recently formed wood, the circle farthest from the central cylinder; it is the physiologically active part of the wood through which the sap rises and so demonstrates high level of humidity. This makes it susceptible to rot and vulnerable to attack by fungi and insects, which find it a convenient place for breeding and development; the sapwood is often removed from timber, especially where weather and rot resistance and durability are required. Generally the sapwood in the trunk of a mature tree occupies a circle a few centimeters deep, though in some species, or in young trees, it may be considerably thicker.

The heartwood is the part of the trunk nearest the center, the older part, which makes up the greater part of the trunk. It is simply a form of the sapwood modified by aging, and differs from it in its greater compactness and darker, more intense color. Heartwood has a lower humidity, and its cell walls are so thickened by deposits of tannins, resins, starchy substances, coloring matter and oils that the light is perceptibly reduced, if not completely shut out from them. This part of the plant is already dead, performing only the functions of support and storage, but for the carpenter it is the most valuable wood, harder and more resistant both to damage from weather conditions and to attack by fungi and insects. The various substances (tannoids or resins) with which it is impregnated alter its color, as in the black of ebony heartwood or the deep red of mahogany, and this adds to its value; in some trees the heartwood may be impregnated with inorganic substances like silica, which gives them an extraordinary hardness such as we find for instance in teak.

In the temperate zone, when spring knocks at the door, the birds sing and the first flowers open in the fields, the trees too begin to renew their growth cycle: it has been said that they "fall in love." This is when the buds open to form new leaves and new twigs and the whole tree feels the need for a greater quantity of nutrients, so to supply this it forms new woody vessels to transport the raw sap which must rise up swiftly within the trunk. The light part of each annual ring is formed from this *spring wood*, characterized by large vessels; the dark part corresponds to the *summer wood*, also (wrongly) called autumn wood. In the latter the vessels, narrower and more numerous, function mainly to support and to transport the water required for transpiration, because so late in the season the tree's crown has already completed its growth and no longer needs the great quantities of rising liquid that help to form the leaf tissues in the spring. This alternation of a light ring with wide vessels and a dark with narrow vessels is what forms what are called annual rings, so that each ring is the wood produced in one year, made up of a wide band of spring wood and a narrow one of summer wood.

Each year, as it grows, the tree enfolds its past in a firm embrace, constructing a new ring of living material around it; the trunk of a tree is the product of labor as old as the tree itself. Thus we can learn from the number of circles how old the plant is, and it is possible from a close reading of their width, their form and their color to reconstruct the tree's whole life story, starting from the climate and any adverse weather conditions to which it has been subjected and reflecting the conditions in which it grew up and any interference by humans or animals that it had to suffer; the annual rings or growth rings are thus an instant and permanent record of all the events that have taken place around the tree. Observations on the appearance of the cross-section of a tree had already been made by Theophrastus and Columella, and it was Leonardo da Vinci, with his encyclopaedic mind, who guessed not only that it was possible to deduce the age from the number of rings, but also that it was possible to learn the climatic conditions in any given period by the differences in their width. Later, H. L. Duhamel du Monceau and Buffon took up the study, and in 1737 they recognized in the ring for 1708–1709 the influence of a cold spell which Linnaeus himself (1745) referred to in the same winter. In the next century De Candolle and Pokorny studied junipers, Scotch Pines and firs and worked out a relationship between growth in diameter and climatic events. But it is to the American astronomer A. E. Douglass that we owe the foundation at the beginning of the present century of a new science, *dendrochronology*, which by close examination of the growth of trees investigates the history of the climate and the trees' reaction to variations in the environment. Evidence of the growth of a tree is afforded by its annual rings, a measurable quantity that can be reproduced on a graph having diametrical growth and time as its coordinates; dendrochronology is based on the study of those two factors. Since the influence of the climate on each ring ensures that it will be as unique as a man's fingerprints, it has become possible by "reading" the wood to establish its year. In this way it has proved possible to construct a diagram for a given period, starting with very old trees felled at a known time, and to go back, matching unmistakable features on the diagrams for older and older specimens of wood by placing the last elements of one series against the first elements of the next (using a tree particularly sensitive to rain, *Pinus aristata*, the Bristle Cone Pine of California) until we have information about a period 7100 years back. A group of scientists at the University of Arizona foresees that it will eventually be possible to investigate climatic conditions of as much as 9000 years ago.

Every tree produces wood of different structure, color and pattern, as the craftsmen who made furniture in centuries past well knew; the character of the wood is influenced by a greater or lesser distance between branches, by the slow or rapid growth of the tree and whether it was young or old when it was felled. When we handle something made of wood, look at it closely, examine it with all our senses, we can see that it has certain special qualities — its "organoleptic" qualities.

Color. Everyone knows about the different colors of wood — daily

we use expressions like "black as ebony" or "ash-blonde." Then, the wood of the Red Fir (so called from the tawny color of its bark) is white, the heartwood of the locust is bronze, oakwood is yellow — the range of colors is almost infinite.

Scent. All woods have an agreeable smell, but it takes on a more or less individual quality according to the resins, essential oils or alkaloids with which the cells are impregnated. The Arolla Pine smells of resin, the Turkey Oak smells of tannin, while the camphor tree smells (naturally!) of camphor. (The Chinese used to make carved boxes from this wood which were highly valued in the West, not only for the extreme delicacy of the carving but also for storing furs.)

Taste. Again according to the substances with which they are impregnated, woods also have a characteristic taste — the laburnum, for example, the poplar, the Red Fir and the Indian Licorice Tree (*Abrus precatorius*).

Texture. What is called the texture of wood is the appearance it assumes as a result of differences between genera in cell size and structure. The texture can be coarse as in oak or fine as in boxwood.

Grain. Alternation of color between the zones of spring and summer wood in the annual rings creates a circular pattern in cross section and various other patterns depending on how the log was sawed. This pattern made by the rings is more marked in some species than in others, clearest in conifers like pines and firs, less clear in certain broadleafs like poplar and birch.

Besides these elements there is also *marbling*, a phenomenon often found particularly in the roots and collar of arboreal plants. The marbled woods of maple, oak, olive and nut trees are valued in high-quality work for their curly, sinuous, irregular pattern. This effect is caused by a deviation from normal, straight upward growth of the woody vessels resulting in diversion or even interruption of the flow of rising sap. This weakens the timber, but with a compensating elegance in the shape, color and variety of the grain. Marbling can also be caused by a tree's reaction to an invasion of parasites, to cuts, to stripping off the bark, to excessive pruning, to frost or to excessive bud production; all these negative factors can add to the beauty and elegance of the wood.

The sum total of these characteristics helps us to make a first classification of the various types of wood, but to obtain a positive identification it is necessary to examine the various elements that compose them in detail under the microscope. It is possible to substitute similar woods for one another, and woods of little value can sometimes be disguised, dyed and treated so as to change their most obvious features in order to make them look like more valuable woods. In such cases examination by microscope or gas chromatograph can give infallible results.

For microscopic study the three basic anatomic sections are used: a *transverse section*, perpendicular to the axis of the plant; a section along a line running from the circumference of the plant to the center, called a *radial section*; and, perpendicular to the radial section, a

Christ crucified; a wooden sculpture from the Valley of Aosta. Here wood is turned into idea and art.

tangential section (tangential, that is, to the circumference of the trunk). The thickness of the microscopic sections (obtained with instruments called microtomes) used for this specialized scientific identification must be at most 0.2 mm (0.05 in).

If we stroke a wooden object we can feel that it is "alive," sometimes perhaps because it suggests an animal's fur or a bird's feathers, but most of all because we feel that it is the product of a living creature which, in its genus and its species, represents an extraordinary entity: the tree within the field of nature. And the lines on it, elegantly engraved, are like the lines by which life has marked our faces.

The Leaf: Source of Life

It has often been said that the leaf is the most wonderful factory on earth, but such a definition needs further clarification. The leaf is *the* factory, the primal source of life, the first link in what is called the alimentary chain, which means that the sun's energy, captured and elaborated by the leaf, completes an infrangible whole when it once more turns into energy in its capacity as food for herbivorous animals, carnivores, and finally man. Leaf tissues through the process of photosynthesis form the organic compounds which will in due course break down, each performing its own task in the creation and maintenance of animal organisms. To perform these functions, unique upon earth, leaf tissues are highly specialized, being

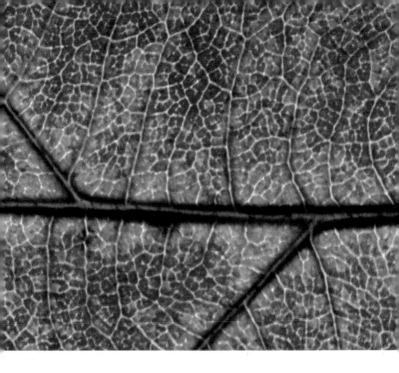

composed of cells containing various pigments; the most important of these, chlorophyll, is formed only in the presence of light and is the substance that colors plants green. Chlorophyll is contained in green corpuscles, the chloroplasts, and has the property of capturing light energy and using it, by means of complex photochemical reactions, to convert carbon dioxide obtained from the atmosphere and added to the raw sap into organic compounds such as sugar and starch. Although photosynthesis is normally carried out by leaf tissues, it can be delegated to stalks, branches and even trunks, which take over the function of the leaves when for one reason or another they are missing or reduced in number, or when they are metamorphosed.

The leaf is an appendage of the stem, which has what are called *nodes* at certain points; the point at which the base of the leaf joins the stem is called the *axil*. Protuberances generally appear at those points, the *axillary buds*, as distinct from the *apical buds* which form at the tip of the stem and are responsible for its growth upwards. The buds are simply embryonic tissues enclosed by leaves that are pressed against the shoot by the uneven growth of the two sides of the leaf itself and so form a sort of hood that protects them both against transpiration and against material damage. From this, as the plant grows, the leaves will develop, and then the shoot, which will produce a new branch. When the leaves reach a certain stage of development a new bud appears at their axil which may remain latent for a long time or may develop quite quickly, forming a new branch with new leaves. There are also, of course, buds that will grow into

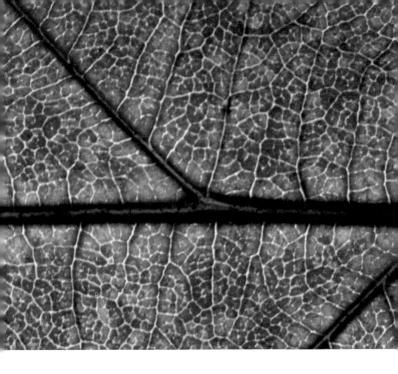

flowers or inflorescences; these are called flower buds. In plants, especially woody plants, in which the buds have to go through a period of quiescence (hibernating buds), the outer leaflets are transformed into protective scales, often accompanied by other protective formations such as hairiness or resin.

There are three main parts to a leaf: the *base*, the *stalk* or *petiole* and the *lamina* or *leaf blade*. The base is the point at which the leaf is joined to the stem; the junction may be simple, but sometimes the base is wholly or partly wrapped round the stem, in which case that part of the base is called the *sheath*. If on the other hand it is firmly attached with a leaf base opposite, the whole leaf is described as *prefoliated*. Sometimes the base is slightly swollen and forms what is called the *pulvinus*, which moves the leaf slightly according to the level of turgor; others form outgrowths called *stipules*, quite small and soon shed on some plants, large and persistent on others, sometimes spiny or scaly, taking over the protective functions of the scale leaves, as for instance in oaks. The stalk is the thin section joining the base to the lamina; it may be missing, in which case the leaf is called *sessile*. It is generally cylindrical or semicircular in form, though there are a number of exceptions; it may for instance serve as a protective sheath for the following leaf, remaining flattened and expanded at the basal end as it grows, with lateral formations that make it look winged. In some cases the stalk can develop into a broad, flat shape so that it looks and functions like a leaf. Such stalks are called *phyllodes*. The lamina or blade is the wide part of the leaf.

Chart illustrating the process of photosynthesis, which takes place in the leaves and other green parts of plants. Photosynthesis makes the development and preservation of life possible on earth.

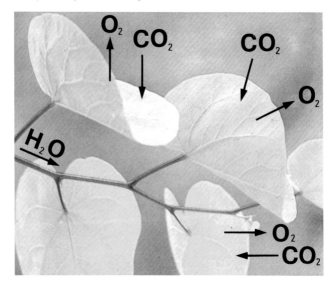

Leaves can be of many different shapes, and there are terms to describe those shapes. Primarily, leaves are divided into simple and compound: the first are those in which the lamina, while it may be deeply indented, has a continuous structure, the second those in which the stalk branches to bear a number of leaflets. In simple leaves it is the shape of the lamina, the base, the margins and the point that decide the terms by which they are described. Thus we have *acicular* (needlelike) leaves, as on some conifers, while in other genera of this order, like the cypresses and *Thuja*, the leaves are scalelike (squamiform). Leaves that are long and straight are called linear; they are called ensiform if they are sword-shaped, falciform if sickle-shaped, like those of the *Eucalyptus*, or lanceolate, oval, elliptical, and so on. The base can be cordate, hastate, sagittate, according to the shape of the lateral lobes next to the point at which the stalk joins the lamina. The margin of a leaf may be entire, undulate, dentate, crenate when the indentations are rounded, lobate (or lobed) if the indentations do not reach the center of the lamina, septate if they pass the center. The point of a leaf can be acuminate (tapering to a point), obtuse, truncated or cuspidate.

These terms may be used in combination with one another, since leaves may have different characteristics in different places; thus we may have ovato-cordate leaves, palmato-lobate leaves, and so forth. Compound leaves may be palmate, having the leaflets arranged round a single point, or pinnate, when they are joined on the two sides of the stalk.

The buds that appear in springtime may hold either flowers or leaves. Left, a leaf bud. Right, a flower bud.

The buds that appear in springtime may hold either flowers or leaves. Left, a leaf bud. Right, a flower bud.

Leaves may be arranged on the stem in one of three ways: alternate, with one leaf to each node; opposite, with two to a node, and verticillate or whorled, with more than two. In the first case the leaves are arranged, first on one side of the stem, then on the other; in the second case they will be growing at an angle of 180° to one another. Differently shaped leaves can grow on the same plant, a phenomenon called heterophylly; sometimes it occurs at different stages of growth, less often it is permanent.

The form of leaves is closely bound up with all their functions and also with their environment. Besides photosynthesis, which is the key to metabolism, the leaf also carries out all the other exchanges with the atmosphere; it is through the leaf that the plant breathes (absorbs oxygen and gives off carbon dioxide plus energy) and transpires. Its epidermic tissues contain stomata, formed from two kidney-shaped cells that make microscopic openings like valves; they are so constructed that variations in their turgor, which depends on the greater or lesser amount of water that they contain, regulate the opening or closing of the tiny valves, permitting or preventing transpiration, through which the plant loses the major part of the water it absorbs so as to allow further absorption by the roots. In nearly all plants the stomata are located on the underside of the leaves, and their functioning is so perfectly regulated that plants living in dry climates have a substantially smaller number of them than those in humid climates, in which they are numerous and prominent; where the humidity is low they may actually be recessed

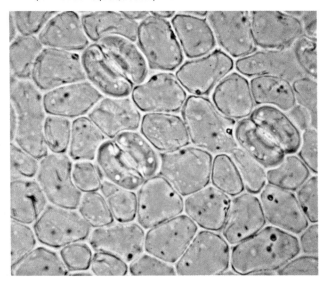

or partly protected by tomentum, soft hairs which can prevent excessive transpiration. This phenomenon occurs both by day and by night, but in green plants it is only observed when there is no light; in the presence of light energy the process of photosynthesis, the most important exchange of gases, is so much more powerful that it masks transpiration completely. While this mechanism is very active in plants that have smooth-textured big leaves, it is reduced in leaves with a leathery cuticle and becomes minimal in plants with needlelike leaves.

The cuticle, an external secretion from the membrane of the epidermic layer, may have special protective features adapted to the plant's habitat and the level of succulence found in the organism as a whole. The waxy secretion called bloom, for instance, not only prevents excessive transpiration but allows water to run off the surface of very succulent plants which might rot with too much moisture. *Tormentum, hairs, nodules, glands* and *thorns* are other protective formations created to deal with adverse conditions, to defend the plant both against over-severe climatic conditions and against too-strong ultraviolet rays such as may often occur high in the mountains.

The plant has a number of defences against atmospheric and climatic agencies: conifers can survive in very cold regions because their needlelike leaves can withstand almost total quiescence accompanied by severe frost and heavy snow; temperate-zone plants are generally deciduous, because the absence of leaves

33

The flower of an Angiosperm is a system of organs which act together to achieve the plant's reproduction. Besides the sexual organs there are accessory organs which function to attract or protect.

ensures a rest period during which their metabolic functions are reduced to a minimum, bringing on a period of hibernation; in other cases the rest period comes at phases of drought during which the plants cannot obtain the water they need for their sap. Where humidity, heat and light are constant, the vegetative rhythm has no breaks and the foliage is perennial, often abundant and soft; the leaves fall only to make provision for the new summer growth, and a layer of woody scar tissue is generally formed at the base of the stalk.

The Flower: Sexuality and Beauty

When we speak of sexuality we almost automatically think of the animal kingdom; but in fact it is inherent in all the more highly evolved living creatures. In a primordial state animals and plants exhibit an exclusively agamic form of propagation by the division of individual cells or the detachment of a portion of the vegetative body. Such forms of reproduction are moreover quite possible even in many plants that already possess sexuality, and in some cases actually predominate despite the presence of sexual organs which would make sexual reproduction perfectly possible; one example is *Lemna*, a little floating aquatic plant which, though it produces microscopic flowerets, normally reproduces in nature by the splitting of the green parts of which it is composed. Sexual cells, called *gametes*, are present in algae and fungi, which by copulation and resultant fertilization can produce a zygote or fertile egg cell which

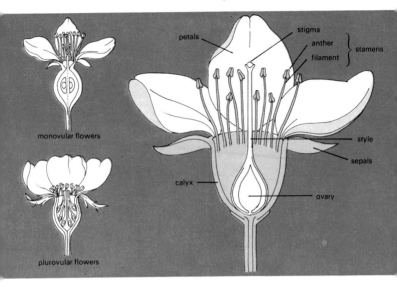

will give birth to a new entity. However, only in the evolution of superior forms do the male and female characters become increasingly evident, up to the point at which we reach the flowered plants.

In the Gymnosperms, many families of which are known today only as fossils, though the great order of Conifers remains almost entirely complete, we find, as their name tells us (*gymnos*, bare; *sperma*, seed), rudimentary forms which, while they belong with the spermatophytes (plants with seeds) have naked ovules, not enclosed within an ovary but attached to open carpellary leaves. The transport of pollen onto the ovule is generally left to the wind (anemophily). The flowers are unisexual, having no perianth; they are often joined in strobiles, or cones (hence the name conifers), formed from layers of bracts which may become woody, as in pinecones.

From the evolutionary point of view the Gymnosperms form the link between the ferns and the true flowered plants, the Angiosperms, in which nature has beyond question created its true masterpieces. In these too the flower is an organ developed from the leaf in which certain parts are modified and adapted to perform reproductive functions; but the ovules are always contained within a closed cavity, the *ovary*, which after fecundation becomes the fruit, while the ovules become the seeds. The essential part of the flower is that which has to perform the sexual function; it comprises the male organs or *stamens* which together form the *androecium*, and the female organs or *carpels* which form the *gynoecium*. Although the majority of flowers are hermaphrodite, with male and female

When insects visit flowers they often carry pollen with them and so carry out fertilization.

elements combined in the one organism, there are many unisexual flowers, in which only one of these elements appears: when they are found on separate specimens the plants are called *dioecius*, while those with hermaphrodite flowers, or those on which unisexual flowers of both sexes coexist, are called *monoecious*. A plant that bears both bisexual and unisexual flowers at the same time is called *polygamous*.

In the great majority of Angiosperms the true sexual organs are enclosed within a floral envelope which serves two purposes, protection and attraction. It comprises the *calyx*, formed by the *sepals*, and in the inner part the *corolla*, the whorl of petals. All these parts together constitute the perianth, the most conspicuous part of the flower, the part that attracts our attention—for the often very strange forms of the corolla, its vivid or delicate colors, are there for the very purpose of attracting attention, not of course the attention of humans, but that of fertilizing insects which help with pollination and so in fertilization. If we look at a flower, in the most general sense of the word, we shall find at its center the gynoecium, formed, as we have said, by the carpels, whose swollen base, the ovary, has an extension called the *style* with a flattened point, the *stigma*, which becomes receptive and slightly sticky when the ovules are ripe and ready for fertilization; the organ as a whole is known as the *pistil*. Around this, generally, are the stamens, composed as a rule of filaments which support a special organ, the *anther*, formed in its turn from two sacs containing the pollen granules, the bearers of the male sex. When the pollen is ready for fertilization it is carried, in many different ways, onto the stigma, in which a pollen tube is formed, as if it were a channel through which the male gametes reach the ovary, where they can fuse with the female gametes contained in the ovule. Fertilization is then complete. In hermaphrodite flowers, of course, there can be self-pollination, particularly where fertilizing agents are scarce or even nonexistent as a result of adverse environmental conditions; in this last case pollination is often entrusted to the wind, or self-fertilization occurs.

However, in a very great number of bisexual flowers there are special devices to avoid this. For instance, stamens and pistils may not ripen at the same time, or the stigma and anther may be located out of reach of one another; in such cases reproduction is only possible by cross-fertilization. And here we come to the role of the insects, and sometimes the birds, who help the pollen from a flower to reach a pistil where the stigma has become receptive (ripe) so that sexual union may take place. But these "bridegrooms" have to be attracted and helped; often they get something in exchange for the service they perform for the species.

Now we can see the object of the transformation of the organs forming the floral envelope. Brilliant corollas opening up to display their colors, corollas partly closed to form a tube where the insect will be powdered with pollen before it can emerge, perfumed corollas to attract nocturnal insects or those in which the sense of smell is more active than that of sight, even corollas which have an unpleasant smell because they prefer to be pollinated by necrophilous insects like flies. Often the insects feed directly on the pollen (although there is always enough left over for fertilization purposes), but in very many flowers they are rewarded with a special secretion, nectar, which they feast on while the pollen is rubbing off onto their wings and body to be carried to the stigma awaiting it. In some cases there are so to speak advertisements, special shapes and color markings to lead the guest to the nectaries, the glands that secrete nectar, so that the insect is obliged to rub against the anthers in order to reach them.

Pollination is also often helped by the position the flowers occupy on the plant; they can grow separately (solitary flowers) or in numbers forming inflorescences. These, different for every species, consist of a certain number of flowers carried on a principal axis, often with a number of branches, and there are names to describe each form in which this branching occurs. First of all there are two big groups: flowers with *cymes*, inflorescences in which the main axis and each of the subsidiary branches terminate in a flower ("definite" inflorescences), and those with *racemes*, in which the axis continues to grow at the tip while the secondary branches grow out from it. In the first group the cymes are known as *monochasious* if single branches appear below the terminal flower, *dichasious* if two lateral branches develop in opposite directions below the flower, *pleiochasious* if there are more than two branches leaving from the same point. Racemous inflorescences are divided into the *spike*, on which the flowers are sessile on an elongated axis; the *capitulum*,

with sessile flowers carried on an axis greatly enlarged toward the tip and smaller below and generally surrounded by bracts; the *spadix*, a spike having an enlarged, fleshy axis on which naked flowers grow; the *raceme* (cluster), which in contrast has the axis elongated, with pedunculate (stalked) flowers growing at different points along it; and the *corymb*, in which all the flowers reach much the same height because the stalks of those growing farthest from the tip grow longest. If the stalked flowers reach the same height but are all growing from the same point, then we have an *umbel*; and finally there is the *catkin*, actually only a spike with a flexible axis, nearly always pendulous, with naked, unisexual flowers. There are also compound or thyrsoid inflorescences, in which the axis branches so that each branch in turn forms a minor inflorescence, generally definite, so that we may have a *compound spike*, a *compound umbel* and a *panicle* or *thyrse* which is really only a *compound raceme*. In trees especially we often find the flowers growing together in inflorescences, because that makes them more immediately visible or perceptible at a distance and so ensures a greater certainty of pollination and a consequent guarantee of survival of the species through reproduction.

The Seed: Perpetuation of the Species

When the tree is covered with flowers it puts on its wedding dress, but as soon as the culminating act of fertilization is completed the seed is formed, the ultimate aim of the plant. is achieved, the conservation of the species is ensured. The seed is in fact the reproductive agency derived from the fertilized ovule; it contains the rough sketch, the outline of the future plant, the embryo, which remains enclosed within the seed in a latent condition, both on the tree and on the ground, for a period of time that varies from plant to plant. Germination will not normally occur until the following spring.

The rigors of winter thus permit germination at the first spring warmth only after a rest period. This is one of the ways in which a plant defends its own offspring, because if the seed were to germinate before it was fully ripe the new plant would have to face the cold too soon, while it was still weak, and would probably succumb to it. This applies of course only to plants in temperate climates; those in tropical and subtropical regions do not need that kind of protection. The period in which they can germinate is relatively short, thus all tropical plants have seeds that must be sown while they are still as fresh as possible.

Often the embryo in the seed is surrounded by a reserve substance, *albumen*, for protection and nutrition. Entrusted to the soil by the plant for the creation of a new being, it is surrounded and protected from the outside by a *seminal integument* or shell, made of dead tissue and derived from the integument of the ovule from which it sprang; or else the outside of it is provided with cells that form a robust cuticle, or with wax, hair, spines, or sometimes outgrowths like wings that serve both as a defence and as an aid to dissemination.

Above: diagrams of ripe seeds. (A) seeds of dicotyledon with albumen. (B) seed of monocotyledon with albumen. (C) seed of dicotyledon without albumen. (D) seed of monocotyledon without albumen. (1) albumen. (2) cotyledon. (3) bud. (4) radicle.
Below: capsules of Paulownia, *which open to release the winged seeds.*

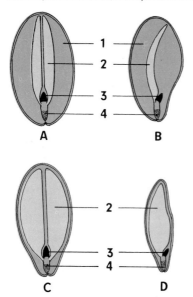

Examples of the transformation of the ovary into the fruit. At the sides: left, capsule; right, drupe. Below: left, nut; right, berry.

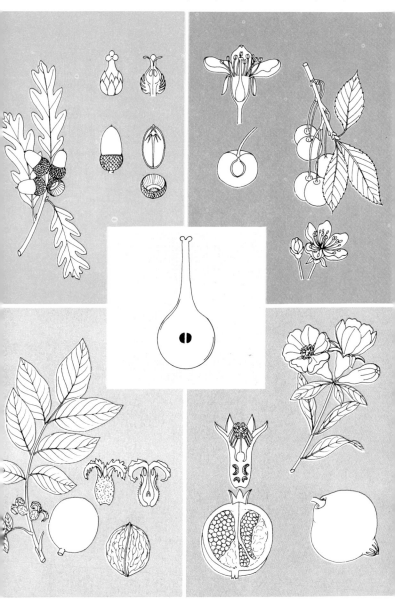

The shape, color and size of seeds vary a great deal, from the countless minute seeds of the orchid to the nuts of the coconut, several centimeters across, and the *Dimorphandra megistosperma*, whose seed may measure as much as 13 cm (7 in). The seed is a feature of all the plants called Spermaphytes (seed plants), but while the older Gymnosperms the seeds are naked and free, in the Angiosperms they are encased within the fruit, which is the transformed ovary, a secondary result of the transformation of the ovules within the ovary.

While the significance of the seeds is quite clear, that of the fruit is rather less so. The fruit is the cradle of the seed, formed from those parts of the flower which remain after fertilization and which on the one hand have a protective function for the seeds themselves and on the other—perhaps more important—facilitate propagation and thus the establishment of the species. Strictly speaking, of course, it is the ovary, more or less modified, that contains the seeds that come from the fertilized ovules, and if we accept that definition, the fruit can only exist in the Angiosperms, because it is only in that group of plants that the ovary exists: Gymnosperms with their naked seeds have no ovaries. Broadly speaking, the fruit is the totality of the parts of the flower, or more precisely of the neighboring organs which, after fertilization, remain to accompany and enclose the seeds until they ripen, afterwards releasing them and separating itself with them from the parent plant. Looked at in this way pine-cones and juniper and yew berries are also fruits, so we may say that Gymnosperms do also bear fruit. This ecological rather than purely morphological interpretation permits easier identification and classification of the reproductive elements, the seeds.

The *pericarp* is generally thought of as synonymous with the fruit (from Greek *peri*, around; *karpos*, fruit). It is formed from the walls of the ovary, modified and enlarged, as distinct from the seed contained in it; but actually the fruit is only complete when it contains the seed. In some cultivated varieties of fruit trees there is a trend toward growing seedless fruit formed after a normal fertilization process, after which the embryo decays. In fruit produced by postfecundative evolution of the ovary, we can distinguish three layers: the *epicarp* on the outside, the *mesocarp* inside that and, nearest the center, the *endocarp*; the different development and consistency of these three layers and their complex mutual relationships, or more precisely their fusion with other parts of the flower, give rise to the great variety of fruits. It is hard to classify fruits, since they differ so very geatly in appearance, in consistency and in the arrangement of their component parts. Their size too varies, from about 1 mm (0.039 in) in the case of the orchids to 1 m (3.3 ft) in the Cucurbitaceae (gourds). There are variations in color, in shape, in surface growths (hairs, ribs, spines), in consistency, in the number of seeds, which may be anywhere from 1 to over 3,500,000. The fruits of Angiosperms are classified according to the carpellary leaves forming the ovary; each one may form a single cavity, or they may be fused together to make a common cavity, the pluricarpellary ovary. Another important point in

The seeds of conifers grow between the scales of the cones.

the classification of fruits is the way in which, and the point at which, the seeds are implanted, and particularly the presence or absence of dehiscence, the capacity to open spontaneously and allow the seeds to emerge.

A traditional classification, based on descriptive terms, divides fruits into *true* fruits, those derived solely from ovaries, and *false* fruits, derived from accessory parts of the flower. A common conventional way of classifying fruits is by their consistency, into *dry fruits* which become membraneous or hard on ripening and *succulent fruits* whose characteristics include a fleshy consistency or a rich sugar content. Among indehiscent dry fruits are the *achene* with dry walls that do not adhere to the single seed; the *caryopsis* (fruit of the Gramineae) in which by contrast the fruit walls are firmly joined to the seed; and the *nut* with its typical hard, woody shell, which also has a single seed but which is derived from a pistil formed by a number of carpels of which only one is not aborted. The *samara* and *disamara* are, respectively, one or two seeds whose fruit has an outer integument that makes a membraneous wing—surrounding the seed in the elm, diverging at an angle in the ash and the maple.

Dehiscent dry fruits include the *follicle*, formed by the strengthening of a single carpellary leaf. The *legume* or *bean*, characteristic of all Leguminosae, also develops from a single carpel, but it opens along two opposite fracture lines, so that the two halves of the fruit are separated and can roll back and allow the seeds to drop. The *silique* is another dry dehiscent fruit; it is derived from two carpellary leaves

43

In the autumn trees with deciduous leaves restore their remains to the earth.

joined together, but the cavity of the fruit is divided in half by a false septum, the replum, and the seeds are attached to that. The *capsule*, finally, is a dry fruit that can assume various forms and has different ways of allowing the seeds to emerge: familiar forms of capsule are acorns, surrounded by a cup at the base; the hazelnut, contained in a membraneous envelope; and the chestnut ("buckeye"), completely enclosed in a hard, spiny shell.

Among the succulent fruits there are more indehiscent fruits than dehiscent. In a *drupe* the seed is enclosed in a resistant shell called the stone, developed from the innermost part of the fruit (the endocarp), while the mesocarp is juicy and the outer part (the epicarp) forms the external membrane commonly called the skin. Drupes include the cherry, plum, apricot and peach, also the almond (though we only eat the stone) and the coconut, in which the mesocarp instead of being juicy is fibrous, which serves to soften the blows when the fruit is floating on the sea and is battered against the rocks.

The *berry*, by contrast, is succulent all the way through. The pulp in which the seeds are contained is bounded on the outside by the skin (the epicarp). Grapes are berries, but the name is wrongly applied to the fruit of the laurel (really drupes) and of the juniper (actually strobiles in which the rather fleshy scales grow together).

Some berries have special names, like the *hesperidium*, the fruit of all *Citrus* trees, in which the true fruit is the peel, made up of an outer layer brightly colored and rich in glands, a spongy whitish mesocarp

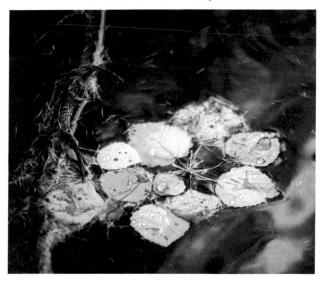

and a membraneous endocarp surrounding the segments. The succulent part we eat is only a secondary tissue developed as a filler.

In the Pomoidae, (a division of the Rosaceae), the typical fruit is the *pome*, the fruit of the pear and the apple and the sorbus. It is a compound fruit: the true fruit is the core, formed from five cartilaginous septa enclosing the seeds surrounded by the fleshy part, which actually comes from the growth of the floral receptacle.

Generally speaking, succulent fruits are not dehiscent, though nature does offer us some attractive exceptions which assist dissemination, like *Impatiens noli-tangere* and *Hura crepitans*, which explodes and hurls its seeds quite a long way. In false fruits it is generally other parts of the flower that contribute to the formation of the fruit, like the sweet edible part in which the little achenes of the *Ficus* are enclosed; in *Anarcardium occidentale* it is actually the stalk of the flower that becomes fleshy. The woody strobiles (cones) of most conifers can be classified as false fruits, and so can the fleshy pseudo-berries of *Juniperus* and the fleshy growths around the seeds of *Taxus* and *Gingko*.

All trees are inexorably joined to the earth. Their roots break up and crumble the rocks, and when the plant dies it surrenders its remains to the earth to enrich it. The leaves rot when they have completed their task of photosynthesis, and after them the wood also rots and its gigantic molecules return to the earth, from which they were first extracted as simple inorganic compounds.

A long process of evolution has been carried out by the plants,

45

from rock to fertile land in which other plants can live. So at the end of its life every tree leaves on our planet a little particle of life, and its testament begins with the words: "You gave me stones; I leave you earth." Man should indeed tremble before cutting down a tree.

The Names of Trees

The object of classifying plants is to assign a name to every one, living or extinct, and to arrange them systematically in a definite order. The overall principles of classification are known by the terms systematics or taxonomy, from the Greek *taxis*, order.

The need for some system that would allow plants to be identified with certainty was recognized by the earliest naturalists, and attempts to devise one were made in the oldest times by both Greeks and Romans, including Theophrastus in the 4th–3rd centuries B.C. and Pliny the Elder (A.D. 23–79). But for centuries the method of distinguishing plants was based purely on descriptive terms so long and so imprecise that it was hard to understand and compare them. As new, hitherto unknown plants were introduced from countries newly discovered the difficulties increased, and many botanists attempted to work out rational classification systems: one of the first was Andrea Cesalpino (1519–1603), who tried to subdivide plants according to the nature of their seeds, and after him Marcello Malpighi, born at Crevalcore near Bologna in 1628, and a near contemporary, Joseph Pitton de Tournefort (Aix-en-Provence, 1656–1708), tried to work out new systems. These and others are called "pre-Linnaean," for the true father of taxonomy was Carl Ritter von Linné, the great Swedish naturalist who lived from 1707 to 1778, and who, as was the custom in those days, wrote his name in a Latin form as Linnaeus. In 1753, after a first attempt on different lines, he published his *Species Plantarum*, in which he worked out a classification based on the plants' reproductive organs—a system therefore described as sexual. At the same time he introduced binomial nomenclature, for his system was so drawn up that for the complete identification of a plant all that was required was the name of the species preceded by that of the genus. The Linnaean system was not perfect, of course, and although it has remained the fundamental base of taxonomy it has been studied, researched and revised many times by such famous botanists as A. L. de Jussieu, who in 1789 divided plants into 15 classes according to the number or absence of cotyledons, while Augustin Pyramus de Candolle (Geneva, 1778–1841) tried to subdivide plants into those with vascular systems and cellular plants with tissues having no conducting vessels, subdividing them further by the way the vessels were arranged and by the morphology of the inflorescence.

An outstanding influence on all subsequent studies of systematics was exerted by Charles Darwin's theories of evolution, from which there arose what was called the philogenetic approach, based on the natural linked series found in the plant world, which among other things minimized the importance given to the concept of originative

Examples of classification. To identify a plant, you need only know the names of the genus and the species.

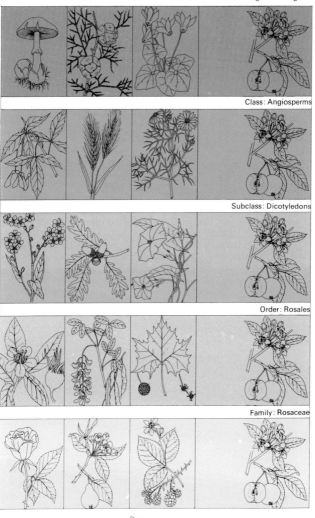

Vegetable Kingdom

Class: Angiosperms

Subclass: Dicotyledons

Order: Rosales

Family: Rosaceae

Apple (*Malus sylvestris*)

species—a concept until then held much more widely and more rigidly. Among the most recent systems, still valid and traditionally followed, are those of H. F. Adolf Engler (1844–1930) and Richard von Wettstein (1863–1931), a supporter of evolutionism and so a follower of the philogenetic approach. Although there is a general tendency today to work out new classification systems based on a variety of biological and chemical concepts, the officially recognized taxonomy divides the vegetable kingdom into *divisions* or types, and thence, in order, into:

Classes *Genera*
Orders *Species*
Families

There are further subdivisions, but thanks to the binomial system we only need to know the names of the genus and the species to identify a plant correctly. The names of plants are now determined by the rules of an International Code of Nomenclature of Cultivated Plants, published for the first time in 1953, although the idea was first mooted as long ago as 1866. One of the difficulties that had to be faced was the fact that, over the centuries, the same plants had often been given different names by different authorities; it was agreed that only names published after the *Species Plantarum* should be valid, and that the nomenclature published first should prevail, those published later remaining as synonyms. This often creates a certain confusion, since names that are no longer valid are in such common use among nurserymen and florists that it is actually the synonym that still prevails. It was laid down that in binomial nomenclature the name of the genus should always be written with a capital letter and that of the species with a small letter, even if it refers to the name of a person or place. There is also provision for the naming of hybrids, both natural and artificial, which until quite recently were given Latin names that often caused confusion with the true species. Today there are several ways of indicating hybrids: basically they are given the names of the two parent species joined by a multiplication sign (e.g. *Forsythia suspensa* × *Forsythia viridissima*), but when they are natural, or show a tendency to breed true, they may be given a name of their own, though still preceded by a multiplication sign and possibly followed by the names of the parents (e.g. *Forsythia* × *intermedia* (*F. suspensa* × *F. viridissima*)). For woody plants this rule is extended to hybrids obtained by pollination; also to chimaeras, the results of grafting two different species when adventitious shoots appear at the point of contact of stock and shoot, formed partly from the tissues of one specimen and partly from those of the other. Such growths are not true hybrids, because their purely somatic origin excludes any real combination of their characteristics; the addition sign is therefore used to indicate them instead of the multiplication sign. Chimaeras are not common, but it is sometimes possible to obtain them experimentally: one of the commonest is + *Laburno-cytisus adamii* (*Laburnum anagyroides* + *Cytisus purpureus*). Varieties within species and hybrids are indicated by "var." or "v." followed by the varietal name. Natural varieties are generally given

Latin names, but the nomenclature code has laid down, very opportunely, that all varieties produced either by artificial or natural cultivation which would not be able to maintain their character if not cultivated should be given the name "cultivar," and that the name given to denominate them should always be an imaginative name which should never be translated from the original language; it should be written in roman type, not italic, and enclosed in quotation marks. So we get *Fraxinus elastica* "Decora" or *Fraxinus excelsior* "Pendula."

All these centuries of effort, all these rules, incorporating activities both scientific and horticultural, may seem a waste of time to many who think that all you need to identify a plant is its popular name. Of course, if we are only concerned with a limited number of plants in a limited area, the popular, common names will do just as well as the scientific, but the distribution of a plant is just what can make its identification uncertain, confused, often quite erroneous. Some popular names of course are perfectly rational (and trees are fortunate in this way on the whole, at any rate as regards the generic names), but others are purely local, often indeed confined to quite small areas; sometimes you only have to go a few miles from one place to another to find a plant known by two different names. So when the transfer passes from one language to another, and since the wild plants in any country will have common names in the local language, he or she needs to know not only the language of the country but often a local dialect to reach understanding. Even if we leave aside the countless plants from tropical and subtropical countries whose popular names may exist in several languages or dialects, what strikes us at once in the study of popular names is that for many of them there are two quite different philological sources: one, Latin, which has produced the names used in Romance-language countries, and the other, Germanic, which has produced the names used in northern Europe and North America, Australia and New Zealand. This applies of course only to names whose etymology is clear and which are used throughout a country, not to nicknames used locally. A good example of this is the genus *Fraxinus* (the original Latin name), which the Italians call *frassino*, the French *frène*, the Spanish *fresno* — all popular names directly derived from corruption of the Latin. But the distribution of *Fraxinus* covers an area reaching as far as the coasts of the Baltic, so the plant has acquired a second set of names of Teutonic origin: *Esche* in German, *es* in Dutch, *ask* in Swedish, ash in English, all derived from the Old German *ask*, which became *aesc* in Anglo-Saxon. This is a clear example of how necessary it is to use a plant's scientific name so as to leave no doubt of its identity, even though sometimes the actual distance between two places where it occurs is not great and the natural environments much the same.

When the surroundings are unpolluted, a luxuriant nature is master even over the works of man.

The Future: Ecology or Disaster?

It is really only in the past decade that everyone has begun to talk about ecology and the protection of the environment, but many voices have been raised in alarm for a good deal longer than that, to denounce the suicidal havoc that men have been wreaking on our planet. From earliest times man's worst enemy has been, not the environment in which he lived, but the selfishness and presumption with which he was determined to dominate everything around him, even to destroy it, without giving a thought to anything but his own immediate advantage. While this could pass unobserved as long as the relationship between man and nature was still in favor of the latter, the danger became more immediate as the human population grew and as *Homo sapiens* acquired and exploited new knowledge with no thought for the future of his own species. The swift advance of industrialization, the increased use of the automobile and the consumption of fuels, above all the spread of urban overcrowding, all happening over nearly the entire surface of the globe, have assumed proportions that bring about more and more damage to vegetation through pollution of the atmosphere. When this phenomenon first began to be observed, these implacable injuries to trees were localized, confined to the areas around the sources of pollution; today they spread over ever vaster areas and constitute the greatest threat to the human race, unless man pauses to reflect a little on the frantic life he leads from day to day. It is true that, in the thousands of millions of years since the earth began to cool and form a crust on its

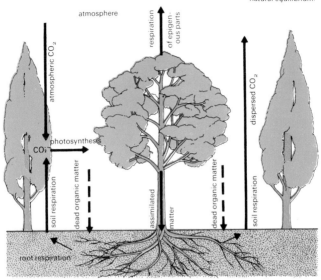

fiery globe, untold cataclysms have occurred and countless species have become extinct, but never so far has the last spark of life been extinguished. Nature can face glaciations, fire, earthquakes, volcanic eruptions, the submersion of continents, but it has no way of warding off the senseless destruction being wrought about by the human intelligence; this polluting factor, this homicidal and suicidal menace will inevitably spread its negative influence over plant life, and consequently over animal life, unless we reflect in time on the extent of it and take proper precautions at once. Today, through what we speak of casually as "pollution," deploring it only in the vaguest way, man is destroying that thin layer of atmosphere which lies between him and infinite space and beyond which no known form of life can exist. When pollution strikes a tree, a field, a hedge, it brings about a deterioration of the soil and the topsoil, upsetting an equilibrium whose complexity makes it particularly vulnerable to toxic substances diffused in the atmosphere; a delicately balanced structure of plants and animals finds itself irremediably damaged, reducing the product of thousands of millions of years of evolution to an empty shell, a dead wandering sphere with no purpose in the universe.

The circle is closing! The green forests delight our eyes; more than that, they have given us oxygen to breathe and used light to create flowers and fruit; the heat of the sun has purified the air, driving off the perennial clouds of unbreathable atmosphere that enveloped the earth. All this we owe to the green plants and not to man's knowledge and intelligence. Neither philosophy nor science, neither splendid

A corner of a poisoned pinewood, destroyed by atmospheric pollution from a nearby petroleum refinery.

cathedrals nor the masterpieces in the museums, neither great captains' dreams of glory nor great idealists' visions of Utopia have done as much for our planet as a dense forest, now reduced to carbon and ashes.

The absorption and diffusion of gases in vegetal tissues are carried out mainly through the stomata and helped by external factors which stimulate vegetative activity (such as high atmospheric humidity, favorable lighting, plenty of water in the soil) and by factors peculiar to the plants (such as the numbers of stomata, width of the intercellular spaces, thicknesses of the cuticle). Gaseous substances attack the vegetation either by the direct action of the toxic gases they contain (e.g. sulfur dioxide, hydrofluoric acid and hydrochloric acid), causing the most obvious, easily recognizable damage, or indirectly, by deposit of substantial quantities of volatile dust full of phytotoxic residues (like lead, copper, tin and arsenic), modifying the structure and chemistry of the soil. In some cases the particles are of microscopic size and can remain in suspension in the air, looking like an opaque mist, which has been formed wherever there are great centers of population; sometimes they act as nuclei for the condensation of water vapor and so alter the composition of the spectrum of the rays of sunlight reaching the earth. The effect of this on plants is to reduce the possibility of assimilation and, in the long term, to deposit dust on the leaf blades, which stunts growth even when it does not directly kill the plants.

Phytotoxic effects can be divided into acute and chronic: the first

Very often the waters of lakes and rivers are polluted by effluents and refuse from industry.

appear quickly, after only a few hours or days, and are shown by patches of dead cells, while the others appear after a rather longer time as a partial destruction of the chlorophyll, a reduction of the vegetative process, a diminution in the width of the annual growth rings — signs of slow poisoning, of a growing disturbance of the plant's metabolism. Among the most harmful gases, the one that has done most damage is sulfur dioxide, which is present in the atmosphere wherever coal and petroleum are used as fuels, such as blast furnaces and factories that manufacture fertilizers, cellulose and soda. Besides the direct damage there are also indirect injuries caused for instance by substantial amounts of toxic substances falling to the ground, leading to changes in the soil itself, which in turn pollutes the water, from which the deadly substances pass by infiltration into the earth and so into the roots; complete stands of splendid pine trees on the coasts of Italy are being reduced to cemeteries full of skeletons by the inadequate control of detergent discharges. The damage done varies according to seasonal conditions, state of growth, length of the attack and meteorological conditions.

A knowledge of the various degrees of resistance to pollution of different plant species in the light of particular seasonal conditions, age and strength of growth can help us to select the plants that will help us to survive. Conifers, for example, apart from the larches, are less resistant than broadleaves, because their needles persist for several years so that poisonous substances can accumulate on them.

Among the various factors that pollute the natural environment we must also include deliberate fires and the culpable carelessness of people who thoughtlessly set brush fires.

Among the conifers, given favorable seasonal conditions, the most resistant trees are, in descending order:

Larix decidua
Taxus baccata
Picea pungens
Picea omorika
Thuja sp.

Juniperus sp.
Pinus Mugo
Pinus nigra
Pinus cembra

Among the *broadleafs* the following, in descending order, are only slightly sensitive to pollution:

Alnus incana
Betula pendula
Ulmus montana
Acer pseudoplatanus

Acer platanoides
Quercus borealis
Populus sp.

Of course these distinctions and comparisons have only relative value because of the different ecological conditions in which the plants are found. We must recognize that, in the right climate, trees like *Albizia julibrissin* are highly resistant and flower extremely well even at the center of big cities.

All the same, it is as well not to put too much faith in such exceptions; and it is essential to make sufficient provision for the future. Precisely because of his intelligence, man seems to be the only animal with sufficient foreknowledge of death as to make him afraid of it; this much it has been possible to learn from observations

and experiments on the rest of the living world, though we have been unable to learn that animals, perhaps even plants, are sensitive to pain. That makes the human attitude psychologically all the stranger: the individual's fear is completely dominated by his selfishness—selfishness which in the end can lead only to destruction.

Today, a felled tree, a plastic bag that poisons the atmosphere when it is burnt, a patch of oil in the sea, a little indestructible detergent—a tree, a plastic bag, a little oil, a handful of laundry powder—how much do they matter?

Tomorrow, they may spell disaster!

CONIFERS

1 ABIES ALBA
Silver Fir

Family Pinaceae.   **Evergreen**
Etymology From the Latin *abire*, to go away, used here in the sense of distance from the ground to refer to the height that some species attain. *Alba* means white.
Habitat Grows in the mountains of central and southern Europe.
Description A tree up to 60 m (195 ft) tall with a straight, columnar trunk and smooth, ashy-white bark with resin sacs when young, later cracking and secreting resin. The leaves (1) grow in two opposite rows; they are 2–3 cm (about 1 in) long, dark green but rather lighter above, with two silver-white stomatic lines on the underside which give the tree its name of Silver Fir. The cones are erect and greenish brown, the scales have a characteristic outgrowth and fall when ripe, leaving the axis bare on the tree. (2, 3) male and female flowers. The little firs of the Apennines are not natural growths; their survival is attributed to cultivation, to the care and protection given them in past centuries by monastic orders such as those of Camaldoli, Vallombrosa, La Verna and Serra San Bruno.
Propagation By seed; shoots can only be obtained if treated with rooting hormones (auxin).
Conditions for growth Prefers climates with high rainfall, limited temperature range and cool, deep soil.

2 ABIES BALSAMEA
Balsam Fir, Balm of Gilead

Family Pinaceae.   **Evergreen**
Etymology From its ability to produce Canada balsam, used as a cement for glass in optical instruments.
Habitat Native to Canada, from Alberta to Labrador and to the Atlantic slopes of the United States. It was introduced into Europe in 1697.
Description *A. Balsamea* can reach a height of 25 m (80 ft). The bark is brownish gray; in young specimens it has resiniferous sacs containing a yellowish oleoresin which thickens with time and is used in microscopy and optics under the name of Canada balsam. The leaves (1) are pointed, 2–3 cm (about 1 in) long and 2 mm (0.08 in) wide, sometimes glossy, sometimes grooved, grayish on the upper side; as with all firs, they leave a round scar on the branch when they fall. The male flowers are greenish yellow tinged with pink, the female are pale yellow. Like all firs, *A. balsamea* has erect cones with overlapping scales. They are 5–10 cm (2–4 in) long, green-gray, dark blue or olive at first, turning lavender-brown. Some varieties are very decorative.
Propagation By seed, the method most commonly used for all species of *Abies*. The cones should be gathered in late autumn and kept dry.
Conditions for growth The tree is hardy and tolerates cold climates well.

3 ABIES CEPHALONICA
Greek Fir

Family Pinaceae. **Evergreen**
Etymology The species is named after the island of Cephalonia.
Habitat Present in all the uplands of Greece and the Peloponnese as far as the Albanian border, and on the islands of Cephalonia and Euboea.
Description A very decorative species, broadly conical, seldom taller than 25 m (80 ft), with branches in regular whorls and dense, smooth, light-brown branchlets. The leaves are 2–3 cm (about 1 in) long, sharply pointed and scented; the upper side is glossy green and on the underside there are two silvery stripes, composed of stomata, separate from the venation. The cones are erect, 15–20 cm (6–8 in) long, rather slender and brownish. The bark is gray brown; it is smooth on young trees but on old trunks it begins to crack into elongated plates. The tree has a denser crown and tolerates the summer heat better than the majority of firs.
Propagation By seed; sometimes by grafting. When the cones open in the spring following the autumn in which they were gathered, the triangular seeds should be sown in a seedbed as soon as possible.
Conditions for growth Tolerates lime in the soil and also fairly arid climates.

4 ABIES NORDMANNIANA
Caucasian Fir

Family Pinaceae. **Evergreen**
Etymology The species is named after the Finnish botanist von Nordmann.
Habitat Native to the western Caucasus and Armenia at altitudes between 400 and 2000 m (1300 and 6500 ft), where it forms pure forests.
Description A very ornamental species, growing to 30 m (100 ft) and sometimes even as much as 50 m (165 ft) in its natural surroundings. The crown is an almost perfect pyramid of glossy dark green. The branches of young trees are downy; the bark of plants in the juvenile stage is gray, smooth and thin, but in mature trees it is rough and cracked. The leaves, 2–3 cm (about 1 in) long, are arranged like a brush and have a blunt, notched point, very sweet scented. The lavender cones, cylindrical-conical, are highly resinous, with broad, awl-shaped scales; they can grow more than 15 cm (6 in) long.
Propagation By seed planted in seedbeds. Following the common rule for the genus, the plantlets are transferred to their home as soon as they are clear of the ground.
Conditions for growth More resistant to drought than other firs. Its late shooting prevents damage from spring frosts.

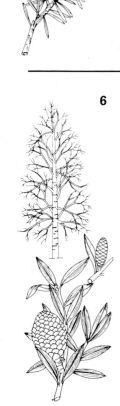

5 ABIES PINSAPO
Spanish Fir

Family Pinaceae. **Evergreen**
Etymology The specific name comes from *pinapares*, the Spanish name for the species.
Habitat Native to a limited mountainous region of southern Spain at 1100–1800 m (3600–6000 ft), where it forms scattered thickets.
Description Although it can grow up to 25 m (80 ft), this is a squat tree, not elegant, with branches growing horizontally and the dark-red twigs joining at right angles to form a little cross. The bark is brown-gray and the leaves (1), about 10–15 mm (0.5 in) long and colored ashy gray, grow all round the branch. The cones (2), erect and cylindrical and tapering toward the top, measure some 10–15 cm (4–6 in); they may grow singly or in groups of two or more, and are lavender-brown. This species can be told from the others by its short needles, growing sparsely round the branches. In particular, it differs from *A. cephalonica* (3) in that the latter has longer and more scented needles, not growing all round the branch, and marginal resin canals.
Propagation By seed.
Conditions for growth Often cultivated in temperate climates. There are varieties, *fastigiata* and *pendula*, as well as others with varicolored leaves, such as *argentea* and *aurea*.

6 AGATHIS AUSTRALIS
Kauri Pine

Family Araucariaceae. **Evergreen**
Etymology From the Greek *agathis*, a ball of twine, since the overlapping scales on the cones look altogether like rolled-up threads.
Habitat Native to New Zealand.
Description An evergreen tree which at first sight might seem to belong to the broadleaves rather than the gymnosperms, its straight, gray trunk grows to heights of 90 m (295 ft) and more. When young, the leaves are linear-oblong, rosy or bronzy in color; when mature they become oval and bright green, up to 5 cm (2 in) in length and well spaced out on secondary twigs. The unisexual flowers grow at the axil of the sessile leaves, the males in solitary catkins, while the females are strobiles, almost spherical, 8 cm (3 in) in diameter, with a single large seed at the base of each scale. From this tree, which was once known by the generic name of *Dammara* from the Malay name of one of its species, a resin is extracted which forms "dammara gum" or "kauri," used for varnishes. Very similar, and less tender, is the Australian species *Agathis robusta*.
Propagation By seed or by cuttings of young branches, taking them with a heel if possible.
Conditions for growth Does well only in mild climates; the mature trees will tolerate sporadic frosts.

7 ARAUCARIA ARAUCANA
Monkey Puzzle Tree, Chile Pine

Family Araucariaceae. **Evergreen**
Etymology The tree is named after a South American Indian tribe, the Araucana, who live in the regions where it grows wild.
Habitat Western slopes of the Andes in Chile.
Description A pyramidal evergreen tree up to 30 m (100 ft) high, with whorled branches, generally five to a node, growing horizontally near the trunk but upturned toward their ends. The secondary branches, erect in the juvenile stage, are remarkably long when fully grown. The leaves (1), about 5 cm (2 in) long, are rigid, ovato-acuminate, closely overlapping so as to cover the branches completely. The plants are dioecious, the male flowers apical and solitary, the females clustered in spherical inflorescences (2) that develop into woody strobiles some 20 cm (8 in) in diameter, with a fairly large seed at the base of each scale.
Propagation By seed, under glass at the end of winter. For fertilization to take place it is necessary to have trees of both sexes growing close together; they seldom fruit in our climate.
Conditions for growth Extremely hardy and re-sistant to frost when mature, the young plants need a humid climate and cool soil and must be protected from intense cold for the first two or three years.

8 ARAUCARIA BIDWILLII
Bunya-bunya

Family Araucariaceae. **Evergreen**
Etymology The specific name commemorates the British naturalist John C. Bidwill (1815–1853).
Habitat Native to Queensland in Australia, where it is called *bunya-bunya*.
Description This conifer, shaped like an inflated cone, can grow up to 50 m (165 ft) tall, but in mild, humid climates, which suit it well in cultivation, it assumes a more massive shape. Very graceful when young, it becomes less ornamental later, with a large part of the trunk showing naked and the lowest branches drooping toward the ground. The secondary ramifi-cations grow alternately in two lines and bear the leaves in two horizontal rows. The leaves are bright green, some 2 cm (0.75 in) long, lanceolate-acuminate, strongly scented at the tips and with parallel, flattened veins. The flowers are unisexual, the males growing as catkins, the females in round strobiles as much as 25 cm (10 in) long which, once fertilization is completed, bear a big winged seed on each scale. The seeds are edible.
Propagation By seed; by cuttings from young branches; by basal suckers.
Conditions for growth Intolerant of frost, except sporadically with adult plants.

9 ARAUCARIA EXCELSA
Norfolk Island Pine

Family Araucariaceae.   **Evergreen**
Etymology The species name comes from the Latin *excelsus*, great, referring both to its splendid shape and to the height it can reach in its natural surroundings.
Habitat Endemic on Norfolk Island, east of Australia.
Description This plant, sometimes called the "indoor fir" because young plants are grown in pots as house plants and look like little fir trees, is a huge tree in its native habitat, growing up to 60 m (200 ft), with erect habit and a thick, strong trunk whose branches grow horizontally, regularly whorled, so that the crown becomes pyramidal. The leaves (1) appear in two shapes; those on the youngest branches are light green and unscented, while those on older branches are shorter and overlapping, with a stiff point. The flowers (2) are unisexual, and the females produce rounded strobiles some 10 cm (4 in) long and 11 cm (4.5 in) broad, with a large, winged seed to every scale. The wood of the tree is used for shipbuilding.
Propagation By seed, but since growth is very slow, propagation by terminal cuttings is generally preferred. The lateral shoots that grow where the cuttings are taken can be used for further cuttings.
Conditions for growth Intolerant of frost.

10 CEDRUS ATLANTICA
Atlas Cedar

Family Pinaceae.   **Evergreen**
Etymology The name is derived from the Latin *cedrus* and Greek *kedros*, a tree that has not been definitely identified but was probably a species of *Juniperus*.
Habitat Native to the mountainous region of Algeria and Morocco, but some writers maintain that in more remote periods of the earth's history the cedar grew wild in Europe. Introduced into Europe in 1827.
Description The tree can reach a height of 50 m (165 ft) with a girth of 1.5 m (5 ft); it has a crown with a completely erect summit. The bark is gray, smooth and shiny for the tree's first 25 years but then begins to crack and form little scales. The leaves (1) are needlelike, short and stiff, flattened and curved, glossy green, joined in little tufts. The cones (2) are short and erect with a depression at the tip, at first yellowish, then violet-purple; they contain seeds with wings 2 cm (0.75 in) long. The timber is excellent for carpentry, with a strong smell that keeps insects away. A very imposing forest tree, it has two more ornamental varieties, *glauca* and *aurea*.
Propagation Only by seed, which must be ripe.
Conditions for growth In its native surroundings it grows on limestone soils, but it has adapted to slightly acid, sandstone soils also. Very resistant to pollution, it does well in mild climates and a humid atmosphere.

11 CEDRUS DEODARUS
Deodar

Family Pinaceae.   **Evergreen**
Etymology The species name is derived from the Sanskrit *devadara*, tree of the gods (whence the common Indian name, *deodar*).
Habitat Native to the Himalayas and Baluchistan, at 1100–4000 m (3600–13,000 ft).
Description Grows up to 50 m (165 ft) high; the crown is pyramidal, with an inclined head when young. The principal branches are mostly horizontal and graceful, with pendulous terminal shoots. The leaves (1) are needlelike, 2.5–5 cm (1–2 in) long and smooth. The cones (2), 7–12 cm (2.75–4.75 in) long, are conical, rounded at the end with no depression, violet at first turning to brown, and covered with smooth-backed scales; they ripen biennially. The Deodar can be recognized from other cedars by its long, soft leaves, the pendulous main branches and the cones with no depression at the tip. It is used in Asia for the construction of temples. In ancient Egypt it was used to make sarcophagi for mummies. Highly ornamental.
Propagation Like other cedars, by seed.
Conditions for growth Temperatures in much of the United States are too low, but the tree's rapid rate of growth and its adaptability have made it popular in California and the South.

---

12 CEDRUS LIBANI
Cedar of Lebanon

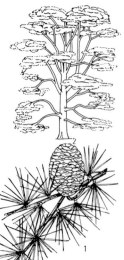

Family Pinaceae.   **Evergreen**
Etymology Named from the country of origin.
Habitat The species is still found in the mountains of Lebanon, and in the Cilicia and the Taurus Mountains at altitudes of about 2000 m (6500 ft).
Description *C. libani* possesses an imposing trunk, often branching, a dense crown with inclined head, mostly dark green, with characteristic flat growth in adult trees. The bark is dark gray. Secondary branchlets are often densely ramified like a candelabra. The terminal shoots (1) are erect or slightly inclined, never pendulous. The flowers open in September or October, which is peculiar to the genus *Cedrus* among the Abietoideae. The cones (2) are 7–10 cm (2.75–4 in) long, initially violet-purple turning to a dark green-gray. They are borne upright on the top side of the branches. The tree is mentioned in the Bible: Solomon's temple and throne room were probably built from it. It is of little economic importance because of its slow growth and its polycormic trunk and is grown for ornament.
Propagation By seed; germination is about 70–80% and the germinative period lasts for two years.
Conditions for growth Frost-free climate. Var. *stenocoma* is hardy in southern New England.

13 CHAMAECYPARIS LAWSONIANA
Lawson Cypress, Port Orford Cedar

Family   Cupressaceae.   **Evergreen**
Etymology   From the Greek, from its similarity to the true cypress; named for the Scottish nurseryman Peter Lawson.
Habitat   Northwestern United States from Coos Bay, Oregon, to the Mad River in California.
Description   This tree, growing as much as 60 m (200 ft) high with a diameter of 120–180 cm (4–6 ft), has a strong, conical crown. Very like the true cypress, so that some authorities regard it as a member of that genus, it differs from them in its remarkably flattened twigs (in the cypress they are cylindrical or rectangular in section) on which the scalelike, entire leaves (1) grow. The small, round strobiles (2), measuring 9 mm (0.33 in), glaucous at first and red-brown after a year when they ripen, have from one to four seeds equipped with wide lateral wings on each scale. Often used for hedges.
Propagation   By seed, directly on the ground when the surrounding conditions permit; but new varieties are obtained by grafting or cuttings, done in the spring. This practice is particularly important to preserve the character of the young plant throughout the tree's whole life.
Conditions for growth   Prefers deep soils. Cannot tolerate extreme temperature changes, dry winds or excessive sunlight.

---

14 CRYPTOMERIA JAPONICA
Cryptomeria, Japanese Cedar

Family   Taxodiaceae.   **Evergreen**
Etymology   The name is derived from the Greek *cryptos,* hidden, and *meros,* part, because the parts of the flower are not easy to distinguish.
Habitat   Native to Japan, forming vast forests in the north of Hondo, and to southeast China. Introduced into Europe in 1844.
Description   A tree that can reach a height of 50 m (165 ft), with a pyramidal crown and straight, slender trunk protected by a red-brown fibrous bark which peels off in long strips. The graceful branchlets, green at first and turning dark red, are sometimes deciduous. The leaves (1), arranged spirally and persisting usually for five years, are 1–2 cm (0.5–0.75 in) long and have a roughly rectangular section. They show bright green in summer, then in autumn a pigment that protects them from the cold gives them a dirty red-bronze color which they keep until the next spring. (2) flowers. The spherical cones (3) are terminal; they ripen in the first year and remain on the tree for many months after dissemination has taken place.
Propagation   By seeds, germinates in seedbeds, or by cuttings, 10 cm (4 in) long, rooted in a coldframe.
Conditions for growth   For good development the tree needs light soils, deep and fertile, and high humidity. Injured by frost.

15 CUPRESSUS ARIZONICA (C. GLABRA)
Smooth Arizona Cypress

Family Cupressaceae.   **Evergreen**
Etymology The Latin name comes from the earlier Greek. The Greek *kuparissos* commemorates a youth of that name, turned into a cypress tree by Apollo.
Habitat Native to the mountains of Arizona and southern New Mexico, at altitudes of 1300 to 2400 m (4000 to 8000 ft).
Description A slender tree growing to a maximum of 20 m (65 ft), with a dense crown formed by short branches covered with a brownish-red bark. The leaves (1), ovate and scalelike, about 2 mm (less than 0.01 in) long, gray-blue and glandular, may exude a white resin and give off an unpleasant smell when burned. The strobiles (2) are small spheres 0.5–2 cm (0.25 in–1 in) in diameter, growing in clusters on stalks; red-brown but with a glaucescent bloom, they are formed of 6–8 pointed scales and ripen in the second year, though they persist a long time on the plant. The seeds are elongated, with narrow wings. This tree differs from other cypresses in the blue color of its foliage and its disagreeable smell.
Propagation By seed. Sometimes grafted to better rootstock to hold it upright against wind.
Conditions for growth Xerophilous; prefers alkaline soils but will adapt to acid.

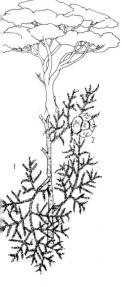

16 CUPRESSUS MACROCARPA
Monterey Cypress

Family Cupressaceae.   **Evergreen**
Etymology The species name refers to the large size of the fruit.
Description A tree that can grow to a height of 25 m (80 ft) and has a thick, dark brownish-red bark, turning light gray in old specimens and breaking off in flat scales. The crown may take various shapes, classified by some authorities as *lambertiana* with a wide top; *fastigiata* with a narrower top; *guadalupensis*, from the island of that name, characterized by bark that breaks off in very thin scales; *farallonensis*, native to the Farallon Islands, with glaucous foliage. The leaves (1), scalelike and lying flat against the branches, light green in the type species, are triangular and aromatic. The strobiles (2) are formed of 10–12 polygonal scales, angular and pointed; they are green at first, then gray, brown, a rather light greenish gray-brown, and finally brownish-violet. The seeds are winged, with little resinous glands. This cypress can be distinguished from *C. sempervirens* by its larger leaves, and from other species by the larger strobiles and the branches set obliquely on the trunk. The tree is very ornamental and can be used as a windbreak.
Propagation By seed; grows very quickly.
Conditions for growth Will not stand severe frosts; likes a humid atmosphere; indifferent to the nature of the soil.

17 CUPRESSUS SEMPERVIRENS
Italian or Mediterranean Cypress

Family Cupressaceae   **Evergreen**
Etymology The specific name marks the persistence of the foliage, giving the crown its dark-green color.
Habitat Grows wild in regions bordering the eastern Mediterranean.
Description A tree 20–30 m (65–100 ft) high, with a great variety of forms of crown, among the most typical being the spreading form of the var. *horizontalis* and the pyramidal var. *stricta*, wrongly called female and male cypress. A very long-lived plant, it has an erect trunk and gray-brown bark, fibrous and furrowed longitudinally. The scalelike leaves (1), growing along the branchlets like tiles, are dark green with resinous glands which secrete *oleum cupressi*, used in the pharmaceutical industry. This plant is monoecious, that is, it has both male and female flowers on the same specimen. The round cones (2), 3–4 cm (1.25–1.75 in) in diameter, are composed of 8–12 scutate woody scales. The wood is resistant to rot and was used in old times to make boxes for the storage of valuable objects.
Propagation By seed.
Conditions for growth Likes warmth, resistant to drought, will adapt to all kinds of soil and of country. Grows from sea level to altitudes of 700–800 m (2300–2600 ft) according to the climate.

18 CYCAS REVOLUTA

Family Cycadaceae.   **Evergreen**
Etymology The name comes from the Greek *kykas*, used by Theophrastus for a plant not definitely identified.
Habitat Originally from eastern Asia, from southern Japan to Java.
Description Though very like a palm, this slow-growing little tree will reach a height of only 3.5 m (11 ft) in ideal conditions. It does not belong to the palm family but to one of the oldest known classes of plants—so old that, apart from the Gingko, the Cycadaceae are the only ones still living; all the others are known only as fossils. The plants have a very slow growth rate, and the trunk becomes scarred by the persistent bases of fallen leaves, often surrounded by a great many suckers. The leaves (1) are as much as 2 m (6 ft) long, deflexed and pinnate, with a number of thin, stiff segments with sharply pointed tips, forming a big crown at the top of the trunk. The trees are dioecious, with very simple flowers (2); the males resemble strobiles made of scales and carry the pollen sacs; the females grow in a big rosette of carpellary leaves with the ovules on the lower part, protected by a thick down.
Propagation By seed or basal suckers.
Conditions for growth Very hardy, resists frost.

19 GINGKO BILOBA
Maidenhair tree

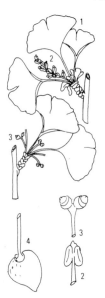

Family Gingkoaceae.   **Deciduous**
Etymology The name comes from the Japanese 'gin-kyo', used in the 17th century and wrongly transcribed. Many modern authorities have adopted the spelling 'Ginkyo'.
Habitat Native to China, where fossils of this plant have been discovered dating from the Mesozoic period. The tree has only been able to survive because it was cultivated by monks.
Description A deciduous tree, dioecious, which reaches a height of 40 m (130 ft); the bark is reddish. Male specimens especially have an elegant shape; female trees are more spreading. The flabellate leaves (1) have the upper margin irregularly toothed, and are divided by a deep incision which cuts them into two lobes; they have a great number of veins, and are glossy green in colour, though becoming golden yellow before they fall. The reproductive elements are insignificant: the male flowers (2) grow as catkins, the stalked females (3) spring from the axils of scale-like bracts and are followed by fruit in the form of false drupes (4) with a fleshy, evil-smelling pericarp.
Propagation By seed, or by cuttings of soft wood, or by grafting in order to avoid female specimens. The tree will take 30 years to reach a height of 10 m (33 ft).
Conditions for growth Very adaptable; tolerates all climates.

20 JUNIPERUS COMMUNIS
Common Juniper

Family Cupressaceae.   **Evergreen**
Etymology The name has kept its original Latin form.
Habitat A species widely distributed in almost the whole of the Northern Hemisphere, from sea level to 3750 m (12,000 ft).
Description Generally bushy or trailing, the plant has arboreal forms which can reach a height of 10 m (33 ft), though the trunk is never more than 10 cm (4 in) in diameter. The branchlets are triangular in section, the bark smooth and glossy at first, becoming gray-brown. The needlelike, aromatic leaves (1), 10–14 mm (nearly 0.5 in) long, are glaucous green. The globose female flowers (2) have a number of sterile scales underneath and three fertile scales above; these last, after fertilization, swell up and grow together to form a round, fleshy body (3), wrongly called a berry (strictly, it should be called a cone). Green at first, then frosted violet-black, they ripen every two years in Mediterranean climates and every three years in cooler climates. They contain three triangular seeds. The resinous, aromatic cones are used in the preparation of medicinal juniper and for flavoring gin; they can also be used for flavoring certain foods, game or venison, for example.
Propagation By seed; a slow grower.
Conditions for growth Hardy, adapts to all soils.

21 JUNIPERUS OXYCEDRUS
Prickly Juniper

Family Cupressaceae.   **Evergreen**
Etymology From the Greek *oxys*, pungent, and *cedrus*, which meant a tree—probably a juniper.
Habitat Mediterranean species, as far as Spain, to Portugal and from Madeira into Algeria; its eastern limits are the Crimea and the Caucasus.
Description Scarcely reaches 8 m (25 ft). The leaves (1), needlelike and whorled, are glaucous and have two white stomatic lines on the lower surface; the upper surface is green. Very much like the common juniper, this species can be distinguished by the strobile (2), which is generally larger, reddish when ripe but sometimes covered with a bloom that makes it look bluish red; it contains two or three seeds. The Prickly Juniper (sometimes called the Red Juniper) is a typical component of the Mediterranean maquis, particularly its subspecies *macrocarpa*, which is notable for its large cones. Juniper wood is compact, hard, sticky and resinous.
Propagation All junipers reproduce by seeds extracted from cones that have been stratified for 18 months; some varieties reproduce from cuttings taken in late summer.
Conditions for growth Will not tolerate too-cold climates. Withstands drought and adapts to lime in the soil.

22 JUNIPERUS VIRGINIANA
Eastern Red Cedar, Pencil Cedar

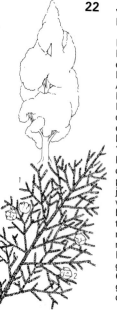

Family Cupressaceae.   **Evergreen**
Etymology The species name records the region of origin.
Habitat Occupies a fairly extensive area in North America, from Hudson's Bay and the Great Lakes to Florida and Texas.
Description Usually of moderate size, but in ideal conditions it can reach a height of 30 m (100 ft); it has deep roots, a dense crown and reddish-brown bark. The leaves (1) are of two types, needlelike and more than 1 cm (0.5 in) long, and scalelike and opposite, overlapping; the latter are those of the adult plant, but it is quite possible to find the pointed needles of a juvenile plant on a plant that is well developed. (2) cone. This juniper, wrongly called a cedar, produces the best of all wood for pencils. It is also used in "cedar" closets because of its fragrance, which is supposedly anathema to moths; and for fence posts, because of its resistance to rot. Oil of cedar is extracted from the wood and used for medicinal purposes and in perfumery.
Propagation From seed, like the other species of the genus.
Conditions for growth This tree is hardy and will grow on most types of soil. It self-seeds so freely it can quickly take over pastures. It grows rapidly.

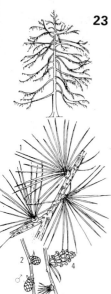

23 LARIX DECIDUA
European Larch

Family Pinaceae.   **Deciduous**
Etymology The name is the same as that used in Latin.
Habitat Grows wild on all central European mountains. *L. laricina* (Tamarack) is the North American variety.
Description This conifer, one of the very few that are deciduous, is a big tree with a straight trunk, whose bark, smooth at first, thickens with age and cracks into plates, gray on the outside and red-brown within. It can grow to a height of 40 m (130 ft), with a trunk diameter of more than 1.5 m (5 ft). The branches are whorled, the terminal shoots pendulous; the leaves (1) grow in clusters of 30–40, about 3 cm (1.25 in) long, and turn a beautiful golden yellow before they fall. The inflorescences, male and female, are carried on the same branches: the males (2) are reddish and covered with scales, the females (3) are small, solitary, erect cones of a yellowish brown, with pointed scales. (4) cone. The wood is heavy, with reddish heartwood smelling strongly of resin; it is extremely durable and is used for boatbuilding.
Propagation By seed.
Conditions for growth Mountainous zones up to 2000 m (6500 ft); also in fresh, damp climates and soils at lower altitudes, as in England. May be attacked by a fungus that causes the disease known as larch canker.

24 METASEQUOIA GLYPTOSTROBOIDES
Dawn Redwood, Water Larch

Family Taxodiaceae.   **Deciduous**
Etymology The name is derived from the Greek *meta*, together or near, and *Sequoia*, referring to their botanical similarities.
Habitat This species, found in the fossil state in Japan in 1941, was discovered living in central China near the Yangtze River shortly afterwards, and from there was introduced into America and Europe.
Description This deciduous tree, which in its homeland reaches a height of 30 m (100 ft), is naturally much smaller where cultivation has only recently begun, though there are already specimens more than 15 m (50 ft) tall. The shape is pyramidal and regular, with branches growing almost horizontally. The bark is grayish and breaks off in strips; the trunk of the biggest specimens is often deeply fissured and reddish. The linear leaflets (1) are green turning yellow and deep red-gold before falling in late autumn. The flowers are unisexual: the female flowers produce globose, green cones (2), somewhat angular, which grow solitary on long stalks. The secondary branchlets fall with the leaves, but the following year's buds persist below them.
Propagation By seed, or by softwood cuttings.
Conditions for growth Hardy; needs high humidity.

25 PICEA ABIES
Norway Spruce

Family Pinaceae.   **Evergreen**
Etymology From the Latin *pix*, pitch, resin, referring
to the great amount of resin produced by some species.
Habitat Covers a vast area, from Scandinavia to the
Balkans, as far as the Alps, at altitudes between 1000 m
and 2300 m (3300 ft and 7500 ft).
Description The genus *Picea* is often confused with
the firs, because of its "Christmas tree" shape. It differs
from the genus *Abies* in having the leaf (1) rectangular
rather than flat in section, in having the cones (4)
pendulous rather than erect and in the fact that the cones
fall complete after the seeds have been released instead
of disintegrating at the moment of dissemination. (2, 3)
male and female flowers. A tree of great size, the Norway
Spruce has a dark-green crown with a generally
triangular look. The reddish bark, which gives the tree the
alternative name of Red Fir, flakes off in scales. The
branchlets are long and pendulous and the branches
dip gracefully as the tree matures. From the Carpathians
to the mountains of Bohemia and in the eastern Alps,
certain groups of spruces grow which are particularly
valuable for violin sound boxes.
Propagation By seed.
Conditions for growth A very fast-growing tree that
tolerates most soils. Requires full sunlight.

26 PICEA OMORIKA
Serbian Spruce

Family Pinaceae.   **Evergreen**
Etymology The species name is derived from the local
name.
Habitat Grows between 600 m and 1400 m (2000 ft
and 4500 ft) in the southwest of the former Serbia and
the west of Bulgaria; may form pure groves.
Description On its own territory the tree can reach a
height of 35 m (115 ft) with a trunk circumference of
1.2 m (4 ft); the crown is typically narrow and pointed,
the bark dark brown, the branches short in relation to the
trunk and pendulous, with reddish branchlets covered
with a black down. The leaves (1) are more or less
flattened with a blunt tip, bright green on the upper side
and grayish on the underside, where two stomatic lines
can be seen. (2) cone. Serbian Spruce is not important in
forestry because of its slow growth rate, but it is used in
gardens as an ornamental on account of the elegance of
its leaves, which look white on the underside, and the
very narrow spike that it forms. The tree was discovered
in the Balkans in 1832 and introduced from there into
other countries in the temperate zone.
Propagation By seed.
Conditions for growth Fairly hardy; prefers limestone soils.

27 PICEA PUNGENS
Colorado Spruce, Blue Spruce

Family Pinaceae. **Evergreen**
Etymology The species name refers to the leaves' sharp points.
Habitat Between 1800 m and 3000 m (6000 ft and 10,000 ft) in the Rocky Mountains and in the south-western United States.
Description Can reach a height of 35 m (115 ft) and a trunk circumference of over 2.5 m (8 ft); the tree has a broad crown, gray-brown bark and strong, hardy young shoots, blue-green at first turning to orange, but always glabrous. The leaves (1), stiff and sharp, sparse and curved, are blue-green and give off a pleasant smell when rubbed. The cylindrical strobiles, 4–10 cm (1.5–4 in) long, have rhombic scales with the upper edge toothed; when young they are a greenish-red color, becoming bright brown when ripe. The bluish color of the leaves is more marked in the smaller varieties.
Propagation By seed, in a coldframe in March, in the open air in April. The strobiles should be gathered before they open and kept in a warm, dry place.
Conditions for growth Very frost resistant; grows well in very wet places, even on marshy ground. With age the tree loses many of its lower branches and becomes rather unsightly—especially in the eastern United States.

---

28 PINUS CEMBRA
Cembran Pine, Swiss Stone Pine

Family Pinaceae. **Evergreen**
Etymology *Pinus* from the Latin, *cembra* from its Italian name.
Habitat Distribution is divided into two sectors: in Europe, in the Alps and the Carpathians, and in Asia, from the Urals to northern Japan.
Description This is the only European conifer to have the leaves (1) triangular in section; they are rather stiff, dark greenish and glaucous, growing in clusters of five. (2) cone. (3) female flower. While the tree is young the crown is slender, with branches that come down to the ground, but later it becomes rounded. The tree grows very slowly; sexual maturity begins after about 40 years. To enable it to live in high mountainous country under exposed conditions, it has strongly developed roots which can penetrate into cracks in the rocks to anchor the plant. The large wingless seeds are edible, and magpies are very fond of them. The heartwood is yellowish brown and the whitish sapwood has many dark-brown knots. The wood is easy to work; used for intaglio work, for rustic furniture and for carving.
Propagation By seed.
Conditions for growth Does well on any kind of soil. Not very sensitive to temperature but needs plenty of water.

29 PINUS EXCELSA
Himalayan Pine, Bhutan Pine

Family Pinaceae. **Evergreen**
Etymology The species name refers to its elegant appearance. It is also called *P. wallichiana*, after Nathaniel Wallich, or *P. griffithii* after William Griffith.
Habitat At altitudes from 1600 to 4000 m (4000 to 13,000 ft) in the southeastern Himalayas as far as Afghanistan; in Burma and Yunnan.
Description Sometimes called the Weeping Himalayan Pine on account of its long leaves (1) (12–15 cm [5–6 in] long), partly pendant and silver-blue, and its long, pedunculate, pendulous cones (2), this is an outstanding ornamental. It grows 25–50 m (80–165 ft) tall, has gray-brown bark which comes off in little scales and young branchlets at first glaucous and frosted, later bright gray-green, finally darkening as summer draws to an end. The thin leaves grow in clusters of five. The male flowers, forming catkins, appear in May; the females have yellow scales with red edges and appear in April at the tip of the twigs. The strobiles, 15–25 cm (6–10 in) long in groups of two or three, open when ripe to release the broad-winged seeds. The wood, which is a source of a high-quality resin, is used a good deal in the countries of origin for building and carpentry.
Propagation By seed.
Conditions for growth Likes a mild climate and humid atmosphere, tolerates a wide range of soils.

30 PINUS HALEPENSIS
Aleppo Pine

Family Pinaceae. **Evergreen**
Etymology The tree gets its specific name from the ancient city in Syria.
Habitat Grows in the Mediterranean region, where it has become widespread as a result of cultivation.
Description Not a tall tree, its trunk is often twisted. It may live 150–200 years. It has a wide crown of a lighter green than the other Mediterranean pines, which looks as if it were formed from a series of flaps owing to the arrangement of the secondary branchlets on the branches and of the leaves that grow at their tips. The bark is ash-gray at first and later becomes reddish-brown. The needlelike leaves (1) are joined in pairs, or more rarely in threes. The cones (2), ovate-conical, contain the little seeds. The wood (light sapwood and reddish brown heartwood) is strong and durable. Thanks to these qualities it was used for shipbuilding, as in the historic Roman ships of Nemi, and for piles and pit-props. Its bark is rich in tannin, used in the dressing of skins and hides and by fishermen to dye their nets.
Propagation By seed sown directly in the ground or in seedbeds in autumn.
Conditions for growth Not very demanding, adapts to all kinds of soil, but needs plenty of warmth and light; tolerates drought.

31 PINUS MUGO
Dwarf Pine, Mountain Pine

Family Pinaceae.   **Evergreen**
Etymology A name of pre-Latin origin.
Habitat A European mountain species, from the Pyrenees to the Balkans.
Description Four varieties are included under this species name: *P. rotunda*, *P. uncinata*, *P. pumilio* and *P. mughus*. Apart from the first named, these can be considered as species. The different varieties of this pine can have all sorts of shapes, from prostrate to erect, with all the intervening forms. *P. montanus* sp. *mugo*, as many authorities classify it, is the smallest of the European pines, often with whippy, prostrate branches, whorled, with the ends turning upward. The linear leaves, glaucous and dark green, pungent, grow in clusters of two or sometimes three. The tree has an important protective function in high mountains, where it does a good deal to consolidate drifting snow, its long branches hindering the movement of potential avalanches. The hard, strong wood, heavy and compact, is of little practical use since the tree is so small. An essential oil which has famous medicinal qualities against catarrh and as a balsam is distilled from the twigs. In the photograph, *P. mugo* is shown in the foreground, in its prostrate form.
Propagation By seed.
Conditions for growth Very resistant to the hard climate of high mountains.

32 PINUS NIGRA
Austrian Pine, Black Pine

Family Pinaceae.   **Evergreen**
Etymology The specific name refers to the color of the crown.
Habitat The species is distributed in quite small isolated areas, from Spain to the Crimea, from Asia Minor to Austria and from Algeria to Morocco.
Description The Black Pine is a tall tree, as much as 40 m (130 ft), very long lived and resinous, generally with a straight, dense crown and whorled branches growing horizontally. The dark-gray bark cracks and breaks up in the oldest trees to form big, rugged hollows. The linear leaves (1) are pointed, 8–18 cm (3–7 in) long, in pairs; they are dark green and very glossy. (2, 3) male and female flowers. The ovate-conical strobiles (4), solitary or in groups of two or four, are brightly colored. This description applies to *P. nigra* in the general sense, but the name covers a number of minor species and geographical races which are not always easily distinguishable; shape, ecology and specific area of growth are decisive. The species is thus a collective one, in which we can distinguish four others: *P. clusiana*, *P. laricio*, *P. nigricans* and *P. pallasiana*.
Propagation By seed.
Conditions for growth This pine needs good light from above and tolerates lateral density.

33 PINUS PINASTER
Maritime pine

Family Pinaceae.   **Evergreen**
Etymology The specific name comes from the Latin, a pejorative form of the domestic pine 'pinus'.
Habitat Eastern Mediterranean and the Atlantic coast of France.
Description Not a long-lived tree. The trunk is usually straight but sometimes curved like a sabre; it can reach heights of 20–30 m (65–100 ft) and a diameter of 1 m (3 ft). The dark green crown is pyramidal in the juvenile stage but spreads rather more in later years. The bark is deeply fissured and has a dark red tinge inside; outside it is a violaceous brown. The leaves (1), acuminate and up to 20 cm (8 in) long, grow in pairs and become denser towards the ends of the branches. The cones (2), growing two or more together round a branch, are 10–20 cm (4–8 in) long, green at first turning bright reddish. A productive tree, resistant to salt, its big, strong roots are able to fix shifting sand very quickly, and the tree is effective in colonizing coastal areas, forming a screen that protects the groves of domestic pines further inland.
Propagation Exclusively by seed.
Conditions for growth Prefers sandy soils with acid reaction; likes light, fears severe cold.

34 PINUS PINEA
Italian Stone Pine

Family Pinaceae.   **Evergreen**
Etymology The specific name refers to the production of pinecones.
Habitat Indigenous to the northern and eastern Mediterranean regions, this tree has been known since ancient times.
Description A majestic tree that reaches a height of 25 m (80 ft), the rounded crown in the juvenile stage widening into an "umbrella" on maturity. The bark is gray-brown and fissured; the scales fall off from time to time leaving light-brown patches. The long, needlelike leaves (2) are paired on a sheath base. The insignificant male flowers grow in catkins and produce an enormous amount of pollen. The strobiles (1) are solitary, composed of woody scales, and among these the seeds form, covered with a blackish powder. The seeds are large and enclosed in a woody shell; the interior, which already contains the embryo, is edible. The seeds take three years to ripen, when the scales open and fall to the ground before the cones, which remain on the branches.
Propagation By seed; bare-root transplants will never succeed. Growth is very slow and the tree can live a remarkably long time, up to 250 years.
Conditions for growth Light, limefree soils; sunny position; does not tolerate prolonged temperatures below −12 °C (10 °F).

35 PINUS STROBUS
Eastern White Pine

Family Pinaceae.   **Evergreen**
Etymology The species name denotes a resiniferous tree. The common name refers to the almost-white wood.
Habitat Widespread in southeastern Canada and the northeastern United States.
Description May exceed 40 m (130 ft) in height. Young specimens have a conical crown with branches down to the ground; with age, the tree loses many of its lower branches and develops a wide, flat top. Young branches emerge covered with hairs, but in their first spring they become smooth and orange-brown in color. The leaves (1) are 10–15 cm (4–6 in) long, bluish-green, flexible, grouped in fives. (2, 3) male and female flowers. The strobiles (4), 20–25 cm (8–10 in) long and often slightly curved, are pendulous when ripe; they release the seeds in September, remaining on the tree themselves until the next spring. Once plentiful and used for all types of construction, today the soft, white, straight-grained wood is primarily reserved for millwork.
Propagation By seed.
Conditions for growth One of the least light-loving pines, tolerates a certain amount of shade. Grows in a wide variety of soils. Subject to damage by the white pine weevil and blister rust.

36 PODOCARPUS NERIIFOLIUS

Family Podocarpaceae.   **Evergreen**
Etymology The name comes from the Greek *podos*, foot, and *karpos*, fruit, from the fruit's fleshy stalk.
Habitat Native to the Himalayan region, but with varieties as far as the Sunda Islands.
Description Large, evergreen tree which can grow to a height of 15–20 m (50–65 ft), with a solid, much-branching trunk and a spreading crown. The leaves (1) are sparse, sometimes whorled but always rather close growing, especially on the secondary branchlets; they are lanceolate-acuminate, narrower at the base, with a short stalk and prominent central veins, glossy dark green, not uncommonly lighter or translucent toward the edge; on maturity they may become slightly curled, and by that time they reach a length of more than 10 cm (4 in). The flowers (2) are unisexual, nearly always solitary. The males are sometimes clustered in brown catkins; the females, greenish, with a succulent stalk, give way to a naked seed which ripens in about two years, with a fleshy, ovoid, greenish growth on a dark stalk about 1 cm (0.5 in) in diameter (3).
Propagation By seed; reproduction by cuttings is difficult.
Conditions for growth Half-hardy; when mature will tolerate occasional frosts. Prefers cool soils.

37 PSEUDOTSUGA MENZIESII
Douglas Fir

Family Pinaceae.   **Evergreen**
Etymology From the Greek *pseudes*, false, and the generic name *Tsuga*, from its resemblance to that genus. The common name is owed to the fact that it was once assigned to the genus *Abies*, and commemorates David Douglas (1798–1834), the greatest of all botanist-explorers, who introduced the seeds into Europe.
Habitat Native to the western part of North America as far as Canada, where it forms great forests.
Description Among the biggest trees in the world, the Douglas Fir can reach a height of almost 100 m (330 ft), with a straight, cylindrical trunk. The bark is grayish at first, smooth and highly resinous, later becoming red-brown and cracking into irregular ridges and fissures. The branches, downy when young, have reddish-brown buds and soft leaves (1) about 3 cm (a little over 1 in) long, with a strong smell of resin. The strobiles, pendulous and ovoid, are solitary and terminal, with light-colored trifid bracts extending beyond the dark scales. (2, 3) male and female flowers. The timber, of great strength, can be obtained in commercially important amounts, since the tree grows quickly.
Propagation By seed.
Conditions for growth Remarkably adaptable, but prefers cool, deep soil; easily grafted.

38 SEQUOIADENDRON GIGANTEUM
Wellingtonia, Giant Sequoia, "Big Tree"

Family Pinaceae.   **Evergreen**
Etymology The name comes from that of the genus *Sequoia*, to which the plant is often assigned, and from the Greek *dendron*, tree.
Habitat A limited area in central California.
Description These are among the tallest and most long lived trees in the world; the trunk can reach a height of 96 m (310 ft) and the age of many trees may be anything between 2000 and 3500 years, though it is not possible to be certain since no specimen has ever died of old age—only as the result of some accident. The general shape is pyramidal; the huge trunk has red-brown fibrous bark and the branches are carried high up, hanging down a little, to crown the gigantic bare trunk. The buds grow from the persistent leaves (1), which are scalelike and pointed, up to 6 mm (0.25 in) long. The male flowers form axillary and terminal clusters, the female apical clusters made up of whorled scales each having 4–7 ovules at the base. The ovoid strobiles (2) ripen in two years; they are erect when young but become pendulous on ripening.
Propagation By seed.
Conditions for growth Despite the small natural distribution area, the trees will thrive in any cool and humid climate.

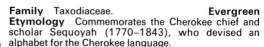

39   SEQUOIA SEMPERVIRENS
Coast Redwood

Family Taxodiaceae.   **Evergreen**
Etymology Commemorates the Cherokee chief and scholar Sequoyah (1770–1843), who devised an alphabet for the Cherokee language.
Habitat   Native to California and Oregon.
Description   Reckoned to be one of the tallest trees, if not the tallest, in the world, the Coast Redwood can grow to 110 m (355 ft). It has an erect trunk with reddish-brown, spongy bark furrowed with deep fissures, which gives the tree its common name. The form is slender, the crown narrow, an irregular pyramid; the leaves (1) are small and needlelike, arranged in spiral rows and having three resin canals. The flowers (2) form at the tip of the shoots. They appear in autumn and open in the spring; the females are composed of 15–20 pointed scales which become small, woody, brown-red strobiles (3), with 4–5 seeds to each scale, ripening in about a year. The beautiful reddish-brown wood is moderately strong and very easy to work, and is widely used — particularly because of its high resistance to decay and termites.
Propagation   By seed, but the tree often puts out shoots from the stump after felling, and even from broken-off knots. Also by cuttings, under glass.
Conditions for growth   Fairly mild climate, in cool soils.

40   TAXODIUM DISTICHUM
Bald Cypress, Swamp Cypress

Family Taxodiaceae.   **Deciduous**
Etymology From the Greek *taxos*, yew tree, and *eidos*, resemblance, from the leaves, which resemble those of other species of *Taxus*.
Habitat   Native from Mississippi to Florida, in swampy regions and along river banks.
Description   This deciduous conifer can grow as high as 40 m (130 ft) and forms a narrow pyramid when young, but in the adult stage the crown becomes less regular and more flattened. The reddish-brown bark has long, shallow cracks. When planted in marshy soil the trunk develops enlarged, fluted, buttresslike roots and strange protuberances ("knees") which take in air for the roots. The leaves (1) are linear and pointed, about 1 cm (0.5 in) long and light green; in the autumn they change from tawny to brown. The alternate shoots do not lengthen the branches but fall together with the leaves. The unisexual flowers are carried on the same plant, the males in pendulous, branching clusters, the females in little strobiles (2). The lumber is especially valued for its excellent resistance to decay and termites.
Propagation   By seed, or by cuttings in ground saturated with water.
Conditions for growth   Fairly hardy; frost tolerant. Requires considerable moisture at the roots but is not demanding about soil.

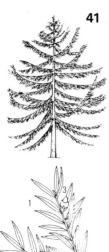

41 TAXUS BACCATA
English Yew

Family Taxaceae.   **Evergreen**
Etymology The specific name is the old Latin name;
the English name is from Welsh *yw*.
Habitat From northern Europe to North Africa and, in
Asia, as far as the Caucasus.
Description An evergreen conifer, dioecious, which
can grow to 10–15 m (33–50 ft), with reddish bark
which is smooth at first but peels off in thin flakes with
age, becoming rather rough. Remarkably long lived. With
time the heartwood is destroyed, leaving the center
hollow. Fossils have been discovered dating from the
Tertiary, and there are specimens about 1500 years old.
The crown is irregular, globose, branching low; the
leaves (1) are linear, sickle-shaped, dark green on top
and growing spirally. The male flowers (2) grow in
clusters; the females produce a "berry" containing a
single seed (3), green at first, turning to bright red. The
leaves and seeds are highly poisonous, but the pulp
surrounding the seeds is harmless and is eaten by birds.
Slow growing; popular for hedges and topiary art.
Propagation By seed.
Conditions for growth Cool, humid climate with
lime in the soil.

42 THUJA OCCIDENTALIS
American Arborvitae, White Cedar

Family Cupressaceae.   **Evergreen**
Etymology The name seems to be derived from the
Greek *thyon* or *thia*, a tree that produced resin or incense;
the resin was burnt as incense during religious cere-
monies.
Habitat This species lives in southeastern Canada and
the northeastern United States, from Nova Scotia to
North Carolina.
Description A tall tree, generally 18–20 m (60–65 ft),
with a pyramidal crown when young, becoming irregular
later; thick trunk divided in two or three at the base, with
horizontal branches curved at the ends and pendulous
branchlets. The leaves, opaque green on the upper
surface and yellowish green below, are small and
scalelike, overlapping and persistent. The strobiles are
ovoid, often growing in groups; they are composed of
5–6 pairs of scales, not pointed, only two pairs of which
are fertile; the seeds are winged. The foliage is compact
and has an aromatic scent due to the presence of a
poisonous oil. The wood, soft and light, is used in
building and as the source of oil of cedar, which is used
for medical purposes.
Propagation By seed; also from cuttings.
Conditions for growth The tree will grow on
different kinds of soil (best if limed), and tolerates
drought, low temperatures and pollution.

43 THUJA ORIENTALIS
Oriental Arborvitae, Chinese Thuja

Family Cupressaceae.   **Evergreen**
Etymology The proper name is *Biota orientalis*, from the Greek *bios*, life; it is not certain whether it was given this name for its capacity to tolerate unlimited pruning or because it was used as a cure for scurvy.
Habitat Native to Manchuria and Korea, but cultivated in all Asian countries.
Description Of modest size, not more than 12 m (40 ft) tall. Both branches and shoots are erect and the former are often no longer than the diameter of the trunk. The bark is thin and red-brown; the leaves (1), persistent, scalelike and opposite, are smaller than those of other species (1.5 mm, or 0.06 in) and have no glands. The strobiles (2), ovoid and fleshy, glaucous green at first turning reddish brown, are formed of 6–8 thick scales that bear downcurved hooks which protect the 1–2 wingless seeds. This tree differs from other species of *Thuja* in having the leafed branchlets smaller and arranged vertically, in the glandless leaves which have a depression along the center, and in the wingless seeds. Nurserymen have produced a great number of varieties.
Propagation By seed and by cuttings.
Conditions for growth Adapts to a wide range of soils but prefers sandy. Tolerates drought and, like all *Thuja*, dislikes stagnant water collecting around its roots.

44 THUJOPSIS DOLOBRATA
Hiba, False Arborvitae

Family Cupressaceae.   **Evergreen**
Etymology So called from its resemblance to the genus *Thuja*.
Habitat Native to Japan, where it grows from sea level to 1800 m (6000 ft).
Description The sole species of the genus. The trunk is curved and divided from the base up, and does not grow taller than 25 m (80 ft); the branches may be horizontal or erect, always flattened, whitish on the underside. The thin bark is red-brown but turns grayer with age. The leaves are persistent, opposite, decussate and bright green above, with whitish patches on the underside. The strobiles are globose, composed of 6–10 wedge-shaped scales, leathery or woody, and pointed, each one shielding 3–5 small, ovoid seeds which ripen in a year. The wood, whitish yellow with a suggestion of pink, is light, strong and durable; it is used for civil and naval construction. The tree can be distinguished from *Thuja* by the larger leaves and bigger light patches on the underside, and by the squat fruit with prominent umbo.
Propagation By seed, which may not germinate readily.
Conditions for growth Fairly hardy, but needs some humidity.

45 TORREYA CALIFORNICA
California Nutmeg

Family Taxaceae.   **Evergreen**
Etymology Named in honor of the American botanist John Torrey (1796–1873).
Habitat Native to California.
Description A large evergreen tree, often more than 20 m (65 ft) tall; the bark is gray-brown and the branching fairly open; the secondary branches are pendulous. The linear leaves (1), up to 8 cm (3 in) long, grow spirally round the branches, but because the short stalks are twisted it looks as if they were opposite; they are glossy dark green on the upper side, pale with two yellow ridges on the underside, and they give off an unpleasant smell if rubbed. The flowers are unisexual: the males are joined so as to form little axillary strobiles, the females consist of a single ovule, with a scaly base. The fruits (2) are long oval drupes and consist of one seed within a hard shell surrounded by a fleshy aril, light green with violet-red stripes.
Propagation By seed; by softwood cuttings (slow); and by grafting.
Conditions for growth Young plants cannot stand frost, and even mature plants only tolerate it if it is occasional and not too prolonged.

46 TSUGA CANADIENSIS
Canadian Hemlock, Eastern Hemlock

Family Pinaceae.   **Evergreen**
Etymology From the Japanese name for the Asian species.
Habitat Native to North America.
Description A coniferous evergreen which reaches 20–35 m (65–115 ft). When mature, the trunk is often branched down to the base. The ramification is sparse and often not whorled, with thin branches; young branches are pubescent. The leaves (1) are glaucescent, 1–2 cm (0.5–0.75 in) long, generally opposite, with two whitish stomatic lines on the underside and a central resin duct; indeed, the whole plant is resinous. The flowers are unisexual; the males form globose catkins, the females are terminal, with scales each carrying two ovules at the base. The strobiles (2) are small and pendulous, with persistent scales and winged seeds. The tree stands pruning well and is often grown as a hedge rather than a tree. There are several varieties, among them the very attractive var. *pendula*, with weeping branches. The wood is soft and has no economic value, but the tannin in the bark is used for tanning hides.
Propagation By seed in the spring or from cuttings of mature wood at the end of the summer.
Conditions for growth Completely hardy, but does not tolerate strong summer heat. Grows particularly well on the banks of rivers, streams and lakes.

47 ARECA CATECHU
Betel Palm

Family Palmae.   **Evergreen**
Etymology Derived from the common name used by the people of the Malabar Coast in southwestern India.
Habitat Has a vast natural distribution area, from southern Asia across the Indonesian Archipelago to Polynesia.
Description A slender palm with erect, rather thin stem, solitary, in its homelands reaching 10–30 m (33–100 ft) in height. It has a crown of big fronds (1) up to 2 m (6 ft) long, pinnate with fairly large segments, dark green, glabrous and irregularly toothed at the tip, with unprotected stalk. Some of the outer leaves are pendulous, but the general habit is erect. The flowers are unisexual, growing in an inflorescence with branching spadix that appears below the fronds, often apart from them. The female flowers (2) grow singly, at the base of the ramification, surrounded by the smaller, white, scented male flowers. The fruit (3) is an ovoid berry, about 5 cm (2 in) long and orange colored; the seed has a smooth skin and contains a dyestuff. These seeds, boiled, sliced and dried and wrapped in the leaves of *Piper betle*, are chewed by all East Indian peoples for their slight inebriating effect.
Propagation By seed.
Environment Exclusively tropical.

---

48 BRAHEA DULCIS

Family Palmae.   **Evergreen**
Etymology Named after Tycho Brahe, the Danish astronomer (1546–1601).
Habitat Native to Mexico.
Description The erect stem reaches 6 m (20 ft); the upper part of it is generally covered with the remains of dried leaves, while the lower part remains smooth and marked by ringshaped scars left by fallen leaves. Often puts out suckers, so that several stems grow intertwined and crowned by a great number of fronds (1). These are palmate, almost round and deeply divided into about 50 segments; they are stiff, often with light filaments, and are borne on flat, convex stalks, pale at the edges, fibrous at the base (which forms a sheath) and having little teeth turned toward the base. The flowers (2) are hermaphrodite, surrounded by white down and enclosed within branched spadices which may be more than 2 m (6 ft) in length, hanging down from among the lowest leaves. The fruits (3), a little more than 1 cm (0.5 in) long, are ovoid, yellow, juicy and edible.
Propagation By seed.
Conditions for growth Thrives in mild climates and may even tolerate occasional frost. The soil should be rich in humus, sandy and moist, the atmospheric humidity should be rather high.

49 BUTIA CAPITATA

Family Palmae.   **Evergreen**
Etymology The name is taken from that commonly used in Brazil.
Habitat Native to Brazil, Uruguay and Argentina.
Description This palm was once included in the genus *Cocos* with the name of *Cocos australis*; in the trade it is still called by that name, but botanists no longer include it in the genus. The stem, scarred by the marks left by fallen leaves, is cylindrical and may reach a height of 5 m (16 ft), with a crown of leaves that may be as much as 3–4 m (10–13 ft) long, the outer ones markedly pendulous, the inner ones semierect, giving the plant the look of a spreading crown. The leaves are pinnate, divided into linear segments, glaucescent and rather stiff, often whitish on the underside, with the base of the stalk forming a fibrous sheath. The flowers are unisexual, in inflorescences having a spadix. The fruits that follow the females are orange-colored drupes the size of a pigeon's egg, with sweet, edible flesh and oily seeds.
Propagation By seed.
Conditions for growth Half-hardy, when adult tolerates frosts if they are not too long or too severe. Requires high humidity.

50 CEROXYLON ANDICOLA
Andes Palm

Family Palmae.   **Evergreen**
Etymology Derived from two Greek roots: *keros*, wax, and *xylon*, wood, whose combined meaning, "wax tree," describes this palm exactly (see below). The name was given to the plant by two famous botanist-explorers, Humboldt and Bompland, who introduced this generic name in 1807 when they published *Plantes Equinoxiales*.
Habitat Grows in the central cordillera of the Andes, up to 3000 m (10,000 ft).
Description The very tall stem, up to 30–40 m (100–130 ft) high and 1–2 m (3–6 ft) in circumference, marked in rings by the scars left by fallen leaves, is covered with a coat of gray wax which oozes out, especially from the leaf nodes, and flows over the trunk, making it look like a marble column. The leaves (1), up to 4 m (13 ft) long, are pinnate with acuminate segments, dark green on top and whitish underneath; the inflorescence (2) has a spadix that forms a beautiful yellow cluster. The fruits (3) are single-seeded berries as big as billiard balls, which turn reddish purple when ripe. The wax produced by this palm has local economic importance.
Propagation By seed, which germinates quite easily.
Conditions for growth Likes surroundings that are fairly warm and humid.

51 COCOS NUCIFERA
Coconut palm

Family Palmae.   **Evergreen**
Etymology The name seems to be derived from the Portuguese *coco*, monkey.
Habitat Widespread and cultivated for centuries throughout the tropics, but believed to be of Indo-Malayan origin.
Description This palm has a relatively slender, flexible stem which can grow to a height of 30–40 m (100–130 ft), marked in rings each year by the scars of fallen leaves and crowned by an apical cluster of huge pinnate leaves (1), 3–4 m (10–13 ft) long. The flowers (2), united in inflorescences with a spadix and bracted, are unisexual with the females below, generally solitary and formed by six twining sepals, while the numerous males grow at the top of each branch. The fruit (3) is the well-known coconut, actually a big drupe containing a sweet liquid which becomes fleshy on ripening and when dried constitutes the copra used as a source of oils and fats. The whole plant is very important economically, both for its fruit and its wood; the shoots, too, are used for food.
Propagation By seed; in nature the trees reproduce easily because the fruits float from island to island.
Conditions for growth Tropical and subtropical only.

---

52 CYRTOSTACHYS RENDA

Family Palmae.   **Evergreen**
Etymology The name is derived from the Greek *kyrtos*, curved, and *stachys*, ear of grain, in reference to the curved inflorescence.
Habitat Native to Sumatra.
Description This palm has a bare stem, erect and slender, sometimes bushing, which can reach a height of as much as 10 m (33 ft). The leaves, forming a big crown at the top of the stem, are pinnate, with linear or sword-shaped segments, generally obtuse at the tip, sometimes bifid; they are grayish on the underside, and the midrib and the base of the leaf are red. The spadix may be more than 1 m (3 ft) long, with roughly alternate branches reaching about 40 cm (16 in) long. The flowers are unisexual, enclosed within the spadix, and the fruits small and ovoid; the stigma persists at their tip.
Propagation By seed.
Conditions for growth Tropical, in warm, humid climates. Small specimens can be cultivated in the hothouse.

53 ELAEIS GUINEENSIS
Oil Palm

Family Palmae.   **Evergreen**
Etymology The name comes from the Greek *elaion*, oil, referring to the oil extracted from the palm.
Habitat Tropical Africa, west and central.
Description The stout trunk, ringed by the scars formed by fallen leaves, may grow to 20 m (65 ft) and is crowned by a big apical cluster of leaves (1) 2–5 m (6–16 ft) long, with spiny stalk and a great many linear-lanceolate, acuminate segments; the outer leaves hang down, the inner are erect, so that the crown appears almost globose. The flowers (2) are unisexual, carried in separate inflorescences; the males have a spiny tip, the females have spadices with rather big stalks, also spiny tipped, and appressate, so that when they ripen they form a dense, round mass of fruit (3) with the spines sticking out of it. There may be as many as 200–300 fruits, drupes 4 cm (1.5 in) long, with a red or blackish fleshy aril surrounding a very hard black nut with a white, soft kernel. An oil extracted from the fruit is used in the manufacture of foodstuffs and soap, and the whitish butter from the kernel is used locally in cooking.
Propagation By seed.
Conditions for growth Tropical.

---

54 ERYTHEA ARMATA
Blue Palm

Family Palmae.   **Evergreen**
Etymology This name was given by the Greeks to one of the Hesperides, the daughter of Night and the dragon Lado, and to the island where she lived, in the extreme Western Ocean; it was given to this palm by the botanist Watson in 1880 when he discovered it in Guadeloupe.
Description These are big, bare-stemmed trees terminating in a cluster of round leaves subdivided into 40–50 segments of silvery blue-green. The stalk has powerful thorns which earn the plant the epithet *armata* in the specific name. The spadices are elongated and the flowers bisexual and sessile, grow in groups of three. The fruit is more or less round, resembling that of *E. edulis*, though it is not edible. An elegant, decorative palm, it is as hardy as it is beautiful, so that it can be grown for ornamental purposes in the warmer zones of temperate climates. This attractive American palm was introduced into European gardens at the end of the 19th century, immediately after it was discovered.
Propagation By seed.
Conditions for growth Needs a sunny position with dry soil. Does not tolerate winter temperatures below freezing.

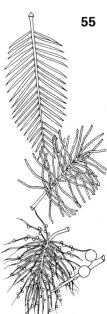

55 EUTERPE EDULIS
Assai Palm

Family Palmae.   **Evergreen**
Etymology The name, generally said to be derived from that of Euterpe, the Muse of music and lyric poetry, probably originated from the Greek *euterpes*, pleasant, attractive, from which the Muse's name also comes.
Habitat Native to Brazil.
Description Supple and slender stem up to 20–30 m (65–100 ft) high, with a feathery crown of drooping leaves, often solitary but also quite often in dense groups. The leaves are sheathed, bare, with long stalks and as many as 60–80 linear segments on either side of the midrib; they are pendulous, up to 3 m (10 ft) long. The little flowers, white and sessile, are borne in the interior of the branching spadices; the little pealike fruits are purple. The seeds are crushed in water to produce a beverage drunk locally under tha name of *assai*, and the plant is very often commonly called the Assai Palm. This plant belongs to the group known as Cabbage Palms, the young shoots of which may be eaten, either cooked or raw in salads.
Propagation By seed, which germinates in a relatively short time.
Conditions for growth Tropical; young specimens under glass.

56 HOWEA FOSTERIANA
Kentia, Curly Palm

Family Palmae.   **Evergreen**
Etymology Also known as *Howeia*; the name comes from the place of origin, the Lord Howe Islands, east of Australia, where the plant is endemic.
Habitat Only two species of the genus are known, both occurring in the Lord Howe Islands.
Description These elegant plants are undoubtedly among the best known of all palms. Young specimens are often grown as ornamental house plants, but in their original home, and if cultivated in congenial climates, they can reach heights of 20 m (65 ft), with a stout stem marked in rings by the scars from fallen leaves. The crown, at the apex, is formed of long leaves which gradually grow bigger as the plant reaches maturity; they are borne on long, thin stalks and are pinnate, with fairly broad, leathery segments. The flowers are enclosed in spadices which appear among the bases of the opposite leaves, and are unisexual; the males have rounded sepals. The fruits are drupes, rather like olives, greenish yellow. They appear in great racemes which ripen some six years after the first flush.
Propagation By seed, which must be imported, since the tree will only fruit in its country of origin.
Conditions for growth Young specimens can be grown in pots as house plants; in the open in summer.

57 HYPHAENE THEBAICA
Doum Palm

Family Palmae. **Evergreen**
Etymology From the Greek *hyphaino*, network, referring to the fibers of the fruit.
Habitat Indigenous to Upper Egypt, the Sudan and Kenya.
Description This is virtually the only palm with a branching stem; it can reach a height of 15 m (50 ft). The branches are dichotomic, continuously bifurcated, each branch bearing a rosette of fanshaped leaves at the tip, not very big, spiny stalked, with pointed segments; the outer leaves are markedly deflexed and pendulous. The stems are thin and smooth, partly covered by the bases of fallen leaves; the general habit is quite different from that of other palms. The flowers are unisexual, and the fruits that follow them are orange-yellow drupes, scented and edible.
Propagation Despite the branching stems, these palms are generally reproduced from seed, in sandy beds with as much warmth as possible.
Conditions for growth The plants are only cultivated in the countries of origin and other parts of tropical Africa. Even young specimens are rarely met in greenhouses, since their thin stems rather spoil them as ornamentals.

---

58 JUBAEA CHILENSIS
Chilean Wine Palm

Family Palmae. **Evergreen**
Etymology The name commemorates King Juba of Numidia, who lived in the 1st century B.C.
Habitat Native to Chile.
Description This genus contains only the one species, also known as *J. spectabilis*. This great palm grows as tall as 25 m (80 ft), with a stout stem covered by the bases of withered leaves and carrying at its head a great crown of long pinnate leaves with linear-lanceolate segments, rigid and forming sheaths at the base. The inner leaves are erect, the outer deflexed. The inflorescences have spadices, with unisexual flowers followed by fruit like little coconuts. (They are called *coquitos* in Chile.) The special feature of this plant is that, if the trunk is incised, it exudes a sugary liquid which will continue to flow as long as the cut is kept fresh; as much as 400 liters (105 gals) of syrup can be obtained in three months from an adult tree. In the tree's homeland the sap is boiled and a syrup obtained from it, called "palm honey," which can be fermented to produce an alcoholic drink.
Propagation By seed.
Conditions for growth Half-hardy; will tolerate occasional frosts when adult, but flourishes only in mild climates.

59 LIVISTONA AUSTRALIS
Australian Fan Palm

Family Palmae.   **Evergreen**
Etymology The name commemorates Patrick Murray,
Lord Livingstone, who as early as 1680 had a garden
with so many rare plants in it that it became the nucleus
of the Edinburgh Botanical Gardens.
Habitat Native to Australia.
Description A slender palm which can reach a height
of 20 m (65 ft) or more. The stem is marked in rings by the
scars left by the bases of fallen leaves, while in the
juvenile stage it is covered by the bases themselves and
by brownish fibers. The huge palmate leaves, leathery
and smooth, which crown the top are almost circular and
more than 1 m (3 ft) in diameter; they are divided into
two distinct parts, with narrow curved green segments
with yellowish central veins and a pointed tip that may be
entire or divided in two. There are big, curved thorns on
the stalk. The flowers are joined in long erect spadices
which become pendulous when, after fertilization, the
oblong yellow or brownish fruits appear.
Propagation By seed.
Conditions for growth Half-hardy, tolerates temperatures near 32 °C (0 °F) provided they are only
sporadic and not prolonged.

60 METROXYLON SAGO
Sago Palm

Family Palmae.   **Evergreen**
Etymology From the Greek *metro*, the pith of the
trees, and *xylon*, wood, referring to the large amount of
internal pith.
Habitat Native to the Indonesian archipelago.
Description These palms are often shrubby, with
several stems which reach a height of about 12 m (40 ft)
and a diameter of 70 cm (27 in). The large, suberect
pinnate leaves (1), with linear, acuminate, opposite
segments, can also be as long as 6 m (20 ft). The flowers
(2), polygamous or monoecious, are carried by long,
branched spadices which form a sort of broadened spike.
The fruits (3) are globose or elliptical drupes some 3 cm
(1.25 in) long, with a single seed enclosed in overlapping scales; they take several years to ripen. Each
stem dies after fruiting, but the stump puts out new
shoots. The pith is extracted by felling the tree before it
fruits, cutting it in strips and washing it out. The starch
remaining is the sago, which is used for food.
Propagation By seed.
Conditions for growth Grown only in the tropics, in
its indigenous distribution area.

61 PHOENIX CANARIENSIS
Canary Islands Date Palm

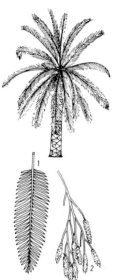

Family Palmae.   **Evergreen**
Etymology A very old name, used by Theophrastus and indicating that the tree was first introduced to the Greeks by the Phoenicians.
Habitat The Canary Islands, though now widespread through cultivation.
Description Perhaps the best known of the ornamental palms, since it can be grown in pots when young, while in the Mediterranean countries the adult trees make a beautiful show in gardens. This is a vigorous tree that can reach a height of 20 m (65 ft). The leaves (1) are pinnate, 5–7 m (16–23 ft) long, with longitudinally acuminate segments, sometimes transformed at the base into long double thorns at the node. The spadices (2) are borne on long stalks, 1 m (3 ft) or more long, and curved; the fruits, about 2 cm (0.75 in) long, are ovoid or spherical, with a yellow skin turning reddish. The tree differs from *P. dactylifera* (**62**) in having a shorter, thicker trunk and wider, stiffer leaf segments; these are bright green.
Propagation Reproduces by seed, but in the tropics propagation by division of suckers is held to retain the useful features of the plant more exactly.
Conditions for growth Temperate to warm, or at least mild.

---

62 PHOENIX DACTYLIFERA
Date Palm

Family Palmae.   **Evergreen**
Etymology The species name refers to the tree's production of the edible fruit, the date.
Habitat Native to western Asia and North Africa.
Description This palm, whose stem, covered with the bases of withered leaves, can exceed 30 m (100 ft) in height, is often confused with *P. canariensis*, which is shorter and more ornamental; but this is the only one of the genus that produces edible fruit. The leaves (1) are pinnate, upturned, glaucous, with linear-acuminate segments and spiny stalks, and form a terminal cluster. The plants are dioecious; the inflorescences are enclosed in a spathe on a branched spadix, and pollination, generally carried out artificially for commercial purposes, is effected by shaking the male inflorescence in the spathe of the female. The flowers (2) are inconspicuous. The fruit (3) is a berry whose pericarp, fleshy and sweet, is the edible part. This palm can put out suckers at the base, but the stem is never branched.
Propagation By seed or basal suckers.
Conditions for growth Easy to cultivate, but needs warmth and humidity at the roots. High temperatures and full sunlight are essential requirements. Hybrids are very common.

63 PHOENIX RECLINATA
Senegal Palm

Family Palmae.   **Evergreen**
Etymology The name given to this species refers to the stem, which becomes serpentine in adult plants.
Habitat Tropical Africa, especially Senegal.
Description This palm, which can reach a height of 8 m (26 ft), with a slender, supple stem, readily produces a number of basal suckers, and unless these are removed to permit growth the main stem remains low. The crown of leaves carried at the top is markedly downturned; the leaves themselves are pinnate, bright green, with stiff segments, acuminate and sharp at the tip, arranged in two rows. The central segment is bifid, the lower ones are spiny, the lowest so modified as to consist solely of long thorns. The plants are dioecious, with unisexual flowers growing in racemes on separate plants; many hybridizations have been attempted, sometimes successfully, especially on the Riviera in France and Italy, where the whole genus finds conditions congenial. The typical fruits are small and red, though on some hybrids they are black.
Propagation By seed.
Conditions for growth Tropical and subtropical climates, including mild climates if the cold is only sporadic and never very intense.

64 ROYSTONEA REGIA
Royal Palm

Family Palmae.   **Evergreen**
Etymology The name commemorates General Roy Stone (1836–1905), who was in Puerto Rico with the American army. The tree was formerly called *Oreodoxa* and is still sometimes so called.
Habitat Has a vast area of natural distribution, from Florida as far as the northern parts of South America.
Description This robust palm grows up to 30 m (100 ft) or more, with a smooth, erect trunk which sometimes has a swelling above the central part, though that feature may be missing. The leaves form an apical cluster; graceful and deflexed, they are unarmed, pinnate, and opposite, with an equal number of segments growing either side of the midrib. The stalk is a half-cylinder, unarmed, forming a sheath, and the whole leaf can reach a length of 3–6 m (10–20 ft). The flowers, small and white, are clustered in spadices with pendulous branches. The fruits are violet-black, globose or oblong, and the seeds are rather small.
Propagation By seed.
Conditions for growth Tropical and subtropical, in warm, humid conditions.

65 SABAL PALMETTO
Caribbean Cabbage Palm

Family Palmae.   **Evergreen**
Etymology The name probably comes from that commonly used in South America.
Habitat Grows wild in the southern United States from South Carolina to Florida, and also occurs in the West Indies.
Description These palms can reach a height of 20–25 m (65–80 ft). The stem is erect and robust, almost always covered with persistent leaf-bases and encrusted with the sheaths of dried leaves. The top is crowned by a large cluster of leaves, pinnatifid with long linear segments, partly deflexed; the long stalk, with its sheath, is erect in the central leaves, curved outward in the outer ones. The segments are thready at the edges, green above and grayish below and deeply indented at the center. The small, white flowers grow on long, branching and spreading spadices, shorter than the leaves; the fruits that follow are drupes, black when ripe and about 1 cm (0.5 in) long. *S. palmetto* is the emblem of South Carolina and is depicted on its state flag.
Propagation By seed, or by basal shoots if they appear.
Conditions for growth Very fertile and well irrigated soil in very mild climates. When adult the plants will withstand sporadic cold.

---

66 SABAL TEXANA
Texas Palmetto

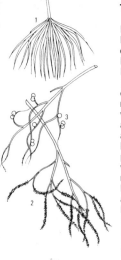

Family Palmae.   **Evergreen**
Etymology The species name comes from the place of origin.
Habitat Endemic in southern Texas.
Description This palm is a robust-looking tree, 15 m (50 ft) or more tall with a trunk about 45 cm (18 in) in diameter, reddish brown on the outside. It is one of the most elegant of the genus, though often the bases of the withered leaves, or even the leaves themselves, remain attached to the stem for a long time. The crown of foliage at the top is dense and rounded; the leaves (1) have a long, reddish stalk and are fan shaped, with ribbed, palmate, deeply incised lamina as much as 1 m (3 ft) wide; the segments are acuminate, pendant and partly rotated, with slightly thready margins. The scented, hermaphrodite flowers (2) grow in inflorescences which are generally longer than the leaves, and greatly branched. They are followed by globose, blackish fruits (3), drupes with prominent micropyle.
Propagation By seed.
Conditions for growth Mild climate and soil with a high organic content.

67 TRACHYCARPUS FORTUNEI
Chusan Palm, Windmill Palm

Family Palmae.   **Evergreen**
Etymology The name comes from the Greek *trachys*, rough, scabrous, and *karpos*, fruit, describing the fruit of the species.
Habitat Native to China.
Description A palm with a strong stem covered with the sheaths of old leaves and with long, dark-brown fibers which make it look shaggy. The leaves, forming a great apical cluster, have a long, unarmed stalk and the circular lamina is divided into numerous sword-shaped, dark green segments. The flowers appear on a number of long, branching spadices, and may be unisexual or hermaphrodite on the same plant; they are small, with three sepals and three petals, and the fruits that follow them are globoid or kidney shaped, blue or bluish, with a deep furrow.
Propagation By seed.
Conditions for growth This palm is one of the most resistant to cold and will even tolerate temperatures below freezing once it is mature. Young specimens, however, must be sheltered in the cool greenhouse in less favorable climates.

68 WASHINGTONIA FILIFERA
Petticoat Palm, California Fan Palm

Family Palmae.   **Evergreen**
Etymology Named in honor of George Washington.
Habitat Native to California and Arizona.
Description These palms, which may grow to 10–12 m (33–40 ft), have erect, cylindrical stems, wider at the base and partly covered with withered leaves which, when they fall, leave a scar on the bark, which is consequently striped in rings. The leaves (1) have long stalks with spines almost halfway up; they are erect at first, but later they bend outward. The linear segments are spread almost like a fan and their margins have a certain number of fibrous threads. The inflorescences are ramified spadices bearing spikes, with thin, supple branches; the bracts are membraneous and glabrous. The little, white, insignificant flowers are followed by fruits (2) that consist of a black drupe with a brown seed, rather flattened.
Propagation By seed, rather slow to germinate. As with the whole family, growth is far from rapid.
Conditions for growth Grows in mild climates, though it can tolerate several degrees below freezing if the frost is sporadic and not prolonged. Where the climate permits, it is often planted as a border to avenues in large gardens.

69 ACACIA HORRIDA

Family Leguminosae.   **Evergreen**
Etymology The specific name denotes the vicious-
ness of the thorns.
Habitat Arid regions of northern and central Africa.
Description The trunk can reach 4–7 m (13–23 ft),
and has sparse, thorny branches that form a fairly regular
rounded crown. The alternate leaves (1) are composed
of 3–7 pinnules, formed in their turn from ten pairs of
linear leaflets with obtuse points, pale green, somewhat
glaucescent. The stipules, transformed into spines,
branch in two; they are robust, white and sharply
pointed, 3–6 cm (1.25–2.50 in) long. The scented,
yellow flowers (2) are arranged in fairly large globose,
rather feathery heads growing from the leaf axils; the tree
flowers in July and August. The fruits (3) are big,
oblong, blackish legumes containing 3–5 seeds. In its
original habitat this species shows how well it can adapt
to a hot, dry climate. It is similar in general appearance to
A. cavenia but can easily be distinguished from it by the
conspicuous long white thorns, especially in young
specimens. In some regions of very low rainfall, in
southern Italy for example, it is cultivated for its
abundant summer flowers.
Propagation By seed and by layering.
Conditions for growth Indifferent to the nature of
the soil. Tolerates drought.

70 ACER CAMPESTRE
Hedge or Field Maple

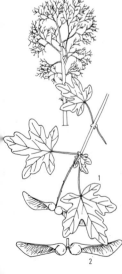

Family Aceraceae.   **Deciduous**
Etymology The name has kept the form of the original
Latin.
Habitat Has a vast natural distribution area, extending
from the north of England, south of Sweden and Russia
over a great part of Europe, as far as western Asia.
Description The tree is 15–20 m (50–65 ft) high,
often with a twisted trunk. The crown is rounded, and the
gray-brown bark cracks into rectangular plates. The
medium-sized leaves (1) are palmate, with 3–5 lobes of
which the central one can in turn be trilobate, dark green
above, paler and pubescent below, and rather leathery;
in autumn, before they fall, they turn yellow and then red.
The flowers are yellowish green, in erect clusters. The
fruit (2) is a characteristic disamara, rather like the blades
of a helicopter; an outstanding example of how far
nature anticipated man with inventions essential to the
propagation of species and their establishment over wide
territories. The samaras of the Field Maple have wings
open horizontally and not narrowing toward the base,
slightly wider toward the tips, 2–4 cm (0.75–1.5 in)
long.
Propagation By seed in seedbeds. The young trees
must remain where sown for two years.
Conditions for growth Grows well in limestone soil.

71 ACER MONSPESSULANUM
Montpellier Maple

Family Aceraceae. **Deciduous**

Etymology The species name attributes this maple to Montpellier, a small city in the south of France.

Habitat Southern Europe and northern Africa.

Description A tree that grows to 6–7 m (20–23 ft), with a wide, spreading crown and yellowish-gray bark, smooth at first but becoming fissured longitudinally. The young branches, supple and smooth, are brownish. The leaves (1), the smallest of any European maple, are glabrous, light green above and dull below, leathery, with the typical shape of three blunt lobes. The flowers (2), small and yellowish green, polygamous, grow in terminal corymbs, which appear before the leaves. The pendulous infructescence is a glabrous disamara with almost parallel wings, 2–3 cm (0.75–1.25 in) long and narrowing toward the base. The wood is the hardest and heaviest of any of the European maples, reddish in color; it is little used commercially. The tree is used to hold dry soil. It can also be grown naturally as a support for vines, or as an ornamental species in parks and gardens.

Propagation By seed.

Conditions for growth A great lover of light. Tolerates drought fairly well. Prefers dry, stony and limy soil.

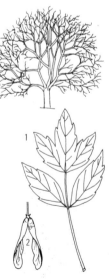

72 ACER NEGUNDO
Negundo, Box Elder

Family Aceraceae. **Deciduous**

Etymology From the Sanskrit and Bengali *nurgundi*, used for a tree that has leaves like those of the Negundo.

Habitat The type species is native to the whole of North America.

Description A tree growing up to 15–20 m (50–65 ft) high, with smooth, green young branches. The leaves (1) are composed of 3–5 ovato-acuminate leaflets, deeply indented, often with the terminal leaflet trilobal. The fruit (2), as in the entire genus, consists of twin samaras set at an acute angle; the wing generally looks curved inward, concave on the side facing the central axis. This very hardy tree was first imported into Europe from its homeland in 1688. Varieties of it are cultivated for the beauty of the crown in parks and gardens; *A. variegatum* has leaves with a broad white border that make its foliage very ornamental. The trees, especially in the type species, can be used as windbreaks, and a sweet liquid can sometimes be obtained by making an incision in the trunk, as with its relative, *A. saccharum* (**267**).

Propagation By seed; but the variegated varieties may also be reproduced by grafting onto the type species.

Conditions for growth Temperate climates with adequate humidity.

73 ACER OPALUS
Italian Maple

Family Aceraceae. **Deciduous**
Etymology Probably from *opulus*, the old Latin name of a type of maple.
Habitat The western Mediterranean region.
Description Normally some 10–15 m (33–50 ft) high, but can occasionally grow as much as 23 m (75 ft). The trunk is often twisted, the crown broad and rounded. The simple palmate leaves (1), the lamina as broad as it is long and cordate at the base, have 3–5 subacute lobes at the tip; dark green, glossy on the upper side and dull below, and leathery, they have a stalk 2–5 cm (1–2 in) long and turn red in the autumn. The polygamous, greenish-white flowers (2) are clustered in pendulous terminal corymbs and appear before the leaves, in April or May. The fruits (3), samaras with the wings set at right angles and broadening at the center, hang down on long stalks. The wood, pinkish white with a silky luster, is compact and sticky; it is much valued for high-quality furniture, for veneers and for musical instruments. The tree is also used for planting along roadsides and for the reforestation of limestone-weathered mountain soils.
Propagation By seed.
Conditions for growth Likes alkaline soils and temperate climate.

74 ACER PALMATUM
Japanese Maple

Family Aceraceae. **Deciduous**
Etymology The specific name refers to the shape of the leaves, like the palm of a hand with the fingers spread.
Habitat Originally from China, Korea and Japan.
Description A tree 5–8 (16–26 ft) tall with a domed crown and glabrous twigs, stalks and peduncles. The leaves (1) are divided into 5–9 lobes, oblong-acuminate, doubly serrated or incised, and always with smooth stalks. In the spring it displays a foliage delicately shaded from green to red, while in autumn it glows with more vivid colors. The flowers are erect, purplish pink, growing in corymbs. The fruits (2) are disamaras with the wings set at an obtuse angle. There are many varieties, and nurserymen have tried to unite the two variable features, the color and shape of the leaves. Very similar is *A. japonicum*, the true Japanese Maple (Full Moon Maple), which differs from *A. palmatum* in having its stalks covered with a light down. No one who wants to couple elegance of shape with brilliance of color, which may vary with the seasons, should fail to plant a Japanese Maple.
Propagation By seed, but to retain the characteristics of the leaves it is best to use cuttings.
Conditions for growth Fertile soil, light and rich in humus. Prefers sun but tolerates some shade.

75 ACER PLATANOIDES
Norway Maple

Family Aceraceae.   **Deciduous**
Etymology The specific name tells us that this species has leaves like those of the plane (**142–144**), but the two species cannot be confused.
Habitat Covers a vast area from the Pyrenees to the Urals and the Caucasus and from Scandinavia and Finland as far as Greece and central Italy.
Description A tree as much as 25 m (80 ft) tall, very much like the sycamore, with which it is often confused but from which it differs in having almost black bark with fine longitudinal fissures that does not split off, and by the simple, deciduous leaves (1) with shallow, open indentations between the lobes, green on both sides and borne on a reddish stalk that emits a milky liquid when broken. The dense foliage turns bright red in autumn. The flowers (2) are small, greenish yellow and fragrant. The fruit is a disamara, greenish yellow even when ripe; it has flattened carpels and broad wings, also flattened, set at a wide angle and not narrowing toward the base. The heavy, homogeneous wood is less white and shiny than sycamore and so of less value. There are a number of smaller varieties, some with leaves that are red for part or all of the summer.
Propagation By sowing seed in October.
Conditions for growth Requires a cool, deep soil.

76 ACER PSEUDOPLATANUS
Sycamore Maple

Family Aceraceae.   **Deciduous**
Etymology The specific name refers to the leaves' resemblance to those of the plane (**142–144**).
Habitat A widely distributed species, from the Pyrenees to the Caucasus and as far as Iran, growing in mountain forests.
Description A tree growing as high as 40 m (130 ft), the most long lived of related species, with a straight trunk and erect branches making a spreading, regular crown, and smooth gray bark that soon cracks into scales. Leaves (1) simple, opposite, deciduous, with five unequally toothed pointed lobes at acute angles, dark green on top and glaucescent on the underside, where some down grows along the veins. The leaves vary a good deal in size and in the depth of the lobes with the age of the tree and the strength of the branches. They are always borne on a long stalk, which does not emit milky sap when broken. The fruits (2) are disamaras with wings set in a V; they grow in clusters on short green stalks (sometimes suffused with red) and appear abundantly when the tree is at least 20 years old. The yellowish-white wood looks light and silky and is valued for the manufacture of fine furniture and as a veneer.
Propagation By seed. If cut, it bleeds profusely.
Conditions for growth Needs fertile soil, cool and deep.

77 ACER RUBRUM
Red Maple, Swamp Maple

Family Aceraceae.   **Deciduous**
Etymology The specific name refers to the color of the foliage.
Habitat From Newfoundland to Florida, and west to Minnesota and Texas.
Description A tree that reaches a height of 25–30 m (80–100 ft); the light bark is smooth and contrasts with the color of the foliage, which turns bright red in the fall. The tall, columnar trunk bears branches close together and rather erect, which gives the dense crown an oval shape. The young branches are glabrous, the small buds reddish green. The leaves (1), on long stalks, have 3–5 oval lobes, triangular with a crenate margin, and glaucous on the underside. The flowers are scarlet, occasionally yellowish, and grow in corymbs. The fruits (2), also red, are the typical disamaras, small, with the pericarp swollen and the wings making an acute angle. This maple is similar to *A. saccharum* (**267**), but differs from it in the red color of the flowers and leaf-stalks and in the more acute angle made by the lobes of the leaves. It also grows more quickly, flowers earlier and colors earlier in autumn. Readily drops branches.
Propagation By seed.
Conditions for growth Likes a cool, moist soil with a high water table.

78 ADANSONIA DIGITATA
Baobab

Family Bombaceae.   **Deciduous**
Etymology The name commemorates the French botanist Michel Adanson (1727–1806), who lived in Senegal for six years and wrote a work on that country's natural history.
Habitat Native to tropical Africa.
Description This distinctively African tree does not grow high, at most 12 m (40 ft), but its trunk is probably the thickest of any in existence, as much as 10 m (33 ft) in diameter. The palmate leaves (1) have 3 leaflets in the juvenile stage and 5–7 when adult; the widely spaced branches form a sparse, spreading crown. The wood is spongy and saturated with water, which enables the tree to withstand drought. The trunk grows without forming annual rings. The thick gray bark contains a strong fiber used in making paper and ropes. The flowers (2) are white, large, pendulous and solitary, carried on long stalks; after a short time the petals curve outward, reflexing to reveal the purple anthers of the many stamens. The fruits (3), oblong and woody, may be as much as 30 cm (12 in) long and weigh several pounds. Its floury, acid flesh is eaten by the Africans and produces a drink like lemonade.
Propagation By seed.
Conditions for growth Very warm, dry climate.

79 AILANTHUS ALTISSIMA
Tree of Heaven

Family Simarubaceae.   **Deciduous**
Etymology From the Moluccan *ailanto*, "tree that can grow up to the sky."
Habitat Originally from China, naturalized in America and Europe, where it was introduced in 1751 by the Jesuit missionary Incarville.
Description A big, deciduous tree with an erect trunk, almost smooth grayish bark and white, compact but rather light wood; the wood and bark contain tannin and other astringents. The branches are spreading and young branchlets are covered with a yellowish tomentum. The alternate leaves (1), unevenly pinnate, are composed of 13–15 lanceolate-acuminate leaflets; they have no stipules. Oil-bearing glands at the base of the leaf give off a disagreeable smell if rubbed, as do the flowers. The plant is polygamous, with small, yellowish-green, five-petalled flowers, male or hermaphrodite; the bisexual ones have a central pistil with 5–6 carpels and 10 stamens, of which 5 are relatively short. The inflorescences are long, dense panicles. The fruit (2) is a reddish, winged samara.
Propagation By seed or by basal suckers, which grow easily; the tree seeds itself freely and can become a pest.
Conditions for growth Hardy and very adaptable. Thrives in cities in meager soil.

80 ALNUS GLUTINOSA
Common Alder, European Alder

Family Betulaceae.   **Deciduous**
Etymology The genus has retained its original Latin name. *Glutinosa* refers to the sticky feel of the young leaves.
Habitat Widespread in Europe as far as Siberia, in western Asia and North Africa, along watercourses with marshy or rocky banks.
Description A tree up to 20–30 m (65–100 ft) high, with an erect trunk, sparse, spreading ramification forming a broad, conical crown, and rough, brown bark that cracks into slender, vertical scales in the summer. The simple leaves (1), obovate and irregularly toothed at the margins, are dark green above and lighter below. The unisexual flowers grow in catkins; the males (2), cylindrical and pendulous, appear before the leaves, while the females (3) are ovoid and erect. After fertilization the female inflorescence is transformed into a stalked infructescence in the form of a little strobile, from which small winged achenes appear when ripe. The wood, homogeneous and opaque, grows harder in water and becomes remarkably strong when permanently submerged, so that it is used for piles and hydraulic works. Its charcoal is used in the manufacture of fireworks.
Propagation By sowing in spring, or by cuttings.
Conditions for growth In flooded, loamy soils.

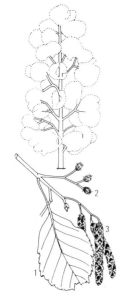

81 ALNUS INCANA
Gray Alder, American Speckled Alder

Family Betulaceae.   **Deciduous**
Etymology The specific name means white haired and refers to the down on the young branches and leafstalks.
Habitat A northern mountain species, spreading from the central and northern regions of Europe to Asia and North America.
Description A tree 10–20 m (33–65 ft) in height, not quite as tall as the Common Alder, with a smooth, shiny, light-gray bark, unlike the Common Alder (**80**), whose bark is dark and rough. The simple leaves (1) have a stalk with a hairy stipule; they are ovate-elliptical in shape, cordate at the base with the margins sharply double toothed, dark green and glabrous on top and whitish gray and pubescent below. They are never sticky, unlike those of the Common Alder. The unisexual flowers grow in catkins; the males, long and pendulous, appear before the leaves, while the females, shorter and lacking a stalk, grow in groups of 2–5. The fruits (2) are tiny achenes growing in strobiles with woody scales.
Propagation By seed, by suckers and also by cuttings (difficult).
Conditions for growth Likes wet conditions as long as there is no stagnant water; resists frost.

---

82 ARALIA ELATA
Aralia, Japanese Angelica Tree, Devil's Walking Stick

Family Araliaceae.   **Deciduous**
Etymology Appears to be derived from the French-Canadian *aralie*, a term used for a species of the genus sent from America to Gui Fagon, French botanist (1638–1718), but there are doubts about this explanation.
Habitat The species grows wild in the Far East.
Description This tree, which can grow as high as 15 m (50 ft), has a slightly spiny trunk, branching from the base and often putting out a number of basal suckers, by means of which it can be propagated. The leaves are compound, more than 1 m (3 ft) long, generally free of spines, with toothed ovato-acuminate leaflets, dark green, generally downy on the underside and almost sessile. The flowers are small and white, growing in umbels or panicles; the tiny fruits that follow them are drupes resembling little blackberries. The tree grows very quickly. There are several varieties, among them some with smooth leaves, some with spiny leaves and a rather elegant *variegata* with the leaves edged in white.
Propagation By seed, in spring; by radical suckers and root cuttings. Propagation by softwood cuttings under glass is more difficult.
Conditions for growth Does well in average soil. Thrives in the city.

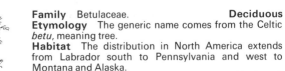

83 BETULA PAPYRIFERA
White Birch, Paper Birch, Canoe Birch

Family Betulaceae.   **Deciduous**
Etymology The generic name comes from the Celtic *betu*, meaning tree.
Habitat The distribution in North America extends from Labrador south to Pennsylvania and west to Montana and Alaska.
Description A tree up to 20–30 m (65–100 ft) high with brilliant white bark that peels off in big strips. The American Indians used to gather it carefully and stretch it on the frames of their canoes. The young branches are downy at first. The oval-acuminate leaves (1) are coarsely double toothed, downy along the veins on the lower side and borne on stalks that are also hairy. They turn yellow in autumn. The unisexual flowers have the male elements (2) growing closely in cylindrical, pendulous catkins, while the females, also in catkins, are smaller and erect. The fruits grow in a cylindrical infructescence which disintegrates when ripe to allow the escape of little samaras with a membraneous wing. The oil extracted from the bark contains methyl salicylate, used to treat rheumatism and inflammations.
Propagation By seed.
Conditions for growth Requires a cool climate. In southern New England, for example, it is almost nonexistent. Needs light; cannot bear shade.

84 BETULA PENDULA
European Birch

Family Betulaceae.   **Deciduous**
Etymology The specific name describes the drooping habit of the young branches.
Habitat Grows in Europe and Asia Minor, at altitudes up to 1300 m (4200 ft) in the Vosges and 2000 m (6500 ft) in the Pyrenees.
Description A tree that can reach a height of 30 m (100 ft) and a diameter of 70 cm (27 in), with a very light, ovoid crown, slender, whippy, rising branches and drooping branchlets that give the crown an attractive appearance. The smooth bark is silver-white in the outermost layer, and has horizontal bands of lenticels characteristic of the birches. The simple leaves (1) are rhomboidal with long points, double toothed, light green and glabrous. (2, 3) male and female flowers. (4) fruit. The yellowish-white, homogeneous wood is used in the manufacture of skis, for clogs, and for small lathe-turned objects. Cellulose is produced from it, and it is also used as a fuel on account of its high calorific value. The leaves contain a yellow coloring matter, and a sugary sap is extracted and fermented to make an alcoholic drink called birch beer.
Propagation By sowing seed early in the spring.
Conditions for growth Light, well-aerated soils. The tree tolerates a certain humidity, likes cool climates and needs plenty of light.

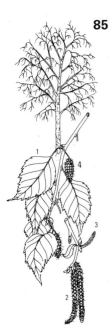

85 BETULA PUBESCENS
Hairy Birch

Family Betulaceae.   **Deciduous**
Etymology The specific name refers to the fact that the young branches are covered with a soft down.
Habitat The distribution extends farther north than that of *B. pendula* (**84**), beyond the Arctic Circle, and as far as the Alps in the south.
Description This birch, together with *B. pendula*, was once grouped under *B. alba*. It differs from *B. pendula* in its habit: the young branches are bigger and do not droop, the young bark is grayish white or yellowish not silvery, the leaves (1) are less sharply pointed and have a fine down on the underside and the stalk, and have no resinous glands. (2, 3) Male and female catkins. (4) fruit. Unlike *B. pendula*, it needs plenty of water; in humid climates it can be found on all sorts of soil, but when the surrounding humidity is low it grows only on marshy, muddy soils. The wood is used for lathe-turned goods and for plywood, and in the production of cellulose bisulphite. The charcoal from this tree is a source of the black pigment in printer's ink.
Propagation By seed, which germinates as soon as it is covered and watered.
Conditions for growth Cold temperature; tolerates marshy ground.

86 BRACHYCHITON ACERIFOLIUM

Family Sterculiaceae.   **Deciduous**
Etymology The name comes from the Greek *brachys*, short, and *chiton*, tunic, from the short, overlapping scales.
Habitat Native to New South Wales and Queensland, in Australia.
Description A tree of remarkable size which in its homelands can reach a height of more than 30 m (100 ft). It is grown particularly for the unusual shape of its leaves and showy red flowers. The long-stalked leaves (1) are palmato-lobate, and each lobe is in turn lobed so as to form a kind of fan; there may be 5–7 segments, and the whole leaf can measure as much as 30 cm (12 in) in diameter. The flowers grow in racemes; they have no petals but are equipped with a very sticky red calyx about 2 cm (nearly 1 in) long, bell shaped, with big, pointed, open, outward-curving lobes at the center of which the staminal column appears with about ten stamens, joined to the pistils. The fruits (2) are big, glabrous and dehiscent follicles on a long stalk.
Propagation By seed or by softwood cuttings under glass.
Conditions for growth Tropical and subtropical; young specimens can be grown in the hothouse.

87 CARPINUS BETULUS
European Hornbeam

Family Corylaceae. **Deciduous**
Etymology The name comes from the Celtic *carr*, wood, and *pen*, head, recalling that the wood was used to make yokes for oxen.
Habitat Central Europe from southern Sweden to Italy, from the Pyrenees to the Caucasus.
Description A tree that can grow to 20 m (65 ft), with a dense, elongated oval crown, erect fluted trunk and smooth ashy-gray bark like that of the beech. The leaves (1), simple and alternate, are oblong-oval, pointed at the tips, with a short stalk and sharply double-toothed margin, dark green on top and paler below, with 10–15 pairs of veins running across the lamina. The unisexual flowers grow in catkins, the males (2) cylindrical, drooping and pendulous, the shorter females (3) at the tip of the terminal shoots. The fruit is a flat, ovoid achene, greenish and furrowed, with a wide, three-lobed, papery bract; it persists on the tree after the leaves have fallen and so helps us to distinguish the hornbeam from the beech, which looks similar though it is quite remote philogenetically. The hornbeam is planted as a shade tree along roadsides, and for hedges.
Propagation By seed, radical suckers or layering.
Conditions for growth Prefers friable, deep soils and dry, sunny hillsides.

88 CARYA OVATA
Shagbark Hickory

Family Juglandaceae. **Deciduous**
Etymology The name is derived from the Greek *karya*, meaning a walnut tree (the form *karyon* was applied to all fruits of similar form).
Habitat North America.
Description A tree that can reach 25–30 m (80–100 ft). The trunk is straight, the branches erect and irregular, the crown narrow. The bark is light gray, and when the tree has reached full maturity, after some 30–40 years, it begins to peel off in curly, shaggy strips; it may be that this is an evolutionary adaptation to keep squirrels away from the nuts, since the strips of stiff bark, with their sharp angles, must certainly constitute something of an obstacle to those animals. The compound leaves (1) have five pointed leaflets, downy and glandular at the base, then glabrous, the terminal one bigger than the others. They turn golden brown in the fall. The flowers are unisexual; the males (2) grow in hairy, pendulous catkins, three together in a characteristic trident shape, while the females appear at the tips of young branches. The fruits (3), which have a sweet, white, edible seed, are flat and angular.
Propagation By seed.
Conditions for growth Hardy, and likes loam soils.

89 CASUARINA EQUISETIFOLIA
Casuarina

Family Casuarinaceae.   **Deciduous**
Etymology The name is thought to refer to the plumage of the cassowary bird, which slightly resembles the leafless branches of this tree.
Habitat The casuarinas are mostly native to Australia, New Caledonia, Borneo (Kalimantan) and Sumatra, extending to the southern part of the Indian subcontinent and the Malagasy Republic.
Description A tree 25–30 m (80–100 ft) high, with bark that peels off in longitudinal strips; from a distance its slender, green branches look like thick pine needles, but a close look reveals that the twigs are jointed and furrowed longitudinally and that they bear tiny, scalelike leaves set in whorls round the nodes. The flowers are unisexual, the males (1) growing in long spikes, the females (2) easier to distinguish because they are arranged in compact clusters about 1 cm (0.5 in) across. After fertilization the bracts below the female flowers grow together to form a woody shell for the seed, and the coiled mass that contains them remains on the tree, conspicuous for its chestnut color.
Propagation By seed or by cuttings from young branches.
Conditions for growth Temperate climate; indifferent to the type of soil.

♂   ♀

---

90 CECROPIA PALMATA

Family Moraceae.   **Evergreen**
Etymology From the name of Cecrops, a legendary king of ancient Athens, who deeded Attica to the goddess Athena for her gift of the olive.
Habitat Native to Indonesia.
Description Slender, solitary trunk reaching a height of 10 m (33 ft), with few branches set near the top, almost horizontal and recurved at the ends; the big leaves are palmate-lobate, with white down on the underside. Trunk and branches are hollow at the nodes, and certain ants of the genus *Atzeca instabilis* raise their larvae in the cavities, digging out the point of insertion of the stalk to gain access; the plant's hospitality is repaid by defence against ants of the genus *Attadiscigera*, the leaf-cutting ants with their powerful jaws. This symbiosis is completed by the ants' feeding on certain small bodies—Müller's corpuscles—which grow at the base of the stalks. The buds and leaves constitute the almost exclusive diet of some American tardigrades, which might never have survived had it not been for the *Cecropias*. The plant grows quickly and can also establish itself as a pioneer on bare ground, covering burnt-over areas.
Propagation By seed or cuttings.
Conditions for growth Tropical.

91 CECROPIA PELTATA

Family Moraceae.   **Evergreen**
Etymology The species name refers to the leaves, with their shield-shaped lobes.
Habitat Native to tropical America.
Description This tree can reach a height of 15 m (50 ft), with a maximum trunk diameter of 50 cm (20 in); the trunk and branches are hollow, and certain Indian tribes cut 2 m (6 ft) lengths from them to use as waterpipes, and as a means of communication at a distance; in Haiti this gives the *Cecropia* the name "Trumpet Tree." The leaves are big, with from seven to nine lobes, downy on the upper surface and glabrous, shining white on the lower, so that they flash like mirrors when they are stirred by the breeze. The undistinguished wood, whitish when new and turning honey colored or brown later, has a coarse texture, is hard to polish and deteriorates on contact with the earth, but holds nails well; in the tree's homeland it is called *imbauba* and is used for lighting fires, heat being generated by friction. The rather caustic sap is used to make a kind of rubber.
Propagation By seed or cuttings of half-ripe wood.
Conditions for growth In practice, rarely cultivated; only occurs in the rain forest.

---

92 CELTIS AUSTRALIS
European Hackberry

Family Ulmaceae.   **Deciduous**
Etymology The name was given by the Greeks to an unidentified tree and was adopted for this genus by Linnaeus.
Habitat Grows wild in the whole Mediterranean region.
Description A deciduous tree that can reach a height of 25 m (80 ft), with a thick trunk and round crown. The young branches are downy, and the bark of the trunk and older branches is smooth and gray. The leaves (1) are oval-lanceolate and sharply pointed, with a short stalk and toothed margin, rough on the upper side, downy underneath. The flowers (2) appear in spring; they are small and greenish, and insignificant, and are followed by small fruits (3), drupes that ripen in autumn, dark purple when ripe, sweet and edible but actually only eaten by birds. This is essentially a foliage tree. The rather light wood is used mostly for small objects and inlaid work.
Propagation Reproduced by seed in autumn and by basal suckers, cuttings and layerings.
Conditions for growth Fairly hardy, can adapt to arid soils and prefers lime, but will not tolerate too intense, prolonged frosts.

93 CERCIDIPHYLLUM JAPONICUM
Katsura Tree

Family Cercidiphyllaceae.   **Deciduous**
Etymology The name is derived from that of the genus *Cercis* and the Greek word *phyllon*, leaf, from the resemblance of the leaves to those of some species of *Cercis*.
Habitat Native to Japan.
Description Often polycormic, reaching a height of anywhere from 10 to 25 m (33–80 ft), depending on whether it is growing in favorable conditions; the form is rather pyramidal, the thin, glabrous branches almost horizontal when mature but drooping when young. The cordate leaves (1), set opposite, with reddish stalks, have palmate veins; they are almost circular, and in autumn, before they fall, they take on colors ranging from deep pink to ivory white. The apetalous flowers are unisexual, solitary and insignificant, and appear before the leaves come out. The male flowers (2) are almost sessile, but the females (3) have a short stalk and from them the little many-seeded pods develop. There is a variety from western China that is much bigger and has a single trunk.
Propagation By seed at the end of winter, or by layering or softwood cuttings in summer.
Conditions for growth Hardy, tolerates a limestone soil and a remarkable degree of cold; can withstand drought.

94 COCCULUS LAURIFOLIUS

Family Menispermaceae.   **Evergreen**
Etymology From the Greek *kokkos*, berry, from the form of the fruit.
Habitat Native to east Asia, in the Himalayan region.
Description An evergreen that can grow to 5–8 m (16–26 ft), with a spreading, rounded, very dense crown. The leaves (1) are glossy, green, oblong-lanceolate, pointed at the tip and narrower at the base, with three conspicuous veins that are distinctive and give the plant the name sometimes used in horticultural circles, *Laurus trinervis*—which is of course quite incorrect. The leaves are alternate and entire, with a short stalk, and join the branch very close together. The yellowish flowers (2) are small and inconspicuous, growing in racemes; the plants are dioecious, so that they can only fruit if specimens of each sex are present. The fruit are drupes. The bark contains an alkaloid called coclaurina. This plant is very tolerant of pruning, even of topiary; it can also be grown as a bush or big hedge.
Propagation By seed, cuttings or layering.
Conditions for growth Half-hardy, can withstand only very moderate, sporadic frosts. Best suited to mild climates.

95 COLUTEA ARBORESCENS
Bladder Senna

Family Leguminosae. **Deciduous**
Etymology The name comes from the Greek *koloitia*, used by Theophrastus for this plant in his *Historia plantarum*.
Habitat Native to southern Europe and North Africa.
Description A polycormic deciduous shrub that reaches a height of 3–5 m (10–16 ft), with erect, bushy habit, especially in the juvenile stage; every part of the plant is rich in tannin. The leaves (1) are imparipinnate, with 9–13 elliptical leaflets, acuminate and slightly downy on the underside. The flowers are rather big, papilionaceous, with a calyx covered with blackish hairs and a corolla with erect standard; the flowers are yellow and grow rather sparsely in axillary racemes. They are followed by fruits (2) consisting of a membraneous pod containing several seeds, which swells up until the walls are almost transparent, growing thinner toward the tip, where the pod is dehiscent.
Propagation By seed, in spring, or by hardwood cuttings in autumn, in sand. The plant grows fairly quickly.
Conditions for growth Half-hardy, can withstand only occasional frost; prefers dry surroundings and a sunny position. Transplanting must always be done with a soil ball, never with bare roots.

96 COTINUS COGGYRIA
Smoke Tree, Venetian Sumac

Family Anacardiaceae. **Deciduous**
Etymology Derived from the Greek *cotinos* and its Latin homonym, which was used for a tree that has not been clearly identified.
Habitat Southern Europe, central China, Himalayas.
Description This tree, not more than 5 m (16 ft) high, has entire, simple leaves (1), rarely more than 7 cm (2.75 in) long, oval, glabrous above and below and turning dark red, almost violet tinged, in autumn. The flowers (2), hermaphrodite or unisexual, have yellowish-green petals which fall early and grow in a panicle with threadlike, branched, downy peduncles. The fruits, small oval drupes, red-brown and shiny since they are glabrous, are beautiful but poisonous; in autumn they remain hanging on the hairy stalks, giving the whole tree a feathery look which has earned it the name of Periwig Tree. It is cultivated as an ornamental in gardens, together with the variety *atropurpurea*, which has reddish-purple leaves and flowers. The leaves of the type species provide a tannin used in the tanning of high-quality leather. The white sapwood and yellowish-red heartwood take a fine polish but can be used only for small objects.
Propagation By seed, suckers, or cuttings.
Conditions for growth Temperate climate; any soil.

97 COUROUPITA GUIANENSIS
Cannonball Tree

Family Lecythidaceae.   **Deciduous**
Etymology From a local Amerindian word; the popular name is Cannonball Tree.
Habitat Native to Guyana, but extends over the whole of Central America.
Description A big tree with smooth, light wood which may exceed 15 m (50 ft) in height; the leaves are deciduous, obovate, with short stalks, and appear on thorny, nonfructiferous branches at the apical point of the trunk. The flowers, waxy and scented, have six petals, pink inside and orange-yellow outside, with a big staminal disk and nectariferous at the center. They grow in dense racemes directly on the trunk or on tangled branches that spring from the thick bark, light colored with chestnut stripes, on the lowest part of the bole. The flowers are followed by large, round fruits, brownish, woody and indehiscent, which ripen in 18 months but often do not fall until a year or more later, when they drop with a loud crash. The ripe flesh has an unpleasant smell; the shell is used locally for making utensils.
Propagation By seed. Germination is difficult.
Conditions for growth Exclusively tropical.

---

98 CRATAEGUS OXYACANTHA
English Hawthorn, May

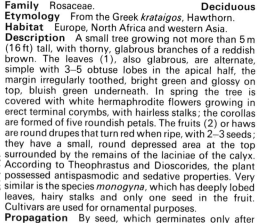

Family Rosaceae.   **Deciduous**
Etymology From the Greek *krataigos*, Hawthorn.
Habitat Europe, North Africa and western Asia.
Description A small tree growing not more than 5 m (16 ft) tall, with thorny, glabrous branches of a reddish brown. The leaves (1), also glabrous, are alternate, simple with 3–5 obtuse lobes in the apical half, the margin irregularly toothed, bright green and glossy on top, bluish green underneath. In spring the tree is covered with white hermaphrodite flowers growing in erect terminal corymbs, with hairless stalks; the corollas are formed of five roundish petals. The fruits (2) or haws are round drupes that turn red when ripe, with 2–3 seeds; they have a small, round depressed area at the top surrounded by the remains of the laciniae of the calyx. According to Theophrastus and Dioscorides, the plant possessed antispasmodic and sedative properties. Very similar is the species *monogyna*, which has deeply lobed leaves, hairy stalks and only one seed in the fruit. Cultivars are used for ornamental purposes.
Propagation By seed, which germinates only after two years.
Conditions for growth Moderate climate; will not withstand excessive humidity.

99 CUNONIA CAPENSIS

Family Cunoniaceae. **Evergreen**
Etymology The name commemorates John Christian Cuno, a Dutch naturalist of the second half of the 18th century.
Habitat Native to South Africa.
Description This tree in its native surroundings grows 6–10 m (20–33 ft) tall and has evergreen leaves, pinnate and leathery, with two or three pairs of oblong, lanceolate leaves, with glossy surfaces, toothed margins and reddish stalks. The white flowers are borne in dense axillary racemes which look like spikes; they are small, with a short calyx tube, five petals and ten very prominent stamens. The fruit is a leathery capsule. Since the tree branches from the base up it can also be cultivated as a shrub, and small specimens can be grown as house plants if the temperature is not too high.
Propagation By softwood cuttings.
Conditions for growth Easily grown in acid, sandy soils high in organic matter. Will not tolerate excessive humidity, needs good drainage and must be sheltered from frost.

---

100 CYRILLA RACEMIFLORA

Family Cyrillaceae. **Evergreen**
Etymology The name was given by Linnaeus in honor of Domenico Cirillo (1737–1799), doctor and botanist of Naples, executed by the Bourbons for his liberal ideas.
Habitat Originally from a fairly restricted area between North Carolina and Florida, now found as far south as the West Indies and Brazil.
Description A tree 5–10 m (16–33 ft) high, in its native habitat and in warm regions it behaves as an evergreen, but elsewhere it is deciduous. It has alternate leaves, entire, lanceolate and glabrous. In summer it produces little white bisexual flowers in racemes at the end of the old branches and at the base of those produced during the year; in autumn the glossy leaves take on vivid colors ranging from orange to scarlet. It also has a pleasant scent. Though it was introduced into Europe, and greatly admired, in the early 1800s, it is not widely cultivated.
Propagation By seed and also by cuttings, using twigs about 8–10 cm (3–4 in) long, rooted in a cold-frame.
Conditions for growth Needs limefree soils, damp and rather shady. Not difficult to establish.

101 DALBERGIA SISSOO

Family Leguminosae.   **Evergreen**
Etymology The name was given in honor of the Swedish brothers Nils and Carl Dalberg, who lived in the 18th century. The first was a botanist and the second explored Surinam.
Habitat Native to India but now introduced throughout the tropics.
Description This is a big tree which in its native surroundings can grow to more than 20 m (65 ft). The leaves (1) are imparipinnate, with five leaflets, alternate and stalked, sharply acuminate and downy on the underside. The flowers (2) are white and papilionate, growing in small panicles; the fruit is a pod. This tree, besides being grown as an ornamental for its large crown, which often starts comparatively low, has been introduced into all tropical and subtropical regions on account of its commercial value. Its timber is elastic and easy to work, being used for all kinds of work calling for strength and durability, including shipbuilding.
Propagation By seed or by softwood cuttings.
Conditions for growth Tropical and subtropical; will not tolerate cold climates. Grows well in sandy soil and will survive in soil that is somewhat arid. A quick grower.

102 DAPHNIPHYLLUM MACROPODUM

Family Daphniphyllaceae.   **Evergreen**
Etymology The name comes from the Greek *daphne*, laurel, and *phyllon*, leaf, from the similarity of their leaves.
Habitat Originally from Japan and China.
Description A small tree that in our climates will hardly grow more than 3 m (10 ft), but taller in the countries of origin. It has a thick trunk with grayish-brown bark and wide, dense ramification which starts low down, with thick branches and secondary branchlets often of a reddish color. The oblong leaves (1) are leathery, glossy, glaucescent on the lower side, with red stalks some 5 cm (2 in) long. The plants are dioecious, with apetalous flowers (2), which once led to its being assigned to the genus *Euphorbia* (from which in fact it is distinguished by its persistent foliage). Both male and female flowers are borne in axillary racemes, having a small calyx and, respectively, 5–18 stems or one bilocular pistil. The fruits are drupes that look rather like olives, but the tree is usually cultivated for its ornamental foliage, since it bears little fruit and its flowers are not conspicuous.
Propagation By seed, if available, or by cuttings of mature wood under glass in summer.
Conditions for growth Half-hardy; tolerates lime in the soil. A slow grower.

103 DIOSPYROS EBENUM

Ebony Tree

Family Ebenaceae. **Deciduous**

Etymology Derived from the Greek *diospyros*, a word compounded from *dios*, divine, and *pyros*, grain, referring to the edible fruit of some species; the specific name is from the Greek *ebenos*.

Habitat Occurs in Sri Lanka (Ceylon), Malaysia, India and Indo-China.

Description A tree that grows very tall, especially in Sri Lanka, though of smaller size in Indo-China. It has gray bark, and the alternate, very short-stalked leaves (1) are ovate-oblong, leathery, entire and glossy. The flowers (2, 3) are sessile, axillary and solitary, and the fruit (4) is an oval berry. The wood is black and heavy, so hard that it is almost impossible to drive a nail into it, of very fine grain and able to take a perfect polish. A valuable wood, it is reserved for luxury goods and veneers; it is also used for the manufacture of musical instruments such as flutes and clarinets and pianoforte keys. Also included under the commercial term "ebony" are many other species of *Diospyros*; and the wood is widely imitated by dyeing black common fine-grained woods, such as pear.

Propagation By seed, which must be planted deeply.

Conditions for growth Tropical.

---

104 DISANTHUS CERCIDIFOLIUS

Family Hamamelidaceae. **Deciduous**

Etymology From the Greek *dis*, twice, and *anthos*, flower, referring to the paired flowers.

Habitat Mountainous zones of central Japan.

Description A small deciduous tree that grows to 3 m (10 ft), often polycormic; the only species of its genus. The alternate leaves (1) on long stalks are entire, almost heart shaped, blue-green on the upper surface and lighter beneath, some 10 cm (4 in) long; before they drop in autumn they take on colors ranging from red to orange. Despite its flowers (2), which grow in pairs united at the ball and set opposite on erect stalks, the plant is grown essentially for its attractive foliage, not unlike that of *Cercidiphyllum* (**93**). The small flowers are dark purple, with a calyx divided into five segments and five slender, open petals; the five stamens are shorter than the sepals. The fruit is a dehiscent capsule with several shiny black seeds in each loculus.

Propagation By seed; germination takes two or three years. Alternatively, by grafting on *Hamamelis* obtained from seed.

Conditions for growth Fairly hardy. Needs a light, acid soil with a high organic content.

105 EUCALYPTUS CAMALDULENSIS
Red Gum

Family Myrtaceae. **Evergreen**
Etymology The name comes from the Greek *eu*, well, and *kalyptos*, covered: the mouths of the flowers are covered by a woody operculum.
Habitat Native to Australia, but naturalized in southern Europe. Introduced into Italy in 1803 under the name of *E. rostrata*.
Description This big tree, called Red Gum from the color of the resinous sap (the name Blue Gum being applied to *E. globulus* [**108**]), can grow more than 60 m (200 ft) high in its country of origin, though it more often stops at 30–40 m (100–130 ft). The bark of the adult trunk is gray, and is shed and replaced; if persistent, it flakes off in thin strips. That of young trees is reddish. The young leaves are ovate, but long leaves appear later, lanceolate and acuminate (1), which may grow as much as 30 cm (12 in) long. The woody calyx is hemispherical, while the operculum, the "lid" which closes the flowers, is conical; when it opens and falls, white stamens emerge. The reddish wood is disease resistant though not very strong, and hard to work when dry. Bees are much attracted by the flowers (2). (3) fruit.
Propagation By seed.
Conditions for growth Hardy, even tolerates salty soils.

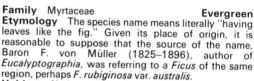

106 EUCALYPTUS FICIFOLIA
Red Flowering Gum

Family Myrtaceae **Evergreen**
Etymology The species name means literally "having leaves like the fig." Given its place of origin, it is reasonable to suppose that the source of the name, Baron F. von Müller (1825–1896), author of *Eucalyptographia*, was referring to a *Ficus* of the same region, perhaps *F. rubiginosa* var. *australis*.
Habitat Native to Australia.
Description From 8 to 15 m (25–50 ft) high, this tree has dark, fissured bark, sometimes fluted. The leaves (1), ovate in the juvenile stage, are longer, oval and lanceolate when adult, leathery and dark green, with lighter central veins. The large flowers (2) are borne in panicles and possess an almost flat operculum; the stamens that emerge when the operculum falls are red, with dark-red anthers. The fruit (3) is pitcher shaped and woody, with red-brown seeds winged on one side. The tree has no economic importance and is grown only as an ornamental, for its mass of showy flowers.
Propagation By seed, with varying results. By grafting if it is desired to maintain the color of the flowers unchanged.
Conditions for growth Barely half-hardy; cultivation is not recommended beyond the Citrus Belt. A slow grower.

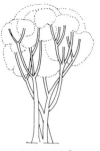

107 EUCALYPTUS GLOBULUS
Blue Gum

Family Myrtaceae.   **Evergreen**
Etymology The name comes from the Greek *eu*, well, and *kalyptos*, covered: the mouths of the flowers are covered by a woody operculum.
Habitat Native to Australia.
Description An evergreen tree that can reach 40 m (130 ft) and more in height, with deciduous bark which comes off in long strips, leaving the trunk patterned in silver-gray. The young leaves are rounded, sessile and opposite, but on maturity they become lanceolate, stalked and alternate and aromatic. The flowers (1) are solitary, sometimes growing two or three together, with short stalks; they consist of a calyx in the form of a truncated pyramid and an operculum ("lid") formed from four petals joined together, which falls at maturity. When the operculum falls, the many stamens and the style emerge to give the flowers a feathery look. Flowering occurs between autumn and spring and is followed by the ripening of the fruits (2), which are angular capsules with a great number of very light seeds. The wood is used mainly for cellulose.
Propagation By seed; germination takes place in 15 days and growth is rapid.
Conditions for growth Can be grown wherever the cold is not intense.

108 FAGUS GRANDIFOLIA
American Beech

Family Fagaceae.   **Deciduous**
Etymology The name is the one the Romans gave to the beech and may be derived frm the Greek *phagein*, to eat.
Habitat This species, growing in the eastern United States, is the American equivalent of the European *F. sylvatica*.
Description A tree 25–35 m (80–115 ft) high, occasionally as much as 40 m (130 ft), with a pyramidal crown and massive trunk; it puts out radical suckers. The thin gray-blue bark makes it attractive even when it has no leaves. As in all beeches the leaves are deciduous and alternate, ovate-oblong in shape and pointed at the tip, medium sized, with a coarsely toothed margin. Hairy at first, they turn bright bluish-green on the upper side and pale green below; they are larger and narrower than the leaves of *F. sylvatica* (**110**). The triangular fruits are covered by a reddish pericarp, 1–3 within a husk called the cupule, which splits into four woody lobes covered by long spines. The American Beech once formed great groves where enormous flocks of the now-extinct passenger pigeon came to feed and to roost.
Propagation By seed or by suckers.
Conditions for growth Likes light, well-drained soils.

109 FAGUS SYLVATICA
Common Beech, European Beech

Family Fagaceae. **Deciduous**
Etymology The name is the one the Romans gave to the beech and may be derived from the Greek *phagein*, to eat.
Habitat The forests of central Europe.
Description The tree can grow up to 30 m (110 ft) high; it has a dense, spreading, oval crown and light, ashy-gray bark with horizontal bands, often with whitish patches due to lichens. The leaves (1), oval or elliptical, are entire and slightly toothed; they turn brownish-yellow or red-brown in autumn and sometimes persist until the end of winter. The flowers are of separate sexes; the stamen-bearing males (2) are grouped in round, stalked catkins, while the females (3) grow in pairs within a covering called the cupule. On ripening, the cupule contains two nuts (4). Called beech-mast, the fruits are eaten by animals (pigs are very fond of them), and not so long ago they were also used as food by humans. The slightly rosy-colored wood, widely used in carpentry, is also used for making bentwood furniture.
Propagation Reproduced either by seed or by rooted suckers, which the tree puts out freely.
Conditions for growth Prefers light soils, well drained and possibly alkaline.

110 FATSIA JAPONICA
Aralia

Family Araliaceae. **Evergreen**
Etymology The name is a Latinized form of the Japanese name.
Habitat Native to Japan.
Description The Aralia, which we generally think of as a house plant and which in mild climates grows as a garden bush, in its native surroundings is a little polycormic tree with bushy habit growing as high as 3–4 m (10–13 ft), often forming a head down to the base. The leaves (1) are glossy green, palmate-lobate, carried on long stalks. The inconspicuous, creamy-white flowers (2) have a small calyx and a corolla that falls before it is ripe; they grow in apical panicles composed of round umbels. Once fertilization is completed, the midrib and its branches grow longer and the flowers are followed by the fruits, which are small berries, green at first, then whitish, finally turning black when ripe.
Propagation By seed, germinating easily as long as it is kept cool; by softwood cuttings; by layering on a woody stem.
Conditions for growth Hardy; resistant to frost if it is only short and sporadic. Prefers half-shade.

111 FICUS BENGALENSIS
Banyan

Family Moraceae. **Evergreen**

Etymology The generic name was used by the Romans for *F. carica* (**203**), the common edible fig, already known and cultivated in ancient times.

Habitat Native to India.

Description This spectacular tree, growing to more than 30 m (100 ft) in height, is unlike any other apart from a few Asian species of the same genus. Aerial roots grow down from its spreading branches; at first they absorb moisture from the air, but on reaching the ground they penetrate it, so that the part still above ground becomes in effect a columnar stem with its own roots, while still remaining attached to the main plant. In this way, complete little thickets are formed from a single tree. The leaves are leathery, ovate, dark green with light-green veins, about 20 cm (8 in) long; the stalks are downy, and so are the new parts of young branches. The fruits are red and round.

Propagation By cuttings of young branches under glass, or by layering on woody branches.

Conditions for growth Tropical; young specimens can be kept in the greenhouse, but they retain a bushy habit and never fruit.

112 FICUS BENJAMINA
Weeping Fig

Family Moraceae. **Evergreen**

Habitat From India to the Philippines, the Malay Peninsula and the Sunda Archipelago.

Description A tree of weeping habit, with slender branches and a fairly thin trunk. In the wild it puts out aerial roots and may be one of the so-called strangulated figs, whose aerial roots grow down to the ground during their epiphytic phase, taking root and enveloping the host plant with a dense network within which the host plant is slowly destroyed. However, that happens only in the depth of the forests; elsewhere the tree may grow as a normal terrestrial plant with no sign of such unusual behavior. The stalked leaves are glossy and leathery, ovate and rather narrow, coming to a sharp point; they can grow up to 12 cm (5 in) long. The small, round fruits are dark red when ripe. There are several varieties, including one from the Philippines, *F. benjamina* "nuda," with small leaves and greeny-yellow fruit, which has deciduous basal bracts putting out aerial roots even when growing as a normal ground plant, behaving like one of the other "pagoda" species of *Ficus*.

Propagation By cuttings, suckers or layering.

Conditions for growth Tropical or subtropical; small specimens are used as house plants or grown in greenhouses.

113 FICUS LYRATA
Banjo Fig, Fiddle-leaf Fig

Family Moraceae. **Evergreen**
Etymology The specific name refers to the shape of the leaves, which suggest a stringed instrument.
Habitat Native to tropical West Africa.
Description Young specimens of this plant are often used as ornamental house plants, but in its natural surroundings the tree can reach a height of 12 m (40 ft), with an erect trunk often divided from the base, and not very spreading branches, with more erect habit. The glossy, leathery leaves are very big, sometimes as much as 50 cm (20 in) long, and have a curious shape that recalls a stringed instrument, with an eared base above which the leaf blade first narrows and then broadens again; the margin is obtuse at the top, with a short, cuspidate point at the tip of the midrib; the margins are sinuate. The inflorescences, typical of the genus, are pyramidal, with unisexual flowers enclosed in hollow receptacles. They are followed by fruit of the syconial type, with a green skin with white dots.
Propagation Difficult by cuttings, easier by layering.
Conditions for growth Needs a minimum temperature of 7 °C (45 °F). Never becomes arborescent in European climates.

114 FICUS RELIGIOSA
Peepul Tree, Bo Tree

Family Moraceae. **Deciduous**
Etymology The specific name comes from Latin *"religiosus,"* sacred. According to legend, it was under one of these trees that Buddha received the enlightenment (*bodhi*) which was to form the basis of his teaching. The tree is often planted beside Indian temples.
Habitat Native to India.
Description This is one of the so-called pagoda figs, a category that includes nearly all those with aerial roots which start from the branches and grow down to and into the ground, where they form new rooted trunks. This plant can grow up to 30 m (100 ft) in height, and its widely spreading branches make a dense crown. The leaves, on long stalks, are cordate at the base, with an entire leaf blade having a remarkably sharp point that forms a sort of cuspidate appendix. The veins of young leaves are rosy; when adult the blade takes on a bluish-green color and the veins turn ivory white. The fruits, small and sessile, grow in pairs at the axils of the leaves, and are purple.
Propagation By cuttings or layering.
Conditions for growth Tropical; young specimens can be raised in the greenhouse.

115 FICUS SYCOMORUS
Sycamore

Family Moraceae   **Deciduous**
Etymology In Greek, *syka* means fig. The species name comes from the Greek *sykomorea*, sycamore, used in the Gospel according to St Luke; but Strabo had used the word *sykomoron* to denote the fruit a century before Christ. It has since been applied as a popular name to many sorts of trees, including *Acer pseudoplatanus* (**76**) and *Platanus occidentalis* (**143**).
Habitat Syria, Egypt, Sudan and parts of tropical Africa.
Description A tree of erect, spreading habit, with a greatly branched, rounded crown, up to 10–13 m (33–43 ft) in height; the trunk is a fulvous yellow. The leaves, partially deciduous—they fall for some months every year—are ovate, with a rough surface and downy veins, glaucescent when young, leathery and olive green when mature. The flowers are greenish. The small, edible fruits are produced in great quantities and, as in all the genus, are syconial. The wood is valuable for its hardness, so much so that in ancient Egypt it was used to make sarcophagi.
Propagation By cuttings or layering.
Conditions for growth Hot, even arid climates; tolerates drought, though it will grow more luxuriantly near rivers.

---

116 FRAXINUS AMERICANA
White Ash, American Ash

Family Oleaceae.   **Deciduous**
Etymology The generic name, which the Romans used for *F. excelsior*, comes from the Greek *phraxo*, closed, since the plant was used to make hedges.
Habitat Native to the eastern United States.
Description A tree 30–40 m (100–130 ft) high, the young branches glabrous and glossy but sometimes covered with a bloom. The leaves (1) are very large, formed from 5–9 pedunculate pointed oval leaflets with an entire margin, which may be slightly toothed at the tip; the glabrous leaf blade is dark green on the upper side and whitish glaucous on the underside, where it is downy. The stalk is yellowish white and furrowed. The unisexual flowers have a calyx but no corolla. The fruits are samaras with one small seed, hanging in dense bunches as in other ashes. *F. americana* is valued for its wood, very similar to that of *F. excelsior* (**118**); it is used in the manufacture of furniture, both large pieces and more delicate work, or cut for veneers. Its big leaves, which turn purple or yellow in autumn, make it ornamental in gardens or parks.
Propagation By seed.
Conditions for growth Prefers rich, highly organic soils.

117 FRAXINUS EXCELSIOR
European Ash

Family Oleaceae.   **Deciduous**
Etymology The Latin specific name means, literally, "higher", compared presumably with *F. ornus* **(120)**, which is common in the woods of Italy and may also have been known to the Romans.
Habitat Widely distributed in the Northern Hemisphere, the ash grows wild in much of Europe at altitudes of up to 1500 m (5000 ft), rarely forming monocultural forests.
Description This tree grows up to 10 m (130 ft) high, terminating in a sparse and irregular crown. The red-brown bark cracks with age. The compound leaves (1) are formed from 9–15 oval-lanceolate leaflets with toothed margin. The flowers (2) are not very conspicuous, having no calyx or corolla; they grow in panicles that are set erect at first but later become pendulous, and open before the leaves appear to facilitate pollination, which is anemophilous. The fruits (3) are samaras, wind scattered by their single wing.
Propagation By seed, gathered from the plant in autumn or at the beginning of winter.
Conditions for growth Needs cool, deep soil; in parks and gardens where the climate is not too cold and dry.

118 FRAXINUS OREGONA
Oregon Ash

Family Oleaceae.   **Deciduous**
Etymology The specific name comes from the State of Oregon, the original home of this ash.
Habitat Western regions of the United States.
Description Grows up to 25 m (80 ft); young branches are often covered with a whitish down and flattened at the nodes. Like all ashes, it bears leaves and buds in opposite pairs, creating a ramification pattern that makes young trees easy to recognize even in winter, when the deciduous leaves have gone. The buds are brown and downy, which distinguishes the tree from the European Ash **(118)**, whose dull-black winter buds are a characteristic feature. The large, compound, imparipinnate leaves (1) are composed of 5–7 leaflets, slightly toothed toward the tip and downy on the underside. The fruits (2) are samaras with a lanceolate wing; they grow in dense clusters.
Propagation By seed, gathered from the plant in autumn.
Conditions for growth Cool, deep soils; temperate climate.

119 FRAXINUS ORNUS
Flowering Ash, Manna Ash

Family Oleaceae.   **Deciduous**
Etymology The specific name comes from the Romans' name for this tree.
Habitat Central-southern and eastern Europe.
Description A tree with a broad, round crown growing to 10 m (33 ft). It produces suckers. The bark is gray and smooth. The imparipinnate leaves (2) are formed of from five to nine ovate-lanceolate leaflets, glabrous on the upper side, downy at the base of the central vein on the underside. The flowers are white and scented, growing in dense panicles which appear after the leaves, in late spring. The fruit (1) is a little, reddish-brown samara with only one seed. The wood, hard and resilient and oily to the touch when worked, is used for tool handles and for sporting goods. The white flowers make this an attractive ornamental tree. The descending sap, when tapped by an incision in the bark, forms a white or yellowish mass of sweet, slightly acid flavor, known as "manna." *F. ornus* is cultivated for this substance, which has purgative properties.
Propagation By seed; by root suckers; in varieties cultivated for manna, by grafting.
Conditions for growth Likes sunny positions and tolerates dry conditions.

---

120 GLEDITSIA TRIACANTHOS
Honey Locust, Sweet Locust

Family Leguminosae.   **Deciduous**
Etymology The generic name commemorates Gottlieb Gleditsch, director of the Berlin Botanical Gardens, who died in 1786.
Habitat Central-eastern United States.
Description A deciduous tree which grows more than 30 m (100 ft) high, with a broad crown. The leaves (1), which appear rather late, are alternate and may be pinnate with 10–12 pairs of leaflets, or bipinnate with 4–7 pairs of leaflets; both forms appear on the same plants and are pubescent along the midrib. The leaflets are oblong-lanceolate, with serrated margin, and turn yellow before they fall. The leaves fall early, so that the foliage is only on the tree for a short time. Long, vicious thorns (2) guard the trunk and branches. The insignificant flowers grow in greeny-yellow panicles, with a small calyx and 3–5 petals. The fruits are brown, indehiscent pods, curved and twisted, up to 45 cm (18 in) long, with depressions between the seeds. They grow very profusely in clusters. Var. *inermis* has no thorns and shorter, red-brown pods. It is an excellent shade tree for terraces.
Propagation By seeds, which are rather hard and must be soaked in water before sowing.
Conditions for growth Completely hardy. Tolerant of most soils.

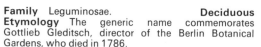

121 GREVILLEA ROBUSTA
Silk-Oak Grevillea

Family Proteaceae.   **Evergreen**
Etymology The name commemorates Charles F. Greville (1749–1809), one of the founders of the Royal Horticultural Society of London.
Description In its native climates this tree reaches a height of some 40 m (130 ft) although, particularly in the North, it is often cultivated in the very young stage as a pot plant. The leaves (1) are bipinnatifid, like big fern fronds, green on the upper side, silvery below. The flowers grow in racemes on the old wood of the previous year's branches; they are apetalous, with a short calyx of four upturned lobes, four stamens with sessile anthers and a long, curved style. They are orange and rather small, but they grow densely on the branches of the inflorescence to form striking clusters. The fruits (2) are follicles, with 1–2 flat winged seeds. The timber is tough and elastic, used in joinery. The flowers are very attractive to bees making this an important honey plant.
Propagation By seed (easy) or by cuttings.
Conditions for growth When adult tolerates temperatures down to −10 °C (14 °F) and withstands drought. Needs acid soil.

---

122 GUAIACUM OFFICINALE
Lignum Vitae

Family Zygophyllaceae.   **Evergreen**
Etymology From the common South American name, *guaiac*, which means wood of life. In Spanish-speaking countries it is called *guayacán*, or holy tree (*palo santo*).
Habitat Native to Central America as far south as Venezuela and Colombia.
Description A slow-growing evergreen that hardly ever reaches 10 m (33 ft), with a broad crown and bifurcated branches swollen at the nodes. The compound leaves (1) are paripinnate, with long, green, leathery, obovate leaflets measuring about 1 cm (0.5 in). The flowers (2) are small, stellate, growing in dense panicles, their blue changing to white before they fall. They often appear at the same time as the heart-shaped fruits, which contain a single large seed, oval and spiny. The brown or greenish wood is very heavy, one of the hardest and most durable in the world, and is used in shipbuilding; it is also very resinous, with a pleasant smell and a slightly acid taste. It has been used for centuries for its medicinal properties—which is how it got its popular name—and contains guaiacic acid and other acids. However, its main use is as timber.
Propagation By seed.
Conditions for growth Tropical. Likes dry, sandy soils and grows mainly along coasts.

123 GYMNOCLADUS DIOICUS
Kentucky Coffee Tree

Family Leguminosae. **Deciduous**
Etymology The name comes from the Greek *gymnos*, bare, and *klados*, branch, referring to the large branches which remain bare from early to late winter.
Habitat Native to the United States, in a central-eastern strip northwest of the Allegheny Mountains.
Description This tree reaches a height of over 30 m (100 ft), and has a stout trunk with a great number of erect branches and a globose crown. The leaves (1) are as much as 90 cm (36 in) long and 45 cm (19 in) wide; alternate, rather irregularly bipinnate, with 3–7 pairs of leaflets; they are oval or ovate and acuminate, and downy in the juvenile stage. The stalks persist after the leaves have fallen. The small flowers grow in greenish-white inflorescences and may be unisexual or polygamous. The fruits (2) are legumes, very large and conspicuous, which persist during the winter; the seeds were once used as a substitute for coffee—hence the common name of Kentucky Coffee Tree.
Propagation By seed or by radical shoots.
Conditions for growth Tolerates severe climates and average soil.

124 HALESIA MONTICOLA
Mountain Silverbell

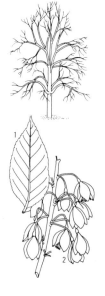

Family Styracaceae. **Deciduous**
Etymology The name commemorates the Reverend Stephen Hales (1677–1761), English inventor and physiologist.
Habitat Grows wild in the mountains of the south-eastern United States.
Description This tree, long thought to be a variety of *H. carolina*, which comes from the same region, is now recognized as a distinct species. It reaches some 25 m (80 ft), with a pyramidal crown, and grows rapidly. The deciduous leaves (1) are entire, stalked but without stipules, oblong-ovate and toothed at the margins, and glabrous; they turn yellow before they fall. The flowers (2) have united petals and grow in axillary clusters in spring on the previous year's wood; they have a small calyx and a fairly big, bellshaped white corolla with four lobes and are generally pendulous. The fruits that follow them are drupes with four big longitudinal wings; the stone contains 1–3 seeds.
Propagation By seed, which must be fresh; by softwood cuttings; by layering.
Conditions for growth Shelter from strong winds. Not demanding about soil.

125 HIPPOPHAE RHAMNOIDES
Sea Buckthorn

Family Eleagnaceae. **Deciduous**
Etymology From the Greek *hippophaes*, used by Hippocrates and Dioscorides for some unidentified spiny plant.
Habitat Central-southern Europe, west and central Asia as far as western China.
Description A deciduous plant of bushy habit which reaches a height of 10 m (33 ft), with gray, spiny branches. On young branches the bark is scaly and light gray, almost silvery. The leaves (1) are linear-lanceolate, gray-green on the upper side, silvery-green below, 2–6 cm (1–2.5 in) long, with a short stalk. The plants are dioecious and the little flowers (2) that appear in spring in short racemes at the axils of the previous year's branches are small, yellowish and insignificant in both sexes. In female trees the flowers are followed by drupelike fruits (3), round and orange-yellow, with a hard ovate stone which contains the seed. The fruit appears in autumn and persists on the bare branches.
Propagation By seed or by cuttings, to produce the desired sex.
Conditions for growth Very tolerant of drought and the saline soils of the seashore. Also grows inland. Often difficult to establish.

126 HOVENIA DULCIS
Japanese Raisin Tree

Family Rhamnaceae. **Deciduous**
Etymology The name commemorates David Hoven, a Dutch senator of the 16th century who helped to finance the expedition of the botanist Thumberg.
Habitat Native to China, Japan and the Himalayas.
Description A deciduous tree, the only species of its genus. The trunk can reach 18 m (60 ft), branches at the top and has deeply fissured bark. The leaves (1) are alternate, with long stalks, glabrous, ovate-acuminate with serrated margin, often almost entire. The flowers (2) are small and white, growing in axillary or apical racemes; the calyx and corolla are divided into five lobes and five petals. The flower stalk, after fertilization and the formation of the fruits, swells up and twists, becoming fleshy; each subdivision carries a little brown, round, indehiscent drupe at the tip containing three flat, glossy, light-brown seeds. Curiously enough, when they are ripe these swollen stems contain a sweetish edible flesh which tastes rather like a raisin, whereas the fruit is not edible.
Propagation By seed or by cuttings of young branches, under glass.
Conditions for growth Half-hardy; can be damaged by frosts if they are too prolonged or too intense.

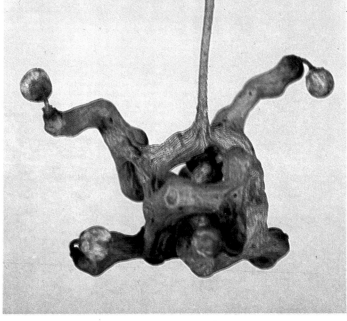

127   IDESIA POLYCARPIA

Family Flacourtiaceae.   **Deciduous**
Etymology The name commemorates Eberhard
Yobrants Ides, a Dutchman at the court of Peter the
Great, who explored Asia in 1691–1695.
Habitat Central-western China and Japan.
Description This is the only species of the genus, a
tree 10–15 m (33–50 ft) in height with horizontal
branches. The leaves (1), deciduous and with a long red
stalk, are alternate, broadly oval, with rounded teeth at
the margins. The plants are dioecious and both the male
and female flowers (2) are greenish creamy white, with
no petals but five or more sepals; the males have a great
number of stamens. The flowers appear in spring in big
terminal panicles. The fruits that follow the female
flowers form large bunches of berries with several
orange-red seeds which persist after the leaves have
fallen. A very decorative tree in winter.
Propagation By seed, which germinates easily but
with no certainty about the sex of the plant. To be sure of
fructification, cleft grafting is commonly used with a
male scion on female stock.
Conditions for growth Likes acid-to-neutral soils.

128   ILEX AQUIFOLIUM
English Holly

Family Aquifoliaceae.   **Evergreen**
Etymology The name is derived from the Latin *ilex*,
which in Classical times meant the Holm Oak.
Habitat Native to Britain and also grows in central-
southern Europe, from the Iberian Peninsula to the
Caucasus and as far as Persia and North Africa.
Description A tree 8–10 m (26–33 ft) high, with a
smooth bark, green in young plants, then gray. The
crown is a pyramidal cone. The leaves (1) are persistent,
oval or elliptical and pointed, with spines at the margins
and the point; they are leathery, alternate, glossy dark
green above but lighter and duller on the underside. The
unisexual flowers (2) are small and white, with short
stalks. The fruit is a bright-red globose or ovoid drupe
which contains four seeds and has purgative properties.
The wood is hard and can be dyed; it may be used as a
substitute for ebony. The bark is sticky and contains
tannin.
Propagation By seed or by cuttings of partially
lignified shoots.
Conditions for growth Not very tolerant of lime.
Likes humidity and therefore grows well only near bodies
of water. It does particularly well in the Pacific
Northwest.

129 JUGLANS NIGRA
Eastern black walnut

Family Juglandaceae   **Deciduous**
Etymology The name is of Latin origin; it was used by Cicero for the species *Juglans regia*, and is derived from 'Jovis glans', Jove's acorn.
Habitat Central and eastern United States.
Description A deciduous tree from 20 to 40 m (65 to 130 ft) in height, with an erect trunk with very dark, deeply furrowed bark and rounded crown. The pinnate leaves (1) are about 60 cm (24 in) long and have 10–20 lanceolate-acuminate leaflets, glabrous on the upper side and pubescent on the under side. The flowers (2) are unisexual, both sexes being carried on the same plant; the females grow in small, sparsely flowering racemes, and both sexes are small and insignificant. The fruit (3) is a drupe in which the seed, enclosed in a woody stone, is surrounded by a fleshy husk. The fruits may be either solitary or paired; they are very much more spherical in shape than those of *J. regia*, and the nut is small and very woody. The tree is cultivated not only for ornament but also for its very beautiful dark red wood, hard and proof against attack by insects. The roots contain a substance called juglone which can poison surrounding trees.
Propagation By seed.
Conditions for growth Hardy; likes well drained soils.

---

130 KIGELIA PINNATA

Family Bignoniaceae.   **Evergreen**
Etymology The name is a latinization of the name used in Mozambique.
Habitat Tropical Africa from the Sudan to Mozambique and the Transvaal.
Description A tree with a stout trunk, often branching from the base, which grows 6–15 m (20–50 ft) high, with spreading branches and pendulous secondary branchlets. The leaves (1) are imparipinnate, with 7–9 oblong leaflets, entire or serrate, smooth on the upper side, often slightly downy below. The lateral leaflets are sessile on the midrib while the apical leaflet grows out as much as 30 cm (12 in) from the final pair; as a result, the crown of the tree does not look very dense. Pendulous racemes bear large, showy flowers (2) with a tubular corolla, yellow at the base and red at the open lobes. The main branch of the inflorescence is very long, and the fruit that grows on it, brownish-gray and cylindrical, hangs from a stalk that may be as much as 1 m (3 ft) long. Some tribes make a drink from it.
Propagation By seed.
Conditions for growth Exclusively tropical.

131 LAURUS NOBILIS
Laurel, Sweet Bay

Family Lauraceae.   **Evergreen**
Etymology The name is the same as the Latin. The Greeks called the plant *daphne* after the legend that the nymph Daphne was turned into a laurel to escape from Apollo. The tree became sacred to that god and was used in festivals in his honor, and when the cult passed to Rome, conquerors and poets were crowned with laurel, a custom that survived for a very long time. Even Napoleon's crown featured a golden laurel wreath.
Habitat Grows wild in the Mediterranean region.
Description This evergreen tree has a maximum height of 8–12 m (25–40 ft) and bushy habit. The lanceolate leaves (1) are glossy green, alternate, leathery and aromatic. The flowers are unisexual, yellowish, growing in small umbels. The plants are dioecious flowering in spring, and the little flowers on the female plants are followed by small black drupes (2), glossy and ovoid or globose, rather like olives. There are several varieties, including *crispa* and *angustifolia*.
Propagation By seed, cuttings, layering and basal suckers.
Conditions for growth Hardy; withstands temperatures as low as − 15 °C (5 °F). Tolerates pruning well, so that it is often used for hedges and even sometimes for topiary art.

---

132 MACLURA PONIFERA
Osage Orange, Bois d'arc

Family Moraceae.   **Deciduous**
Etymology Named after William Maclure, American geologist (1763–1840). The popular name is derived from that of an Indian tribe now living in Oklahoma. Its French-American name refers to its use in making bows.
Habitat Native to North America.
Description A tree with a globose crown, which can reach a height of 10 m (33 ft) or more. The whole plant contains a thick latex. The branches have powerful axillary thorns; the leaves (1) are alternate, oblong with wavy margins, and turn yellow before they fall. The flowers are unisexual, the stalked males (2) in pendulous racemes, the females (3) in globose inflorescences with short stalks. The fruits are syncarps composed of a great number of little drupes making up a nonedible globe as big as a large orange, yellowish green when ripe. The hard wood is used for fence posts. A dyestuff, morindin, is extracted from both the wood and the bark.
Propagation By seed, which must be fresh, and by root cuttings.
Conditions for growth This is an undemanding tree that withstands bitter cold and drought. It is widely used to form windbreaks and impenetrable hedges, especially in the Middle West.

133 MALALEUCA DIOSMIFOLIA

Family Myrtaceae   **Evergreen**
Etymology The name comes from the Greek 'melas', black, and 'leukos', white, because the trunk and old branches have a dark bark while that on the young shoots is white.
Habitat Native to Australia.
Description A small evergreen tree which can grow up to 3 m (10 ft) high, but which often remains shorter because the trunk is so twisted. Branching almost down to the base, it is spreading, with rather pendulous branches, especially the thin and pliant young branches. The leaves (1), small and linear, almost needle-like, are stiff, attached to the branches alternately but in a spiral, not in two straight rows; at most a centimetre (half an inch) long, they are very aromatic. The flowers (2), white, small, and densely growing, appear in cylindrical spikes; since growth continues at the tip of the spike in young shoots, the mid-rib itself becomes part of the branch. After the flowers come the little, sessile, pitcher-shaped fruits—capsules containing many tiny seeds; they persist for a very long time.
Propagation Reproduction by seed results in very slow growth, and propagation by cuttings is to be preferred.
Conditions for growth Half-hardy; flourishes in temperate climates.

134 METROSIDEROS ROBUSTA
North Island Rata

Family Myrtaceae.   **Evergreen**
Etymology The name comes from the Greek *metra*, pith, and *sideros*, iron, referring to the hardness of the wood. In the forests where it grows wild it is called Rata.
Habitat Native to New Zealand.
Description A tall tree that can reach a height of 30 m (100 ft), with an irregular trunk; away from its native surroundings it remains much shorter. It is one of the so-called strangulated trees which begin life as epiphytes and put out roots which, as soon as they touch the ground, take root there and surround the host tree until they completely destroy it and establish themselves in its place. Specimens growing on the ground are not so tall, but produce a wood so hard and durable that it has come to be called ironwood. The leaves are opposite, small, elliptical or lanceolate and very leathery, with a strong central vein. The red flowers are carried on very large terminal cymes, and have a cuplike calyx and a great many prominent stamens. The fruit is a capsule.
Propagation By seed, layering, or cuttings.
Conditions for growth Mild climates where the minimum temperature does not fall below 4 °C (39 °F), though when adult the plants can withstand short, sporadic frosts.

135 MORUS ALBA
White Mulberry

Family Moraceae. **Deciduous**
Etymology The name of the genus is the same as that used by the Romans.
Habitat Native to China, but reached Europe in ancient times.
Description A tree 10–18 m (33–60 ft) high, with an irregularly branched trunk forming a spreading crown. The bark, gray at first, later becomes brown and cracks longitudinally. The leaves (1), deciduous and light green, have a channelled stalk with deciduous stipules; the leaf blade, ovato-acute and three lobed, is smooth and light green on both sides. The flowers are unisexual, the males (2) growing in cylindrical catkins with a short stalk, the females (3) in subglobose catkins. The fruit (4), white, pink or violet, resembles the Black Mulberry's and is sweet even when unripe. Introduced into the Mediterranean probably during the 12th century together with the silkworm, which lives exclusively on its leaves, the tree was a characteristic feature of the Italian landscape when silkworm breeding was both an industry and a home craft. There is now a variety *pendula* which is grown in gardens.
Propagation By seed or cuttings, but mostly by grafting.
Conditions for growth Cool soil and sunny position.

---

136 MORUS NIGRA
Black Mulberry

Family Moraceae. **Deciduous**
Etymology The specific name refers to the dark color of the fruit compared with that of the related *M. alba* (**136**).
Habitat Native to Asia Minor and Persia, this tree too was introduced into the Mediterranean region many years ago.
Description Generally similar to the White Mulberry, but more robust, with thicker, rougher trunk and branches, the tree can reach 10–15 m (33–50 ft) and has a denser crown. The leaves (1), with a shorter, not deeply channelled stalk, are markedly cordate at the base, undivided or with 3–5 lobes, stiffer and of a darker green on the upper side, while the underside is downy. The flowers (2) are unisexual. The fruits (3) are larger than those of the White Mulberry, composed of a number of little violet-black drupes and, unlike the White Mulberry, sour until fully ripe. The tree is grown for its fruit, which is used to make slightly tart jams and jellies. The foliage is rough and not much used for feeding silkworms.
Propagation By seed, cuttings, layering or grafting.
Conditions for growth Has the same requirements as the White Mulberry, but is more frost resistant and can be grown at altitudes up to 1000 m (3300 ft).

137 NOLINA LONGIFOLIA

Family Agavaceae.   **Deciduous**
Etymology The name was given in honour of P. C. Nolin, author of works on agriculture, who lived in France in the mid-18th century.
Habitat Originally from Mexico.
Description A woody, slow-growing plant which becomes arborescent with time and can grow as much as 3 m (10 ft) tall. The thick trunk, covered in a very thick corky bark, has rather few erect branches, each with a cluster of long leaves (1) at the tip, linear and acuminate, with saw-toothed margins. The young branches in the centre are erect, but on maturity they become extroflex and later completely pendulous, remaining persistent for a long time even after they are withered. The creamy white bell-shaped flowers (2) are very small, growing in long, dense, erect panicles from the spreading ramification; they may be unisexual and polygamous. The fruit (3) contains from one to three seeds.
Propagation By seed, which is very slow-growing; if suckers appear they are a preferable means of reproduction.
Conditions for growth Mild climate, with only sporadic cold spells, never intense or prolonged.

138 OSTRYA CARPINIFOLIA
Hop Hornbeam

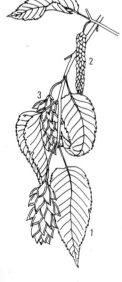

Family Corylaceae.   **Deciduous**
Etymology The name comes from the Latin and was used by Pliny for a species of hornbeam.
Habitat Southern Europe as far as Asia Minor and the Caucasus.
Description A tree growing up to 15–18 m (50–60 ft), with a straight trunk, an irregular outline and a compact crown, conical and less spreading than that of the hornbeam. The smooth, reddish bark has whitish transverse bands of lenticels when young, but becomes blackish red and rough with age. The simple, deciduous leaves (1) are ovate-oblong, rounded at the base and pointed at the tip, double toothed at the margin, dark green and glossy on the upper side, paler and hairy on the underside, with 11–17 pairs of secondary veins, not very conspicuous themselves but making the surface of the leaf look pimply at their intersections. The unisexual flowers grow in catkins, the males (2) cylindrical and pendulous, 2–3 to each precociously flowering cluster; the females (3) shorter and stumpy, erect at first, then also pendulous, appearing at the same time as the leaves. The infructescence is rather like that of the hop.
Propagation By seed; cuttings rooted in autumn; can also be grafted on *Carpinus betulus* (**87**) stock.
Conditions for growth Prefers soil limed, rich and cool. Requires a mild climate.

139 OSTRYA VIRGINIANA
Hop Hornbeam

Family Corylaceae.　　　　　　　　　　**Deciduous**
Etymology The specific name denotes the origin of the species in Virginia.
Habitat The distribution covers the eastern United States.
Description A tree 15–18 m (50–60 ft) high, with a straight trunk whose bark is smooth and reddish when young and later becomes cracked. The young branches are covered with straight hairs. The oblong-ovate leaves (1) are subcordate at the base and have rather inconspicuous veins subdivided into a tertiary venation. The pointed buds have small, light-green, glabrous bud-scales. (2, 3) male and female flowers. The fruits are small, smooth achenes, each one enclosed and protected by bracts fused at the margins when ripe to form a brown bladder; in this species the fruits form clusters up to 7 cm (3 in) long. The vesicles that contain them facilitate dissemination, which is carried out by the wind. The hard, strong wood is one of several commonly called ironwood.
Propagation By seed, cuttings, layering in summer, or grafting.
Conditions for growth Indifferent to soil type but prefers well-drained, sunny positions.

140 PHELLODENDRON AMURENSE
Amur Cork Tree

Family Rutaceae.　　　　　　　　　　**Deciduous**
Etymology Derived from the Greek *phellos*, cork, and *dendron*, tree, since the bark is corky.
Habitat Japan, Korea, northern China and Manchuria.
Description A tree 12–15 m (40–50 ft) tall, with thick, spreading branches and a distinctive form. The bark, deeply fissured, thick and corky, is light gray at first but becomes darker. The leaves (1) are more than 30–50 cm (12–20 in) long, compound, imparipinnate and alternate, composed of 5–11 oval leaflets with long points at the tip, and ciliate. Seen against the light they show transparent dots due to oleiferous cells which contain aromatic elements; when rubbed between the fingers they smell of turpentine. Light green in autumn, they turn golden yellow before they fall. The small, whitish flowers, insignificant and unisexual, open in late spring and grow in corymbs. The fruits (3) are black drupes the size of a pea, ripening in the autumn; they too smell of turpentine when rubbed. The wood, with white sapwood and brown heartwood, is used in China for making furniture, gunstocks and small tools.
Propagation By seed or cuttings taken in July.
Conditions for growth Likes limestone soils but adapts to all kinds; temperate climates.

141 PHYTOLACCA DIOICA

Family Phytolaccaceae.   **Evergreen**
Etymology From the Greek *phyton*, plant, and *lacca*, a
Latinized form of the Amerindian word *laek*, shellac, from
the coloring property of the fruit.
Habitat South America, particularly from Brazil to
Argentina; locally called *ombú*.
Description A big tree that can exceed 15 m (50 ft),
with a very dense, spreading crown, evergreen but
semideciduous in colder climates. The trunk grows as
much as 2 m (6 ft) in diameter, greatly swollen at the
base, with roots that readily come to the surface and put
out numbers of arborescent suckers. The leaves (1) are
green, elliptical and markedly acuminate, with narrow
stalks. The plants are dioecious; the flowers (2) grow in
racemes, often pendulous, the males having 20–30
stamens and a whitish calyx, the females a big calyx and
rounded ovary. The fruits are fleshy berries, joined at the
base and yellowish. The tree grows rapidly and lives no
one knows quite how long, since the very pithy trunk
does not form annual rings.
Propagation By seed.
Conditions for growth Mild climates; injured by
severe frosts but will grow in salt air near the ocean.

---

142 PLATANUS OCCIDENTALIS
Sycamore, Buttonwood

Family Platanaceae.   **Deciduous**
Etymology The species name refers to the tree's
origin in the Western Hemisphere.
Habitat Native to eastern North America.
Description A tree 40–50 m (130–165 ft) high, with
a bare cylindrical trunk whose diameter can be as much
as 3 m (10 ft); the stout, widely spaced branches form a
broad crown. The grayish-brown bark flakes off to reveal
a light-brown inner bark. The deciduous palmate leaves
(1) have three (sometimes five) lobes; the middle one,
wider than long, is separated at the base from the lobes
on either side of it by shallow, wide incisions. The
globose inflorescences (2), small, hanging balls, are
usually solitary, sometimes grouped in twos or threes.
The seeds, thin, prismatic achenes, remain on the tree
throughout the winter. (3) fruit. Its greater size, its leaves
with wider, shallower lobes and its nearly always solitary
fruits distinguish the "western" plane from the "oriental." Long lived, up to 600 years. The wood's intricate
grain makes it hard to cut and consequently suitable for
use as butcher blocks.
Propagation By cuttings (easy), and by seed.
Conditions for growth Likes cool, deep alluvial
soils; will not adapt to acid or marshy soils. Constantly
sheds leaves, branches and bark.

143   PLATANUS ORIENTALIS
Oriental Plane, Eastern Plane

Family Platanaceae.   **Deciduous**
Etymology The specific name refers to the origin of the tree.
Habitat Originally from the temperate zones of western Asia, now grows wild in Sicily and southern Italy, Greece and Turkey.
Description This is a tree up to 30—35 m (100—115 ft) high, with a straight, cylindrical trunk covered with a whitish bark which peels off in wide, thin strips. The stout branches form a broad, rounded, dense crown with big palmate-lobate leaves (1), slightly hairy when young, then glabrous. The long leafstalk grows thicker at the base to form a protective cap for the bud. The unisexual inflorescences (2, 3), which open in April—May, are typical globose, pendulous capitula carried on long stalks (4), which when ripe open to release the seeds, achenes surrounded by a down that helps with dissemination. This fast-growing species is frequently cultivated for onament or as a shade tree on roadsides or in city parks. The light, half-hard wood has a certain commercial value.
Propagation Reproduction by seed is common, but cuttings of two- to three-year-old branchlets are preferable.
Conditions for growth A sunny location; prefers fertile, deep, cool, rather moist soils.

144   POPULUS ALBA
White Poplar

Family Salinaceae.   **Deciduous**
Etymology The name is derived from *arbor populi*, the people's tree, the name the ancient Romans used for the same plant.
Habitat Distributed from central-southern Europe to western Asia and North Africa.
Description Under ideal conditions this tree can reach a height of 30 m (100 ft). It has a gray to gray-green bark on a generally erect trunk; when young it has bands of lenticels, later it becomes fissured and rough. The adult leaves (1) have a short stalk with ovate or elliptical leaf blade, sinuate or bluntly dentate at the margin, with a gray tomentum on the underside and intense green above; on young shoots the leaves are roughly triangular or palmate-lobate, with a long stalk. The flowers are lateral catkins, the males (2) cylindrical with the stamens and anthers purple at first turning to yellow, the females (3) much shorter, with a pink stigma. The fruit is a glabrous capsule. The wood is mediocre, only used for planking and packing cases or as supporting parts in furniture manufactured from finer woods.
Propagation By seed, radical suckers or cuttings.
Conditions for growth The species likes lime and resists drought.

145 POPULUS DELTOIDES
Cottonwood, Necklace Poplar

Family Salicaceae.   **Deciduous**
Etymology The specific name refers to the shape of
the leaves, which, especially when young, form a triangle.
Habitat Native to North America.
Description A tree 25–30 m (80–100 ft) high with a
deeply fissured bark and very broad crown; its thick
branches are angular and brownish when young. The
buds are big, pointed and downy, the leaves (1) very big,
deciduous, alternate and simple; they are delta shaped,
wider than they are long, with straight, slightly heart-
shaped base and fairly pointed tip; the stalk is long and
flat, with two or three characteristic glands. The leaf
blade is dark green on top, paler below and hairy at the
margin; the leaves are pubescent when young. The unisexual flowers grow in catkins, the males denser, the
females as much as 20 cm (8 in) long. The "cotton" is
shed profusely in spring. This fast-growing poplar
reaches its full height in 20 years; it provides abundant
wood for the production of cellulose. Cottonwood
groves on the American prairies provided settlers with
shade and wood for building. Its hybrids with the
European Black Poplar have proved very useful, particularly for their rapid growth and disease resistance.
Propagation The type species by seed, hybrids by
cuttings.
Conditions for growth Cool, fertile, aerated soil.

---

146 POPULUS EURO-AMERICANA

Family Salicaceae.   **Deciduous**
Etymology The name of this group refers to their
origin.
Description This is a denomination covering all the
hybrids obtained by crossing the European black poplar
(*Populus nigra*) with the American cottonwoods
(*Populus deltoides*), which were once known by the
rather too general names of Canadian, Carolinian or
Virginian poplars. Within the scope of this species, or
rather of this now generally accepted standardized
hybrid, individual types are denoted by fancy names or
by initials or numbers indicating pre-selected clones; the
trees are grown throughout the world on a vast scale for
the intensive production of wood. What distinguishes
the Euro-American poplars is the greater size of their
leaves compared with those of the black poplar and the
almost invariable presence of one or two large and very
conspicuous reddish glands at the base of the upper side
of the leaf just where it joins the stalk. Young leaves and
stalks are coppery in colour, or at any rate suffused with
red.
Propagation Often by vegetative methods, to ensure
maintenance of the selected clones.
Conditions for growth The trees prefer light soils,
deep and well watered, or the soils of river banks or
alluvial plains.

147 POPULUS NIGRA var. ITALICA
Lombardy Poplar

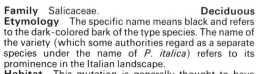

Family Salicaceae.   **Deciduous**
Etymology The specific name means black and refers to the dark-colored bark of the type species. The name of the variety (which some authorities regard as a separate species under the name of *P. italica*) refers to its prominence in the Italian landscape.
Habitat This mutation is generally thought to have originated in western Asia and to have been introduced into Italy in ancient times.
Description Distinguished by its tapered columnar shape, as much as 40 m (130 ft) high. It differs from the type species in its often polycormous trunk, its thinner, erect (almost vertical) branches and its leaves (1), which are rhomboidal-ovate but smaller and more rounded, with a stalk tinged with pink. The unisexual flowers grow on separate trees—there are male and female Lombardy poplars. The male flowers (2) grow in elongated catkins given a reddish look by the large number of red anthers, while the more graceful females (3) become longer when ripe and are greenish. (4) fruit. The tree is widely cultivated for avenues and for lining streets and canals, but is short lived and breaks up in storms.
Propagation Only from cuttings, since the vast majority of Lombardy poplars are male.
Conditions for growth Warm summers, likes sun.

---

148 POPULUS TREMULOIDES
Quaking Aspen

Family Salicaceae.   **Deciduous**
Etymology The specific name refers to the resemblance this poplar bears to *P. tremula*, from which it differs in its distribution.
Habitat A very large area in North America, from Labrador to Alaska and, further south, from Pennsylvania to southern California.
Description This tree, which can grow to a height of 25–30 m (80–100 ft), is also called the False Aspen, because both in its silhouette and in the morphology of some of its parts it recalls *P. tremula:* For example, its bark, which for a long time remains light and smooth, greenish gray or whitish, but becomes rough and dark gray at the foot of the trunk in old trees, recalls that of the aspen. Young branches, however, are reddish brown, smooth and fragile; the buds are sticky. The leaves (1), deciduous and alternate, are rounded, cordate, more pointed than the aspen's and with a more finely, and perhaps more irregularly toothed margin; the long stalk is thin and flattened at the sides. (2) flowers. (3) fruit. Planted in groups, it is a fast-growing ornamental. A favorite tree of beavers, who eat its inner bark and construct lodges and dams from the logs. In the West, often a nurse tree for more commercial timber.
Propagation By cuttings, which root easily.
Conditions for growth Prefers light, friable soils.

149 QUERCUS CERRIS
Turkey Oak

Family Fagaceae.   **Deciduous**
Etymology The species name is from the Latin for fringe and refers to the hairy cups of the acorns.
Habitat From southeastern Europe to western Asia.
Description A fine, majestic tree, as much as 30–35 m (100–115 ft) high, with a trunk 13 m (4 ft) in diameter. It has a graceful shape with a dense, dark crown. The bark is deeply fissured and blackish, the young branches are angular, greenish gray and rather hairy. The alternate simple leaves (1), rather leathery, are often oblong and have a very variable outline with 7–8 pairs of unequal lobes; they are deciduous, falling late, made grayish by tomentum on both sides when young, turning dark green and rough to the touch on the upper side when adult. The flowers are unisexual, the males (2) growing in pendulous cylindrical catkins, the females single or in groups of 2–5, with short stalks. The fruit—the acorn—is an elongated ovate achene (3) protected for one-third or one-half its length by a cupule made of linear scales, brown and downy. The wood, rosy with a slight lavender tinge, is heavy and hard but apt to split; after treating with creosote it is used for railroad ties or barrel staves.
Propagation By seed, planted when barely ripe.
Conditions for growth Likes hot climates, tolerates drought.

---

150 QUERCUS FRAINETTO
Hungarian Oak

Family Fagaceae.   **Deciduous**
Etymology The species name is a local name for this oak from the Balkans.
Habitat The Hungarian Oak is confined to a limited area in the Balkans and southern Italy.
Description A tree up to 30 m (100 ft) high, sometimes as much as 40 m (130 ft), of a very graceful shape. The bark is smooth, not fissured for the first ten years, after that cracked in little flat, dark gray scales. The alternate, simple leaves (1) are large and deeply lobed at the margins, with 7–9 pairs of lateral lobes, themselves lobulate toward the tip. They resemble the leaves of the English Oak (**156**) but are bigger and more deeply lobed and have stipules that are deciduous, falling late. The flowers are unisexual, the males growing in slightly downy catkins, 4–5 cm (about 2 in) long, and the females in very downy spikes. The acorns (2), on short stalks, ripen in October and have a hemispherical cupule with a great number of awl-shaped scales. Ever since ancient times the oak has stood as a symbol of strength and perseverance, loyalty and heroism; a crown of oak leaves with acorns, called *corona civica*, was awarded to a Roman soldier who saved a comrade's life in battle.
Propagation By seed; remarkably fast growing.
Conditions for growth Must have light, fertile soil.

151 QUERCUS ILEX
Holm Oak, Holly Oak

Family Fagaceae.   **Evergreen**
Etymology The specific name is that which the Romans used for this same tree.
Habitat A Mediterranean species, whose distribution extends from the southern European coasts to North Africa.
Description A tree that grows up to 25 m (80 ft), with a not-very-tall trunk which may reach or exceed 1 m (3 ft) in diameter and a broad, oval, dense crown. The bark, gray and smooth when young, cracks into little, almost square scales in older trees. The leaves (1), persistent for two or three years, are simple, alternate and leathery; the leaf blade is very variable in shape and size, with toothed, spiny margins in young specimens but entire on old trees; the edge is glossy on the upper side while the underside is white and fluffy from the presence of stellate hairs. These are easily saturated with water vapor and so reduce transpiration, one of the tree's adaptations to the Mediterranean climate. (2) flowers. The acorns are small, half covered by the cupule, which is made of downy scales; they are a favorite food of pigs, giving their meat a special flavor.
Propagation By seed or by root suckers.
Conditions for growth Grows well even in limestone subsoils.

152 QUERCUS PETRAEA
Durmast Oak, Sessile Oak

Family Fagaceae.   **Deciduous**
Etymology The specific name denotes that this oak likes stony places with good drainage.
Habitat Central and southeastern Europe.
Description A tree up to 30–40 m (100–130 ft) high with a thick trunk and a broad, dense, fairly regular crown. The bark is gray, smooth for the first 20 years then fissured longitudinally. The alternate leaves, simple and deciduous, are stiff and leathery in the adult state and have a generally oblong outline with 5–8 roundish lobes, glossy green below and borne on a long stalk. Those leaves of the Sessile Oak that grow in the shade are different from those exposed to the sun: they are less persistent, contain more chlorophyll and have fewer stomata. The tree is called "sessile" because the female flowers, and hence the acorns, are virtually without stalks. The wood is valuable and is used for roof timbers, parquet flooring, furniture and shipbuilding. The precise alternation of porous spring wood and dark summer wood allows reconstruction of the tree's history and the weather conditions during its growth.
Propagation By seed, where the tree is to grow.
Conditions for growth Sensitive to humidity both in the atmosphere and the soil. Will not tolerate wet soils and is damaged by late frosts.

153 QUERCUS ROBUR
Common Oak, English Oak

Family Fagaceae.   **Deciduous**
Etymology The specific name is a Latin word used to describe all hard wood, especially that of the oak.
Habitat All over Europe except for the extreme north, and in part of the Mediterranean region.
Description A majestic tree which can reach a height of 50 m (165 ft), with a stout trunk and large, irregular crown. The alternate, simple, deciduous leaves (1), herbaceous rather than leathery, are ovate-oblong in the adult state, narrower at the base and broader toward the tip, with 5–7 pairs of broad lobes separated by roundish bays; the color is dark green and glossy on the upper side, paler below. (2, 3) male and female flowers. The acorn (4) is ovate-oblong and pointed, partly enclosed by a cupule of appressed scales, overlapping and slightly tomentose. The wood (whitish sapwood and darker heartwood) is a favorite with shipbuilders and for use as roof timbers. the so-called Slavonian Oak used for making casks for the aging of valuable wines and brandy, comes from the Common Oak and not from the Sessile Oak (**155**), which grows in Slavonia. The wood is easy to work and long lasting.
Propagation By seed.
Conditions for growth Light and fertile alkaline soils. Withstands frost.

---

154 RAVENALA MADAGASCARIENSIS
Traveler's Tree

Family Musaceae.   **Evergreen**
Etymology From the local name.
Habitat Native to Madagascar (Malagasy Republic).
Description A large, arborescent plant as much as 10 m (33 ft) in height, whose trunk is formed by the bases of the leaves, lignified and marked in rings at the points where the old stalks were attached. The distichous leaves open like fans; they are borne on long sheathing stalks, closely overlapping, so that water collects in their hollow base; this is the feature that gives the tree its popular name—travelers could drink from it in need. The leaf blade is very big, with a strong, pale-colored vein in the center from which parallel secondary veins branch off and reach to the margin, so that the leaf is easily torn by the wind. The white flowers grow in spikes, with axillary bracts like spathes, the fruit is a trilocular capsule covered with a blue aril. The tree is often grown for ornament.
Propagation By basal suckers or by seed, from which it grows slowly.
Conditions for growth Completely tropical; small specimens can be kept under glass at not less than 15 °C (59 °F).

155 RHAMNUS ALATERNUS

Family Rhamnaceae.   **Evergreen**
Etymology Derived from the Greek *rhamnos*, which meant this same tree.
Habitat Distributed all around the Mediterranean, from Spain to the Crimea, Asia Minor and North Africa.
Description A tree growing at most to 10 m (33 ft), with persistent, leathery leaves; it forms part of the maquis forest of the Mediterranean region, in which the vegetation reacts to the hot, dry summers by a thickening of the leaf cuticle, so limiting transpiration; it is found together with the *Pistacia lentiscus* and *Phillyrea* spp. The bark, smooth and gray at first, turns blackish brown and rough; the leaves (1), ovate-lanceolate and acuminate, cartilaginous and toothed at the margin, are glossy dark green on the upper side and pale on the underside. The small, greeny-yellow flowers (3), clustered in axillary racemes, have an unpleasant smell when they open in March–April. The fruits (2) are rounded drupes the size of a pea with three seeds in each fruit. Red at first, turning to black when ripe, they are a favorite food of birds. The wood is used in cabinetmaking and has a distinctive smell when cut.
Propagation By seed, or by cutting or layering.
Conditions for growth Hot and dry; withstands salt spray.

156 RHUS CORIARIA
Sumach

Family Anacardiaceae.   **Deciduous**
Etymology The generic name comes from the Greek 'rhous', the ancient name of the sumach.
Habitat Western Asia and Mediterranean Europe.
Description A small tree, 3–4 m (10–13 ft) high, with thick, pithy branches; the deciduous leaves (1) are imparipinnate, with sessile leaflets, oblong-elliptical, dentate and hairy on the lower side, with a stalk which is also velvety. The yellowish-white, insignificant flowers (2) grow in dense panicles. The fruits (3) are hairy drupes, purple-brown when ripe. The foliage and young shoots are rich in tannin, used in the dressing of delicate leathers like Morocco, and in dyeing. The branches are harvested with their leaves in July–September, and the product, called sumach, is sold as leaf or in powder form. In Sicily the tree is grown on poor, dry land, but to a much lesser extent now than formerly. Sicilian sumach contains up to 35% of tannin and is highly valued in the international markets. The bark contains a yellow or orange dyestuff. In the East the fruits are pickled in vinegar and eaten like capers.
Propagation By cuttings or by radical suckers.
Conditions for growth Very hardy; likes hot, dry climates.

157 RHUS TYPHINA
Staghorn Sumac

Family Anacardiaceae. **Deciduous**
Etymology From the fruit's resemblance to *Typha* (the cattails).
Habitat Native to the eastern United States.
Description This is a tree 4–10 m (13–33 ft) tall, with a spreading crown, stout branches growing sparsely and young shoots covered with a dense fur which makes them look velvety. The deciduous leaves, up to 60 cm (24 in) long, are imparipinnate, composed of 11–13 leaflets with a toothed margin, downy at first, becoming glabrous; in autumn they take on a whole range of colors from orange to purple. These little trees very quickly colonize pastures and open country, which they light up with their brilliant colors. They are occasionally grown in American gardens for the beauty of their foliage, especially in the variety *laciniata*, which has deeply incised leaves. The insignificant yellowish flowers grow in erect terminal panicles which persist even after fertilization, when the fruits appear, transforming them into compact, hairy cones which are also very decorative.
Propagation Woody cuttings; layering or radical suckers.
Conditions for growth Grows well on any sort of soil and in any position. Tolerates unfavorable conditions and the polluted air of big cities.

158 SALIX ALBA
White Willow

Family Salicaceae. **Deciduous**
Etymology The name has retained its original Latin form.
Habitat Europe, central Asia and North Africa.
Description A tree up to 20–25 m (65–80 ft) tall, with a maximum diameter of about 60 cm (2 ft). The crown is spreading, composed of long, rising branches, the old ones silvery gray, the young branchlets long and flexible with a reddish-green or brown bark. The bark of the trunk is gray and cracks with age. The leaves (1), with narrow stalks lacking glands and bearing deciduous stipules, have lanceolate, acuminate blades 7–10 cm (3–4 in) long, narrowing toward the tip with the greatest width in the lower half, finely toothed margins, and glandular; they are green and slightly glossy on the surface, lighter below, and their appressed hairs make them look silvery and silky. The flowers appear at the same time as the leaves, the males (2) up to 7 cm (3 in) long with two stamens to the yellow anthers, the females (3) thinner and lightly stalked. Flowering occurs in March–April. The fruits are subsessile, glabrous capsules; the seeds have a white pappus.
Propagation By seed (easy); also by cuttings.
Conditions for growth Needs a good supply of water.

159 SALIX BABYLONICA
Weeping Willow

Family Salicaceae. **Deciduous**
Etymology The specific name suggests that the tree may have come from Babylon, possibly a way station between Europe and the tree's true home in central Asia. Other authorities connect the name with the Jews' bitter complaint during the Babylonian captivity: "We hanged our harps upon the willows in the midst thereof" (Psalm 137).
Habitat Native to central Asia.
Description A tree growing to 8–10 m (25–33 ft), with a distinctively shaped crown due to the presence of long, thin, pendulous young branches which may droop down to the ground. The leaves (1), borne on a short stalk, are narrowly lanceolate, with a long pointed point, serrated at the margin and very often glaucescent on the underside. (2, 3) male and female flowers. Widely grown in parks and gardens, especially near lakes, where the tree looks most romantic when reflected in the water. Rather rare as a true species; those commonly seen are most often hybrids.
Propagation Only by cuttings of female trees.
Conditions for growth Prefers light soils, cool and moist.

160 SALIX MATSUDANA
Corkscrew Willow, Contorted Willow

Family Salicaceae. **Deciduous**
Etymology The specific name commemorates the Japanese botanist Sadahisa Matsudo (1857–1921), who wrote a flora of China.
Habitat This species is distributed in China, Manchuria and Korea.
Description A tree 10–12 m (33–40 ft) high, much valued for its ornamental qualities. The way it grows makes it very easily recognizable, especially in the variety *pendula*, in which pendent young branches add grace to the light, spreading crown, but most of all in the variety *tortuosa*, in which the branches are twisted spirally and interwoven in the most complex way, almost as if an artist had arranged them. This peculiarity has given the tree the name of Corkscrew Willow. The deciduous leaves are lanceolate, glabrous, olive green on the upper side and silver gray on the underside. The flowers appear in spring, in catkins, each sex separately. Much used in Japanese-style gardens, the tree is popular with landscape gardeners because it grows quickly, has leaves that appear early and shows a distinctive character.
Propagation By cuttings.
Conditions for growth Temperate climates and cool soil.

161 SALIX NIGRA
Black Willow

Family Salicaceae.   **Deciduous**
Etymology The specific adjective is the Latin for black.
Habitat Distributed widely in North America.
Description A tree up to 10–12 m (33–40 ft) high, whose scaly bark often becomes rough. Young branches have little scars at the base left by twigs that have broken off in the wind or rain. The narrow lanceolate leaves (1) are minutely serrated at the margins and green on both sides; the buds are small. The unisexual flowers grow in catkins, the males (2) rather short, 2–5 cm (1–2 in) with 3–5 stamens, the females even shorter, having flowers with a short but clearly visible style. Unlike other genera that bear small flowers in catkins, the pollination of willows is not always anemophilous but may also be entomophilous, since the flowers have nectariferous glands that attract insects.
Propagation Willows have seeds with long, silky hairs which help in natural dissemination. Since the species grows along watercourses, broken twigs are generally carried by the water until they are trapped at a bend, where they put out adventitious roots in the mud, performing a sort of natural vegetative reproduction. Also by cuttings.
Conditions for growth Likes cool soils and temperate climates.

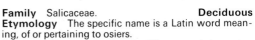

162 SALIX VIMINALIS
Osier

Family Salicaceae.   **Deciduous**
Etymology The specific name is a Latin word meaning, of or pertaining to osiers.
Habitat Common in all parts of Europe and also grows in northwestern Asia and the Himalayas.
Description Normally 4–5 m (13–16 ft) tall, it can reach a maximum height of 10 m (33 ft); the long, pliable branches are covered with a yellow bark. The leaves (1) may be narrow lanceolate or linear, with irregular margins and yellowish central veins; they are deciduous, alternate and short stalked, green above and covered with a silvery down below. The flowers (2, 3) growing in large catkins, have free stamens; the fruits are sessile capsules covered with down. The tree flowers from March to April. It produces very long, pliable and strong shoots (withies) which hardly branch at all and so can be used with the bark still on. Grown in osier beds, the species is a good producer both quantitatively and qualitatively. The withies can be woven and are used commercially for making baskets, garden furniture and cradles; in wine-making regions, before plastics were invented, demijohn cases were made of wickerwork.
Propagation By seed, by cuttings, by layering.
Conditions for growth Likes cool, moist soils.

163 SAMBUCUS NIGRA
European Elder

Family Caprifoliaceae. **Deciduous**
Etymology The name has kept the original Latin form, probably derived from *sambuca*, a musical instrument made from elder wood.
Habitat The species is widely distributed in Europe and Asia, and may grow in the Alps at altitudes up to 1500 m (5000 ft).
Description The elder is a small tree, growing to no more than 3–5 m (10–16 ft), although exceptional specimens have been met as tall as 12 m (40 ft) and 40 cm (16 in) in diameter. The bark of both trunk and branches is light gray, with warty brown lenticels; with age it cracks and takes on a horny, pimply look. The deciduous, opposite leaves (1) are pinnatisect, composed of 3–7 ovate-acuminate, toothed leaflets, light green and downy; the stalk is thick, short and widening at the base. The strongly scented hermaphrodite flowers grow in large terminal inflorescences with a flat surface. The fruits (2) are violet-black drupes with red juice, containing three oval brown seeds. The branches contain a great deal of white pith which is used in microscopy to enclose small sections, enabling them to be sliced more easily to the desired thickness of a few microns.
Propagation By seed or by hardwood cuttings.
Conditions for growth Prefers cool soils.

164 SASSAFRAS ALBIDUM
Sassafras

Family Lauraceae. **Deciduous**
Etymology Perhaps American Indian.
Habitat Eastern United States to the Brazos River in Texas.
Description A tree that can reach a height of 20 m (65 ft), with an erect trunk, rugged bark and a generally conical shape. The leaves (1) exhibit a remarkable heterophylly at all stages; entire ovate leaves can coexist with bilobate or even trilobate leaves; they are light green on the upper side and glaucescent below. The plants are dioecious. In the males the insignificant flowers (2) have nine stamens; the flowers of both sexes are apetalous, with a greenish-yellow calyx, and grow in clusters that appear before the leaves. The fruits that follow the female flowers after fertilization ripen in autumn and are small, dark blue drupes borne on red stalks and attached to the remains of the persistent calyx. The whole plant is very aromatic. It was used for a long time in pharmacy for its essential oils, which were extracted mainly from the roots, and as a source of flavoring for root beer. Nowadays the essence is used in perfumes and cosmetics.
Propagation By radical suckers.
Conditions for growth Intolerant of alkaline soils. Short-lived.

165　SCHINUS MOLLE
California Pepper Tree

Family　Anacardiaceae.　　　　　　　　**Deciduous**
Etymology　Derived from *skinos*, the Greeks' name for *Pistacia lentiscus*, because, like that tree, many species are resinous or produce mastic gum.
Habitat　Native to Peru.
Description　This tree can reach a height of 10–15 m (33–50 ft). It has a knotted, sometimes twisted, trunk with rugged reddish-black bark. The crown is composed of pliable branches of pendulous habit, with persistent long and slender leaves (1), alternate, composed of up to 25 imparipinnate dentate leaflets. The trees are dioecious, with panicles of little greenish-yellow flowers (2), followed by small rose-red fruits (3), drupes, which appear in autumn and persist until winter in pendulous clusters. Their resemblance to the little fruits of the Black Pepper (*Piper nigrum*), and the strong, distinctive smell that comes from every part of the tree, especially from the leaves when rubbed, account for the common name; the whole plant is in fact rich in volatile essential oils which smell very much like the true pepper. The tree is easily infested by the Scaly Cochineal insect.
Propagation　By seed; grows rapidly.
Conditions for growth　Dislikes frost but very tolerant of sun and of periods of drought, so that it is very suitable for mild maritime climates.

166　SCHINUS TEREBINTIFOLIUS

Family　Anacardiaceae.　　　　　　　　**Evergreen**
Etymology　The specific name denotes that the leaves resemble those of *Pistacia terebinthus*.
Habitat　Tropical America.
Description　This tree does not grow more than 6–8 m (20–26 ft) high, with a diameter of 40–50 cm (16–20 in) at chest height. It has leathery imparipinnate leaves. The species is seldom seen in European horticulture, though it was imported into Europe from Brazil in 1830; however, it is cultivated in some tropical regions because the resin collected from the trunk has some practical applications and is sold locally under the name of "mission balsam." In Brazil the wood is highly thought of, and often goes under the name of *aroeira do campo*; it is dark yellow, turning to red, with irregular darker patches. Compact and very hard, it is almost impervious to rot even in structures continually exposed to the weather, in the wettest climates. Its attractive coloring makes it very desirable for the manufacture of luxury furniture. The bark is used in dressing leather, and a dye is also extracted from it.
Propagation　By seed.
Conditions for growth　Tropical and subtropical.

167 SOPHORA JAPONICA
Pagoda Tree

Family Leguminosae.   **Deciduous**
Etymology The name is derived from an Arabic word for some tree not definitely identified, but presumably similar.
Habitat Originally from China, it is also widely cultivated in Japan.
Description A deciduous tree that can reach a height of over 20 m (65 ft) and whose trunk, as it grows old, often becomes curiously twisted and knotted. The first specimen planted in Europe, in Kew Gardens, in the second half of the 18th century, has actually assumed a semiprostrate posture. The branches are wide and the crown looks rounded. The leaves are compound, imparipinnate, with 7–9 stalked lanceolate acuminate leaflets, dark green and slightly downy on the underside. The flowers, creamy white, appear in long panicles; the individual flowers are 1 cm (0.5 in) long and papilionate, rather like those of the pea; the fruits are little berries strung together like a necklace. Flowers and fruit contain a yellow coloring matter. The variety *pendula*, of weeping habit, is particularly ornamental.
Propagation By seed. The varieties are grafted on seed stock by cleft grafting.
Conditions for growth Fairly hardy; needs a sunny position. Growth is quite rapid.

168 SOPHORA SECUNDIFLORA

Family Leguminosae.   **Evergreen**
Etymology The species name comes from the Latin 'secundiflorus', from the flowers which are turned to one side.
Habitat The tree comes from the southern United States, from Texas to New Mexico.
Description An evergreen growing up to 10 m (33 ft) high, with a slender trunk and erect ramification that tends to make it look tall; the compound leaves (1), 15 cm (6 in) long, have 7–9 rather slender leaflets, elliptical and rounded or emarginate at the top, covered with a silky down when young, almost sessile, with a wedge-shaped base. The violet-blue, strongly scented flowers (2) are papilionaceous, more than 2 cm (nearly an inch) long; they grow in terminal racemes about 10 cm (4 in) long and are all turned to one side. They appear in spring, unlike those of the species *S. japonica*, which flowers much later, at the end of the summer. The fruits (3) are moniliform, woody pods with a whitish tomentum; the scarlet seeds contain a poisonous alkaloid called sophorine.
Propagation By seed.
Conditions for growth This is rather a delicate species, needing a mild climate where the cold is only sporadic and never prolonged.

169 SORBUS ARIA
Whitebeam

Family Rosaceae.   **Deciduous**
Etymology The name comes from the Latin 'sorbum', meaning the fruit of the service tree.
Habitat The species has a European distribution.
Description A tree up to 12–15 m (40–50 ft) tall, generally with an erect, cylindrical trunk but sometimes growing irregularly; the tall crown is pyramidal and densely branched; the bark, grey with whitish patches, especially when the plant is young, turns red-brown later. The roots grow strongly, wide and deep, anchoring the plant firmly to the ground. The elliptical or elliptical-ovate leaves (1) are up to 14 cm (5½ in) long, double-toothed, very occasionally lobed, but not deeply; they are glossy green above and covered with a characteristic tomentum below. The white hermaphrodite flowers (2) grow in erect, downy, white corymbs. The fruits (3) are subglobose pomes, orange or scarlet, with a yellow, floury flesh which is sweetish and edible. The tree is often cultviated for its fruit, which can be used for distillation; also as an ornamental.
Propagation By seed, which takes two years to germinate.
Conditions for growth Temperate climate, from sea level up to 1600 m (5000 ft).

---

170 SORBUS AUCUPARIA
Mountain Ash, Rowan

Family Rosaceae.   **Deciduous**
Etymology The specific name means bird catcher, from the Latin *avis*, bird, and *capio*, catch.
Habitat The plant grows in almost the whole of Europe and in western Asia.
Description A tree of medium size (14 m–45 ft), sometimes no more than a shrub. The trunk is cylindrical and slender, the crown rounded and open. The bark, yellowish-gray at first, later becomes blackish, thick and fissured longitudinally. The wood has a fine grain, and the heartwood a beautiful reddish color; it is sometimes used for lathe-turned objects. The leaves (1) are compound, with 5–13 irregularly shaped leaflets, entire at the base and sharply toothed further up. They are reddish in the fall. The flowers (2) appear in May–June; they are small and white, growing in corymbs. The fruits (3) are small red pomes about 1 cm (0.5 in) across, in large, showy clusters.
Propagation By seed, which may take as much as two years to germinate.
Conditions for growth Since it is hardy at low temperatures, the tree is cultivated as an ornamental in mountainous places for the beauty of its fruit, which persists on the tree for a long time. It can also be used for reforestation.

171 SWIETENIA MAHAGONI
Mahogany

Family Meliaceae.   **Evergreen**
Etymology The name commemorates Gerard von Swieten (1700–1772), botanist, and physician to Maria Theresa of Austria.
Habitat Native to tropical America.
Description An evergreen tree which grows more than 30 m (100 ft) high, with a graceful trunk branching profusely at the top. The leaves (1) are long and pinnate, composed of 4–5 ovate-acuminate leaflets. The flowers (2) are small and yellow-white, growing in axillary panicles, and are followed by large fruits (3) which open at the base to release a number of winged seeds. The wood, for which the tree is highly valued, is in very great demand both for its beauty and for its hardness; it has been used since 1500 for quality carpenter's work. The sapwood is yellow, while the heartwood has a beautiful brown color. If they are well grown, the branches are often preferred to the trunk because of their close grain. The tree is now growing rare, and the name mahogany is given to less valuable woods with similar properties.
Propagation By seed, or by cuttings rooted in a hotbed.
Conditions for growth Exclusively tropical, though very young specimens can be kept alive for a time in a greenhouse.

---

172 TAMARIX GALLICA
French Tamarisk

Family Tamaricaceae.   **Deciduous**
Etymology The old Latin name survives. It is generally thought that the Romans named the tree after the river which they called Tamaris, now the Tambro, which had great numbers of these trees growing along its banks.
Habitat From the Canary Islands to Sicily and Dalmatia.
Description A small tree, 3–6 m (10–20 ft) high, branching densely from the base up. The long, thin branches have conspicuous lenticels, and so does the bark of the trunk, which is smooth and dark ashy gray. The tiny leaves (1), almost scalelike, are lanceolate and overlapping, and bluish green. The flowers (2), pink, small and very numerous, grow in spiky racemes 2–4 cm (1–1.5 in) long, most densely at the ends of young branches in May–August, when they form long plumes. This coastal tree will also survive in places where the winter is quite severe; it grows well on sandy soil and is valuable for fixing dunes. It is grown in gardens for the attractive flowers on its drooping branches and for the minute blue-green foliage. The fruit is a three-sided pyramidal capsule.
Propagation Easily reproduced from cuttings.
Conditions for growth Temperate climate, sandy, moist soil.

173 TAMARIX PENTANDRA
Tamarisk

Family Tamaricaceae.   **Deciduous**
Etymology The specific name refers to the flowers' five very conspicuous stamens, the red of the anthers standing out against the rosy corolla.
Habitat Native to Mediterranean Europe, though it is sometimes confused with species from China and Japan.
Description This tree can reach a maximum height of 5 m (16 ft) ; the trunk and branches have lavender-tinged bark. The blue-green alternate leaves (1) are sessile, small and scalelike. The inconspicuous pink flowers (2) grow in racemes that appear at the beginning of the summer and form plumes at the tips of the branches. This species, which nurserymen call *T. hispida aestivalis,* also has a variety *rubra,* whose flowers are of a deeper color.
Propagation Reproduction can be carried out with woody cuttings at the end of winter without any special difficulty, in the open, on the spot where the tree is intended to grow. Propagation by seed is carried out in spring or autumn but is not very effective.
Conditions for growth Very hardy, well adapted to maritime conditions. Likes a sunny position.

174 TECTONA GRANDIS
Teak

Family Verbenaceae.   **Evergreen**
Etymology The generic name comes from a Malayalam (Malabar Coast) word, *tekka,* which also gives the name teak to the wood.
Habitat Native to eastern Asia, India and Indonesia.
Description In its native forests this tree can reach a height of 60 m (200 ft). It has a slender trunk, a round crown and ovate leaves (1) up to 60 cm (24 in) long and 30 cm (12 in) across, very downy on the underside. The bluish-white flowers (2) grow in panicles 35 cm (14 in) across, but many of the flowers are sterile. The plumlike fruits have few fertile seeds ; they are heavy and compact, offering little for the wind to catch hold of. The grayish bark surrounds a light sapwood that is vulnerable to termites and rot caused by fungi ; the heartwood, in contrast, is immune, and during seasoning changes color from yellowish to chestnut with darker streaks, retaining some of its pleasant smell. The wood of this tree, known commercially as teak, is widely used not only for its durability and hardness but above all for its low coefficient of contraction ; it does not absorb moisture and is easy to work and polish. It is used for making furniture, parquet floors and veneers.
Propagation By seed.
Conditions for growth Tropical, hot and humid.

175 TILIA AMERICANA
Basswood, American Linden

Family Tiliaceae.   **Deciduous**
Etymology The name is derived from the Greek *ptilon*, wing, on account of the big bract below the inflorescence.
Habitat As the specific name tells us, the tree is native to North America. It was introduced into Europe in 1752.
Description Many species can interbreed, so that it is easy to find natural hybrids; the classification of linden is consequently a hard task. The American linden is a beautiful tree which in its natural range reaches a height of 40 m (130 ft) or more. The leaves (1) may be as much as 22–23 cm (9 in) long; simple, alternate and broadly ovate; toothed at the margin and the base asymmetrically cordate, terminating in a sharp point. The yellowish-white flowers appear at the beginning of summer, clustered at the end of a stalk which also bears a wide, membraneous bract important in dissemination. Like all the genus, they have five sepals and five petals, also five staminoides, not found in any of the other species. (2) fruit. The wood is soft, white and easy to work. The American Linden is grown as an ornamental, especially for the shape of its slightly trilobate leaves. It is an important honey plant.
Propagation By seed, by layering or by cuttings.
Conditions for growth Grows in any sort of soil.

---

176 TILIA CORDATA
Small-leaved Linden or Lime

Family Tiliaceae.   **Deciduous**
Etymology The specific name refers to the shape of the base of the leaf.
Habitat A European species whose vast distribution extends from Spain to the Caucasus; not found in mountainous regions, but frequently occurs in the hills.
Description This tree, with its ovoid, dense crown, reaches a height of 25 m (80 ft). It has a thick, short trunk with many thick branches; the bark is smooth and brown at first, later blackish and marked by thin longitudinal cracks. The small deciduous leaves (1), with stipules, have a roundish blade, asymmetrically cordate at the base; they are dark green and glossy on top, blue-green below, with clusters of reddish hairs at the axils of the slightly raised veins. The ovoid buds have two bud-scales, often reddish, and not hairy. As in all trees that produce suckers, the leaves are large. The hermaphrodite flowers (2), in clusters of 3–12 on each inflorescence, are yellowish white, with little scent; after fertilization they produce small grayish fruits with a fragile endocarp and very conspicuous ribs.
Propagation By seed; also by suckers.
Conditions for growth Likes cool, deep, moist loam.

177 TILIA INTERMEDIA
Intermediate lime

Family Tiliaceae.   **Deciduous**
Etymology The specific name indicates characteristics intermediate between those of *T. cordata* and
T. platyphyllos.
Habitat Found as a natural hybrid in many parts of
Europe where the parent species grow.
Description This species differs from *Tilia cordata* in
its leaves (1), which are not glaucous on the under side
and have more or less parallel tertiary veins; in the
flowers (2), which are more strongly scented, and in the
fruits (3), which are larger, with a stronger endocarp and
more prominent ribs. It differs from *Tilia platyphyllos* in
having buds, shoots and stalks without hairs and in the
leaves, which are glabrous on the under side as well as
the upper. In the past a textile fibre was made from the
bark, or rather from the bast, particularly in Germany and
Russia, where limes are abundant. Limes are first-class
trees for parks and gardens; they stand up well to
pruning.
Propagation By seed, which may germinate after one
year.
Conditions for growth Like its parent trees, fears
intense frost and drought when juvenile.

178 TILIA PLATYPHYLLOS
Broad-leaved Linden

Family Tiliaceae.   **Deciduous**
Etymology The specific name refers to the leaves,
which are wider than in other lindens.
Habitat Found in central and southern Europe.
Description This is a tree as much as 35 m (115 ft)
high and 2 m (6 ft) in diameter, with a straight, slender
trunk and broad crown with many stout branches,
generally fairly densely covered with green-to-reddish
hairs. The buds have three hairy bud-scales. The leaves
(1), normally about 10 × 8.5 cm (4 × 3.5 in), are green on
both surfaces and slightly velvety below, with little tufts
of white hairs at the axils of the veins and along the stalk,
which is also hairy. The flowers (2) are larger and more
strongly scented than those of *T. cordata* (**177**) and
joined in groups of 2–7. The fruits appear in October;
they are large and grayish, and have a thick wall with five
prominent ribs. This species is very long lived. As with all
lindens, the wood is white and soft, with a silky look and
an even grain; small medullary rays can be seen with the
naked eye. The wood is easy to work and is a favorite
with woodcarvers.
Propagation By seed; also by cuttings.
Conditions for growth Not very demanding, but
prefers light soils and relatively humid surroundings.

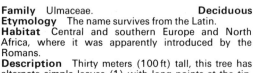

179 ULMUS CAMPESTRIS
English Elm

Family Ulmaceae.   **Deciduous**
Etymology The name survives from the Latin.
Habitat Central and southern Europe and North Africa, where it was apparently introduced by the Romans.
Description Thirty meters (100 ft) tall, this tree has alternate simple leaves (1) with long points at the tip, asymmetrical at the base, with a toothed margin. The flowers (2) appear before the leaves and have red-purple anthers. The fruit (3), which also appears early compared with the leaves, is a broad-winged samara well adapted for dissemination. The bark is smooth and brown-gray when young, later becoming cracked. It is fibrous, and gardeners use it to make ties for grafts. The leaves make excellent cattle food on account of their high protein content; for this reason the English Elm is preferred to other species where grass is sparse and cattle are grazed off trees. It is also widely grown as a roadside ornamental. The elm has a prolonged rest period, which protects the woody buds from late frosts even though, as a result of early flowering, the production of seeds is sometimes adversely affected by long cold periods.
Propagation By seed; also sometimes by suckers.
Conditions for growth Grows well in cool, deep, fertile soils, but also readily adapts to clay soils.

180 ULMUS LAEVIS
Fluttering Elm

Family Ulmaceae.   **Deciduous**
Etymology The specific name refers to the hairs that surround the wing of the samara.
Habitat Central Europe, from the Pyrenees to the Caucasus.
Description The tree has an irregular, open crown; it reaches a height of 20–25 m (65–80 ft) at most. The bark is gray-brown and scales off with age. The leaves are oval or roundish, highly asymmetrical at the base, and have a double-toothed margin; they are light green above and an even paler color below where they are pubescent. The stalked flowers (1), growing in pairs, are hermaphrodite. The fruits (2) are emarginate samaras with a densely ciliate edge. The plant does not produce seeds until it reaches sexual maturity, after 30 years; although seeds are formed every year, they only appear in abundance every two or three years. The wood is of less value than that of other species. Elms are regarded as among the trees most resistant to pollution and poisonous gases. The "tree of liberty" planted in Paris during the French Revolution, and renewed in memory of it, is an elm.
Propagation By seed; also by cuttings and by layering.
Conditions for growth Likes fertile, aerated, cool soil.

181 ULMUS MONTANA
Mountain Elm

Family Ulmaceae. **Deciduous**
Etymology The specific name indicates that this tree grows at greater altitudes than the Field or English Elm (**179**).
Habitat Widespread in northern Europe as far as Scandinavia, in central Europe and western Asia.
Description A tree of rapid growth, reaching a height of 25 m (80 ft); it has an irregular trunk which does not grow as thick as that of the English Elm. The bark is smooth when young, but later becomes cracked and scaly. The shoots are covered with hairs and set in no particular order, unlike those of the English Elm, in which they alternate. The leaves (1) are larger (9–15 cm; 3.5–6 in), asymmetrical at the base and sharply acuminate; the upper side is dark green and rough to the touch, but the underside is lighter. The stalk is shorter than the English Elm's. The hermaphrodite flowers (2) appear on the branches before the leaves. The pale-green fruits (3) have an emargination which never reaches the central seed; they turn chestnut brown before dissemination in July.
Propagation By seed (easy), by suckers and by layering.
Conditions for growth Likes light, deep soil. Adapts to both lime- and sandstone soils.

---

182 ZELKOVA CRENATA
Zelkova

Family Ulmaceae. **Deciduous**
Etymology The generic name is derived from that given to the tree in the Caucasus.
Habitat Eastern Mediterranean, Caucasus.
Description This is a beautiful tree, up to 30 m (100 ft) tall, with a thick trunk that divides into numerous slender vertical branches. The smooth, gray bark comes off in little scales rather like that of the plane. The small, alternate leaves (1) have short stalks, a toothed margin and downy veins on the underside. The insignificant green flowers (2, 3) are unisexual but are all borne on the same plant; they open in April at the same time as the leaves and are strongly scented. The fruit (4) is a small nut about the size of a pea. A slow-growing tree, it produces a hard, compact, resilient orange-yellow or golden-brown wood, used for high-quality furniture and in ships and railroad cars, as well as for gunstocks. Introduced into Europe in 1760, it can be distinguished from the elm, which it somewhat resembles, by its smooth bark (the elm's is rough and fissured).
Propagation By seed or by grafting onto elm stock.
Conditions for growth An undemanding species; prefers temperate climates.

183 ANNONA CHERIMOLA
Cherimoya

Family Annonaceae.   **Deciduous**
Etymology The name is a Latinized form of the name *anon*, used for one of the species in Haiti.
Habitat Native to the Andes in Peru.
Description This little tree, some 5–7 m (16–23 ft) in height, is of shrubby habit; it is often branched down to the base, with the young branches covered in a reddish tomentum. The obovate-lanceolate leaves are stalked, alternate, slightly pubescent on the upper side and tomentose and glaucescent below. The heavily perfumed flowers are solitary, not borne at the leaf axil but often opposite to the leaf on the same node, sometimes even in pairs. The stalks are downy, the calyx gamosepalous; there are six petals, three external and three internal, the former oblong and keeled, greenish or reddish outside and white inside, the latter very small, scaly and flesh pink or lavender. The fruit, for which the plant is cultivated, is a red, tuberculate syncarp of variable shape, generally like a big strawberry, with a white, edible flesh which is easily separated from the seed.
Propagation By seed or by grafting.
Conditions for growth Requires well-drained, humusy soil. On the island of Madeira, Espaliered trees produce fruits of enormous size.

---

184 ANNONA SQUAMOSA

Family Annonaceae.   **Deciduous**
Etymology The specific adjective means 'scaly', referring to the appearance of the fruit.
Habitat Tropical America, but now cultivated throughout the tropics.
Description A small, deciduous tree, 5—6 m (16–20 ft) high, with spreading branches and zig-zagging branchlets; juvenile parts are downy, adult parts covered in bark with sparse hairs and lenticels. The leaves (1) are generally lanceolate-acuminate, pale green, with a downy stalk, alternate, with stipules. The flowers (2) grow in clusters and have six petals arranged within each other; the three outside are fairly big, oblong-linear, yellowish-green dotted with violaceous red, the three inside ones small, ovate and keeled. The fruit (3), the size of an orange, is globular; it is formed from the fused carpels. The outside is greeny-yellow and scaly or pimply, and the flesh is edible, very sweet and scented. The juice is widely used to make a drink. There are many local names, including 'atta' and 'ahate'; in English-speaking countries the fruit is called 'sweetsop'.
Propagation By seed or grafting; a common method is eye-grafting, as with citrus fruits.
Conditions for growth Tropical, but the varieties with hard fruit can withstand long transportation.

185 ARBUTUS UNEDO
Strawberry Tree

Family Ericaceae.   **Evergreen**
Etymology The generic name preserves the old Latin word.
Habitat Grows wild in the whole Mediterranean region, from the Iberian Peninsula to Asia Minor; also in Killarney, Republic of Ireland.
Description This little tree, which except in ideal conditions remains at the shrubby stage, can reach a height of 5 m (16 ft), or in rare cases as much as twice that, but it grows very slowly. The bark is reddish, especially that of the branches, and cracks as it grows old; the plant is evergreen, with small, glossy leaves (1), elliptical and acuminate, narrowing at the base. The pitcher-shaped flowers (2), white and often suffused with pink or green, grow in terminal racemes carrying only a few flowers. The fruits (3), like round berries, contain a great number of seeds in a fleshy pulp; the outside is pimply, and turns from green to yellow and orange, and finally to red when fully ripe, when they are edible. The flowers appear in the autumn or the beginning of winter, when the previous year's fruit is ripe, thus enhancing the tree's ornamental value.
Propagation By seed (slow); reproduction by cuttings or layering is very difficult.
Conditions for growth Avoid planting in alkaline soils.

186 ARTOCARPUS COMMUNIS
Breadfruit Tree

Family Moraceae.   **Evergreen**
Etymology The name comes from the Greek *artos*, bread, and *karpos*, fruit; the fruits are eaten cooked and are commonly called breadfruit.
Habitat Native to the Sunda Islands. Long cultivated in Asia and nowadays also in America and the West Indies.
Description A tree growing to a height of 20 m (65 ft), with a sticky latex. The leaves (1) are big, leathery, deeply lobed and bright green, with strong pale veins. The flowers are unisexual, the males (2) growing in yellowish clubshaped catkins and the females (3) in round, prickly inflorescences. The big fruits that follow are formed of a fleshy mass (syncarp) rich in starch, which forms a valuable foodstuff. The fruit is covered with sharp prickles, but varieties have been obtained that are only reticulated, and even varieties without seeds. At the end of the 18th century an attempt was made to introduce the tree into the West Indies, but the hardships of the voyage provoked the crew of H.M.S. *Bounty* to mutiny against their commanding officer, Captain Bligh. The task was completed some time later. The durable wood is used for boxes and for building boats.
Propagation By softwood cuttings in the hothouse.
Conditions for growth Exclusively tropical.

187 BERTHOLLETIA EXCELSA
Brazil Nut

Family Lecythidaceae.   **Evergreen**
Etymology The name commemorates Claude-Louis Berthollet (1748–1822), French chemist.
Habitat Native to the Amazon and the Rio Negro in Brazil, where it forms great forests.
Description A tall tree, growing to 30–40 m (100–130 ft), with a trunk more than 1 m (3 ft) in diameter, with a scaly bark. The crown is rather round in shape, not very broad, and grows at the top of the trunk. The leaves (1) are alternate, leathery and green, as much as 50 cm (20 in) long, with secondary veins that branch from one another without reaching the margin. The bisexual, creamy-yellow flowers (2) are borne in panicles; they have a gamosepalous calyx which splits in two when the buds open, and six petals. The fruit is a capsule, globoid or elongated, about 10 cm (4 in) in diameter and woody on the outside; it contains about 20 triangular seeds with a rough skin, stiff but thin. They are edible, and may be eaten fresh or dried like other nuts. An oil is also extracted from them.
Propagation By seed.
Conditions for growth Tropical, in hot, damp climates.

---

188 CARICA PAPAYA
Papaya, Paw-paw

Family Caricaceae.   **Evergreen**
Etymology From the Latin *carica*, edible fig, on account of the similarity of the leaves.
Description An evergreen tree of modest size, up to 6–8 m (20–25 ft) tall, with a fleshy trunk with soft wood and gray-brown bark marked by the scars of fallen leaves. It does not form branches. The leaves (1) grow in a big cluster at the top of the stem. They are about 50 cm (20 in) wide and grow on hollow stalks of about the same length. The plant flowers on the stem and is normally dioecious, with funnel-shaped male flowers and female flowers with five separate petals; both sexes are small and yellow. There are hermaphrodite forms (2) in cultivation. The fruits (3), yellowish and edible, are like little melons when they are ripe, with a thin skin, pulpy orange flesh and a central cavity containing blackish seeds the size of a pea and covered with a gelatinous aril. Grown mainly for the fruit, all parts of the tree also contain a latex from which papain, a digestive enzyme, is extracted.
Propagation By seed, or by hardwood cuttings.
Conditions for growth Grows in almost any soil provided it is well drained. Screen from wind. Both male and female trees are required for good production. Bisexual trees produce fewer fruits of lesser quality.

189 CASIMIROA EDULIS

Family Rutaceae.   **Deciduous**
Etymology The name commemorates Casimiro Gomez de Ortega (1740–1818), Spanish botanist, director of the Madrid Horticultural Gardens.
Habitat Mexico.
Description This tree, grown for its edible fruit, which tastes very much like a peach, can reach a height of over 15 m (50 ft) and has a thick trunk with greenish bark thickly covered with characteristic white lenticels; the colour later changes to an ashy grey, but the little light grey pimples remain. The alternate leaves (1) are digitate, composed of 3–5 lanceolate-acuminate leaflets that are bronzy in the juvenile stage, green when adult, and borne on a long stalk. The flowers (2) are small and greenish; they appear in spring in short axillar panicles and have a calyx with 4–5 lobes and a corolla with 4–5 oblong, concave petals. The fruit (3) is a drupe shaped rather like a quince. The skin is thin and yellowish, the flesh cream-coloured, sweet and scented. There should normally be 5 seeds, but smaller numbers are sometimes found.
Propagation By seed; varieties by grafting.
Conditions for growth Mild climate; rarely fruits outside its natural surroundings.

---

190 CASTANEA SATIVA
Spanish Chestnut

Family Fagaceae.   **Deciduous**
Etymology From the Greek *kastanon*, chestnut.
Habitat Widespread in Europe.
Description This is a tree of notable growth, reaching a height of 20–25 m (65–80 ft), sometimes even 30–35 m (100–115 ft). It is exceptionally long lived—up to 1000 years—so that it reaches a remarkable diameter. The crown is wide and rounded. After 20 years the bark forms raise gray-brown ridges in a right-hand spiral. The large, oblong-lanceolate leaves (1) have a crenate margin and the main and secondary veins are distinctly raised. The flowers (2) are unisexual, the males growing in erect catkins while the females, numbering 1–3, are joined in a distinctive cupule.
Propagation Reproduced by seed planted in a nursery or after preparation by stratification.
Conditions for growth This tree once formed the basis of the economy of many hilly regions around the Mediterranean for its highly adaptable timber (used among other things for building houses) and for the chestnuts (widely used as a food). Today there is much less cultivation, both because the tree is subject to two serious diseases, the ink disease and bark canker, and on account of the profound economic and social changes that have taken place in the regions in question.

191 CERATONIA SILIQUA
Carob, St. John's-bread

Family Leguminosae.   **Evergreen**
Etymology From *keras*, horn, referring to the shape of the pod.
Habitat Native to Syria and Asia Minor; now spread widely in the Mediterranean region.
Description An evergreen tree that can grow to 15 m (50 ft), with a short, thick trunk and spreading branches forming a dense crown, a welcome provider of shade in the hot, dry areas in which it grows. The bark is red-brown. The compound leaves (1), paripinnate with 3–5 pairs of leaflets, glossy dark green above and glaucescent turning to red-brown on the underside, have small deciduous stipules. The flowers (2), small and greenish, grow in spikes with a short stalk and appear on old branches or directly on the trunk. The fruits are big lavender-brown pods, flat and pendulous, up to 20 cm (8 in) long and 2 cm (nearly 1 in) wide. They contain 10–16 glossy brown seeds in a sweet pulp. They are called St.-John's-bread or locust beans because it is believed they were the "locusts" that the Baptist is described as eating in St. Mark's Gospel. The word carat is derived from the Arabic word *quirat*, meaning carob seed, since these were used as the first unit of measurement for barter in the East.
Propagation By seed, in autumn or spring.
Conditions for growth Well-drained limestone soil.

192 CITRUS AURANTIUM
Seville orange, bitter orange

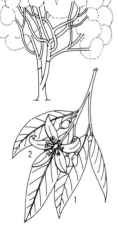

Family Rutaceae.   **Evergreen**
Etymology The name is of Latin origin.
Habitat While the tree is certainly of oriental origin, it is hard to date its introduction into Europe; different varieties were brought in at different times, probably by the Arabs.
Description This is a little tree not more than 2–5 m (6–16 ft) high, with a compact, conical crown which is made spherical by pruning; the trunk is grey, smooth and slightly nodular. The glossy oval evergreen leaves (1), of leathery consistency, have a distinctive winged stalk. The hermaphrodite flowers (2) grow in clusters in spring; they have 5 fleshy white petals and are heavily perfumed, and like those of other species of the genus are used for the extraction of an essence. The well-known fruit is a special kind of berry called a 'hesperidian' (from the garden of the Hesperides, with its golden fruits) with a thick peel full of oilbearing glands; the pulp is formed from big cells of bitter-sweet coloured liquid.
Propagation New plantlets can be obtained by grafting, at 3–5 years of age, those of the bitter orange obtained from seed, which turn out more resistant to the attacks of certain parasites.
Conditions for growth This is a typical temperate climate plant. It cannot withstand winter frosts and will not grow readily on soils that are too chalky or too clayey, but does well on those of medium consistency, light and porous.

193 CITRUS LIMON
Lemon

Family Rutaceae. **Evergreen**
Etymology The name comes from the Arabic and Persian *limun*, used indifferently for all citrus fruits.
Habitat According to G. Gallesio (1772–1839), a botanist and pomologist of Liguria, the first description of the lemon, which had been introduced from India two centuries earlier, is found in Arabic writings of the 12th century. More recent research has identified lemons in the ruins of Pompeii.
Description A small tree, 3–6 m (10–20 ft) high, with an open crown and thorns on the branches. The leaves (1) are elliptical-acuminate with a crenate margin. The flowers (2) are highly perfumed, white inside and streaked with violet outside, with 20 stamens, separate or fused. The hesperidian-type fruit is oval, with a pale yellow peel and greenish-yellow, juicy, sour flesh containing the ovoid seeds. Its high vitamin C content makes the lemon an excellent remedy for scurvy. The juice is used to make refreshing drinks, also in the manufacture of liqueurs and in perfumery and cosmetics. An essential oil extracted from the peel is used as a flavoring.
Propagation By grafting; cannot be used as a stock because it is vulnerable to cankers and dry rot.
Conditions for growth Needs mild or warm, semi-arid climates.

---

194 CITRUS MAXIMA
Shaddock, Pomelo

Family Rutaceae. **Evergreen**
Etymology The specific name refers to the size of the fruit, but it is not easy to make a clear distinction between this species and *C. paradisi*, the grapefruit (**195**).
Habitat Introduced into Florida by the Spanish in the 16th century.
Description The cultivated shaddock is a tree of 10–12 m (33–40 ft), with a spherical crown and regular branching. The ovate leaves (1) are soft, deep green, with a winged stalk that bears a weak, flexible thorn at the axil. The axillary flowers (2), solitary or in clusters, are very big and clear white on both sides of the petals. The fruit, a spherical or globose hesperidium, can grow as much as 15 cm (6 in) in diameter and weigh as much as 2–3 kg (4–6 lb); it is yellow, with a slightly bitter pulp enclosing the big, rough seeds. The fruit is much appreciated for its tonic qualities; refreshing and stimulating to the palate, it is rich in vitamins A, B and C. An essential oil much like that obtained from the orange is extracted from the peel both by crushing and by distillation.
Propagation By grafting or by seed.
Conditions for growth Very sensitive to cold. Likes light, well-drained soil.

195 CITRUS MEDICA
Citron

Family Rutaceae. **Deciduous**
Etymology The specific name records its supposed origin from the land of the Medes, i.e. modern Iran.
Habitat Native to the eastern Himalayas, it was known to the ancient Romans as the 'Medes' apple'. It came from Persia to Greece and thence into the Latin world.
Description A tree 3–4 m (10–13 ft) high with an irregular crown. The leaves (1), which have a thorn 3 cm (over an inch) long at the base, are large, ovate and toothed; the stalk is not winged. The flowers (2), white and scented, have the outside surface of the petals suffused with violet; they grow in clusters of 3–12. The fruits (3), 20–30 cm (8–12 in) long, are ovoid, but bigger and more nodular than those of the lemon, with a thick, pale yellow juice and thin pulp, rather sour. The citron, one of the Citrus fruits, has a number of not very well known qualities—refreshing, antiseptic, anti-putrefactive, diuretic, antiscorbutic, even active in biliary fermentations. What is perhaps better known is an anti-emetic potion made from the juice of the citron and an aqueous solution of potassium bicarbonate.
Propagation By cuttings; less commonly, by grafting on Seville orange.
Conditions for growth Temperate climate, warm and not humid.

196 CITRUS NOBILIS (C. RETICULATA)
Mandarin, Tangerine

Family Rutaceae. **Evergreen**
Etymology The species name refers to the delicate flavor. Mandarin comes from *mandara*, the name by which it was first known in France and on Réunion Island.
Habitat The tree is native to China and southern Vietnam.
Description A tree growing to a maximum height of 3–4 m (10–13 ft), with dark, glossy, lanceolate leaves (1), smaller than those of other *Citrus* trees and lacking the winged stalk. The flowers (2) are small, white and highly scented. The fruits (3), flattened spheroids of a bright orange color, have a thin peel that comes off easily. The flesh is sweet and juicy, with a pleasant smell, and contains a large number of seeds. The essential oil of mandarin obtained from the peel is used in perfumery and as a flavoring and in liqueurs, candies and medicines. The tree is also cultivated as an ornamental pot plant. There is a well-known hybrid called Clementine, obtained by crossing *C. nobilis* with the Seville Orange (**275**).
Propagation By seed, from which hardy specimens are obtained; by layering; or by grafting on Seville Orange stock.
Conditions for growth Likes temperate climates with fertile, well-drained soil.

197 CORNUS MAS
Cornelian Cherry

Family Cornaceae.   **Deciduous**
Etymology The name is the same as the original Latin, meaning horn, probably referring to the hard wood.
Habitat Central-eastern Europe as far as Asia Minor.
Description Not a very tall tree, reaching some 6–8 m (20–26 ft). The branches are red brown, the bark brownish yellow and rich in tannin; it cracks off in scales. The deciduous leaves (1) are simple, oval, entire but slightly wavy at the margin, opposite, green and almost glabrous on the upper side, lighter and hairy on the underside, with curved veins converging toward the pointed tip. The yellow hermaphrodite flowers (2) grow in umbels and appear before the leaves. The fruit (3) is a scarlet ellipsoidal drupe, edible and with a pleasant acid flavor (though some will eat it only with sugar); it contains a bony seed. The homogeneous wood, called cornel wood (light-brown sapwood and reddish heartwood), is very hard and durable; it is used for machine parts subject to intense wear and tear such as the spokes and teeth of gears, or for lathe-turned work. The seed gives oil for burning or for soapmaking, and the whole plant contains a yellow dye.
Propagation Usually by seed, but also by cuttings.
Conditions for growth Prefers limed soil and temperate climates.

---

198 CORYLUS AVELLANA
European Filbert, Hazelnut

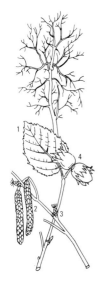

Family Betulaceae.   **Deciduous**
Etymology The name comes from the Greek *koris*, helmet, referring to the leafy covering of the fruit.
Habitat Europe, Asia Minor and Algeria, to 1 200 m (4000 ft).
Description A small tree that may reach a height of 7 m (23 ft). not very long lived. It generally branches from the base up; its bark is gray-brown and quickly peels off. The deciduous leaves (1) are ovate-cordate, alternate, irregularly toothed, soft and velvety as soon as they appear from the bud, bright green above and paler and tomentose below. The flowers are unisexual. The males (2) grow in pendulous cylindrical catkins in the autumn, the females (3) are erect and scarcely visible, showing themselves only by the red stigmas that can be seen at the moment of flowering, in winter. The fruits (4), round achenes growing 2–4 together, are surrounded by a bell-shaped envelope, irregularly dentate. They ripen in September and are edible, containing an excellent oil which is also used for culinary and industrial purposes. The wood, half hard and resilient, but not very durable, is used for walking sticks, barrels, lathe-turned objects and inlaid work.
Propagation Tip-layering; by radical suckers; seed.
Conditions for growth Protect from bitter winds. Prefers deep, well-drained, fertile soil. Remove suckers.

199 CYDONIA VULGARIS
Quince

Family Rosaceae.   **Deciduous**
Etymology The generic name was given to the tree by the Romans, who called it the apple tree. From the Latin *cydoneus*, an adjective derived from Cydon, an ancient city of Crete.
Habitat Native to eastern Asia; cultivated in ancient times.
Description A small tree 3–5 m (10–16 ft) high and slow growing; the trunk bears many branches, often short and twisted. The leaves (1), alternate, short stalked, oval and entire, 8–10 cm (3.25–4 in) long, are green on the upper side and downy gray on the underside, with deciduous stipules. The solitary flowers (2), 5 cm (2 in) in diameter, have a tomentose, persistent calyx, round petals that are white inside and pink outside, and numerous stamens. The fruit (3), a pome, is large and usually pear shaped but sometimes apple shaped, with a hollow at both ends and sometimes pointed toward the stalk; it is golden yellow, scented, with hard flesh that is astringent even when ripe. It is unpleasant to eat fresh but is excellent for preserves.
Propagation Reproduced by cuttings or by division of the roots; like all fruit trees, by grafting.
Conditions for growth Prefers fairly compact soils, light, rather rich and lime free.

200 DIOSPYROS KAKI
Oriental or Japanese Kaki Persimmon

Family Ebenaceae.   **Deciduous**
Etymology From the Greek *diospyros*, composed of *dios*, divine, and *pyros*, grain, from the edible fruit of some species. The species name is derived from the Japanese word for plant, *kaki-no-ki*.
Habitat Originally from the Far East.
Description A deciduous tree 6–12 m (20–40 ft) tall, with a conical crown and brown, cracked bark. The leaves (1) are entire, oval-elliptical and leathery, dark green and glossy on the upper side, often downy on the underside, about 15 cm (6 in) long; they turn red before falling. The axillary flowers, hermaphrodite or unisexual, are solitary; they have a small, whitish corolla, while the calyx, with four big, leafy lobes, is persistent. The fruits (2) have a short stalk and are round berries, slightly hollowed at the base, the size of an apple; the smooth, fairly bright orange skin has a bloom, and the juicy orange-yellow flesh is sweet when completely ripe. There are many varieties, some seedless.
Propagation By seed; but to maintain the qualities unchanged it is usual to graft on *D. virginiana* (**201**).
Conditions for growth Very adaptable as regards soil types. Should be staked when making very rapid growth in early age.

201 DIOSPYROS VIRGINIANA
Native Persimmon

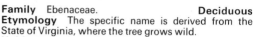

Family Ebenaceae. **Deciduous**
Etymology The specific name is derived from the State of Virginia, where the tree grows wild.
Habitat Native to North America.
Description A deciduous tree that reaches a height of 15 m (50 ft), with a stout trunk with cracked, blackish bark and strong, wide, horizontal or pendulous branches. The leaves (1) are ovate or elliptical and acuminate, of moderate length, glossy green on the upper side, glaucous or pale on the underside. The unisexual flowers, greenish-yellow, have short stalks; the males generally grow in small clusters, the females are solitary and a little larger. The calyx is persistent and forms the base of the fruit, which is a globe about the size of a plum, green at first but turning yellow or orange when ripe, often with a reddish tinge. The fruits (2) are flavorful and sweet, though bitter and very astringent until they have been subjected to frost. They contain 3–4 large seeds.
Propagation By seed. The tree is grown as stock for *D. kaki* (**200**).
Conditions for growth Prefers deep, humusy, well-drained soil.

202 ERIOBOTRYA JAPONICA
Loquat

Family Rosaceae. **Evergreen**
Etymology The name comes from the Greek *erion*, wool, and *botrys*, bunch of grapes, because the flowers grow in woolly panicles.
Habitat Native to the Far East.
Description An evergreen tree 6–7 m (10–13 ft) high, with erect spreading branches that form an open crown, almost like an umbrella, when the tree is adult. The leaves (1), light and downy in the juvenile stage, later become big and leathery, almost sessile, glabrous on the upper side and covered with rust-colored tomentum on the reverse; the margins have widely spaced teeth. The flowers (2), about 1 cm (0.5 in) long, are white and have a scent of bitter almonds; they grow in terminal panicles, but remain almost hidden by a thick, reddish-brown fur. The plant flowers in autumn and the fruits (3) ripen in spring; they are globose or ovoid, with a thin orange-yellow skin and the lobes of the calyx persisting at the top. The yellowish flesh has slightly acid juice, and there are a few large, brown, shiny seeds. The edible fruits, for which the tree is cultivated, are mostly eaten raw; a great number of cultivars of fine quality have been produced.
Propagation By seed; varieties by grafting.
Conditions for growth Prefers a rich, rather heavy soil but grows well under less ideal conditions.

203 FEIJOA SELLOWIANA

Family Myrtaceae. **Evergreen**
Etymology The name commemorates the 19th-century Brazilian botanist de Sìlva Feijoa; the name of the genus has recently been changed to *Acca*, but the old name is still universally accepted.
Habitat Native to tropical America, from Brazil to northern Argentina.
Description Reaches a height of 5 m (16 ft) and is of rather shrubby habit; an evergreen tree cultivated both for its flowers and for its edible fruit. Branched down to the base, its secondary branchlets are covered with a whitish down. The small, opposite leaves (1) are entire, elliptical, glossy green on the upper side and silvery grey below. The axillary flowers (2) appear at the end of spring, solitary or in clusters; they have four waxy petals, white on the outside, purple to carmine inside. The fruits (3) are oblong, about 5 cm (2 in) long, with the persistent calyx at the top; the skin is dark green and leathery turning brown. The juicy flesh, white and scented, contains many seeds; the fruit can be eaten raw but is also used for candied fruits and jellies.
Propagation By seed, but reproduction by cuttings gives quicker results.
Conditions for growth Although this is a tropical tree, it was successfully introduced on to the Italian and French Riviera in 1890.

---

204 FICUS CARICA
Common Fig

Family Moraceae. **Deciduous**
Etymology The generic name is the old Latin name.
Habitat Native to Southeast Asia, but now grows wild in the Mediterranean region.
Description This species has been known and cultivated since the remotest antiquity; indeed, it is mentioned in the Book of Genesis. The wild species differs morphologically from the cultivated, which grows to 5–8 m (16–26 ft). The big leaves (1) are borne on long stalks; they have 3–5 lobes and are irregularly dentate, rough on top, velvety below. The flowers, female only in the cultivated species, are enclosed within a greenish inflorescence, rather pear shaped, which has an opening at the tip. Reproduction in such cases is by partheno-genesis. In the wild fig, however, pollination is carried out by the fig wasp, *Blastophaga psenes*, which brings the pollen to fertilize the female flowers. The fruits are purple, green, yellow, bronze or brown, depending on the variety. Some varieties produce two crops a year.
Propagation By cuttings, or by division of suckers.
Conditions for growth Requires protection from late frosts. Soil should be of good quality and well drained. Needs full sun. In cold climates, trees can be wintered over by bending them over and covering with soil, or grown in tubs which are brought indoors.

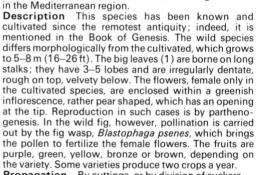

205 FORTUNELLA MARGARITA
Kumquat, Nagami

Family Rutaceae.   **Evergreen**
Etymology The name commemorates Robert Fortune
(1812–1880), a Scottish naturalist who travelled
extensively in China and introduced a great number of
Far Eastern ornamental plants to the Western
Hemisphere.
Habitat Native to southern China.
Description A little tree that in its native surroundings
reaches a height of 3–4 m (10–13 ft), though in our
climates it often remains shorter than that. An evergreen,
it has leathery, lanceolate leaves, narrowed at the base
and coming to a point at the tip, glossy green on the
upper side and paler, with glandular spots visible, on the
underside. The flowers are small and solitary, growing in
little clusters; white and rather fleshy, with five petals,
they are scented and appear in the spring. The fruits that
follow them are oval or oblong, 2.5–3 cm (about 1 in)
long, a rather yellowy orange, the skin dotted with
translucent oleiferous glands, the flesh slightly acid. The
fruits are edible and are eaten whole, including the skin;
they have a distinctive, pungent aroma.
Propagation Generally by grafting on *Poncirus
trifoliata* (the Trifoliate Orange).
Conditions for growth One of the hardiest *Citrus*
trees. Plant in good, well-drained soil.

---

206 JUGLANS REGIA
Persian Walnut, English Walnut

Family Juglandaceae.   **Evergreen**
Etymology *Regia*, Latin "royal", was probably
applied because of the delicious flavor of the nuts.
Habitat In the United States the Persian Walnut is
grown primarily in California. The Carpathian Walnut is
more widely planted and hardy to Zone 5.
Description A tall tree that can reach 25 m (80 ft) in
height and 1.5 m (5 ft) in diameter. The trunk has a
silvery-gray, smooth bark. The branches form a nearly
round head of large, compound, alternate leaves (1)
formed of 5–9 oblong-lanceolate, acute or acuminate
leaflets that are shiny green on top and slightly lighter
underneath with a slight perfume. In spring the tree
produces male flowers (2), brownish green, in pendulous, slender clusters, and females (3) in groups of
1–4 at the ends of young shoots. The fruit is a drupelike
nut whose green husk is rich in tannic acid. The enclosed
nut has a thin, smooth shell containing two sweet, edible
seeds that often break out whole. The high-quality wood
is used for fine furniture.
Propagation Primarily by grafting; also by seed.
Conditions for growth The tree must be protected
from late spring freezes and cold winter winds. Prefers
well-drained, deep, humusy soil. Although self-fruitful,
best nut production results when two different varieties
are planted together.

207 LITCHI CHINENSIS
Litchi, Lychee

Family Sapindaceae.   **Evergreen**
Etymology The name is Chinese.
Habitat Native to the south of China, but also grown in India and other tropical countries.
Description In its native surroundings the tree reaches a height of 10 m (33 ft), though it often remains shorter. It has pendulous branches densely covered with pinnate leaves (1) composed of 2–4 pairs of lanceolate-acuminate leaflets, glossy green on the upper side and glaucous below. The flowers (2), in apical panicles which may grow as long as 30 cm (12 in), are whitish, small and insignificant, and are followed by edible fruits (3) which are borne in large clusters. They consist of big seeds with an aril formed from white, gelatinous flesh, translucent and juicy, with a flavor and scent not unlike those of a very good Muscatel Grape. The nodular exterior is at first rosy red, turning to brown and finally hardening as the fruit ripens. Some fruits are yellow. There are many cultivated varieties, and the seed is generally smaller in the grafted varieties.
Propagation By seed, but growth is slow and the plants do not fruit until 7–9 years after planting; the favorite varieties are obtained by air-layering or grafting.
Conditions for growth Prefer well-drained, acid, humusy soil. Protect from wind.

208 MALUS COMMUNIS
Apple

Family Rosaceae.   **Deciduous**
Etymology This tree still preserves its old Latin name.
Habitat This is probably a species of European origin, improved by hybridization and spread by cultivation.
Description A small tree up to 6–8 m (20–26 ft) high. The young branches sometimes have thorns, the short-stalked leaves (1), deciduous, simple, toothed at the margin, of leathery consistency, slightly tomentose underneath, with 8–16 raised veins. The hermaphrodite flowers (2), composed of five petals, are generally white flushed with pink on the outside, with 15–50 stamens and yellow anthers; they grow in groups of 3–6 in corymbs at the tips of young branches. The fruits (3) are pomes, round, flattened and hollowed at the ends, with a crisp flesh and skin of various colours; the seeds, one or two, are contained within the cartilaginous core round which there is a fleshy receptacle. The cultivated apple includes a group of hybrids of various species, among them *Malus sylvestris* from central Europe, whose little fruits were eaten by Neolithic man, and *Malus dasyphylla* from western Asia. This last is the species that has been cultivated longest among the European species. The countless varieties now cultivated have resulted from cross-breeding.
Propagation By layering, but most commonly by grafting.
Conditions for growth Temperate to cold zones.

209 MANGIFERA INDICA
Mango

Family Anacardiaceae. **Evergreen**
Etymology The generic name is derived from *mango*, the Indian name for the fruit, and the Latin *fero*, bear.
Habitat Native to India, Burma and Malaysia, but now growing in most tropical countries.
Description An erect, widely branching tree, which can reach a height of 30 m (100 ft), the mango has leathery, lanceolate, dark-green leaves (1), sometimes with waxy margins, up to 35 cm (14 in) long, on a short stalk. The yellowish or reddish scented flowers (2) grow in panicles and may be either male or hermaphrodite on the same inflorescence. They are followed by the fruits (3), ovoidal drupes 5–20 cm (2–8 in) long, slightly flattened at the sides, which turn yellow or red when ripe; the flesh is delicious and very nourishing. There are many varieties, since the mango, cultivated in Asia for over 4000 years, is today widely grown in tropical America, the West Indies and Africa. The fruit of plants grown from seed has a disagreeable smell and the flesh is fibrous, but many first-class varieties have been obtained by grafting.
Propagation By seed, to obtain the stock on which to graft selected varieties.
Conditions for growth Grows in any good, well-drained soil; in sun (for better fruit production) or partial shade. Protect from wind.

210 MUSA X PARADISIACA
Banana

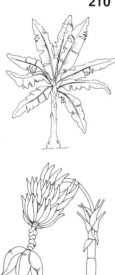

Family Musaceae. **Evergreen**
Etymology Probably derived from an Arabic word. Linnaeus adopted the name to dedicate the genus to Antonio Musa (63–14 B.C.), physician to the emperor Augustus.
Habitat Hybrid, mainly derived from Asian species.
Description This plant, 3–9 m (10–30 ft) high, should not strictly be defined as a tree. Like the palms, it has a stalk formed from the persistent bases of the closely sheathing leaves, so does not bear branches; the roots are rhizomatose, almost always stoloniferous, and new suckers grow from their buds even if the aerial parts have died. The leaves have a short, sheathing stalk and big oblong blades, with a strong central vein and many parallel secondary veins which extend up to the margin, so that the leaf tissue often tears in the wind; the leaves are set spirally and form an apical cluster. The flowers grow in a spike, with lavender-colored lanceolate axillary bracts and yellow flowers which develop fruit without fertilization, since the hybrid is sterile. There are many varieties.
Propagation By basal suckers, in spring.
Conditions for growth Requires full sun; rich, humusy soil with a pH of 7 or somewhat less; protection from wind.

211 PERSEA AMERICANA
Avocado Pear

Family Lauraceae. **Evergreen**
Etymology The generic name comes from the Greek *persea*, used for an Egyptian tree which has been variously identified.
Habitat Native to Central America but today spread throughout many tropical and subtropical countries.
Description An erect tree up to 20 m (65 ft) high, with a spreading, globose crown, the avocado has persistent leaves (1), entire, elliptical or lanceolate and acuminate, with a short stalk, leathery and strongly veined. The little greenish flowers (2) grow in dense terminal panicles and are followed by fruits which are big, fleshy, pear-shaped drupes; their skin is green, smooth or rough according to the variety. The seed, large and generally also pear shaped, is bipartite. There are many varieties, bearing fruits that differ slightly in shape, color and size; the buttery flesh is very rich in vitamins and protein as well as fats, with very little sugar.
Propagation By seed, not completely covered (new plants appear between the two valves); by budding; by cuttings and layering. In commercial practice the plants are grafted to obtain uniform types and quicker fruiting.
Conditions for growth Protect from strong winds. Grows in any good soil, but it must be very well drained.

---

212 PISTACIA VERA
Pistachio

Family Anacardiaceae. **Evergreen**
Etymology The name is that used by the Romans, apparently derived from the Persian through the Greek *pistake*, used by Nicander in 200 B.C. and certainly by Dioscorides.
Habitat Native to the Middle East.
Description In ideal conditions the tree can reach a height of 10 m (33 ft); it is deciduous, with a dense, spreading crown. The leaves (1) are pinnate; downy in the juvenile state, they become leathery later, with 1–5 pairs of acuminate leaflets. The plants are dioecious and have resin canals; young branches are reddish. The apetalous flowers (2, 3) have 1–5 sepals, and the females are followed by the fruit, ovoidal drupes with a rough exterior containing an edible green kernel much used as a flavoring and in pastry. The inflorescences are small panicles, and the fruits grow similarly. At least 1 male plant is needed to pollinate 5–6 females.
Propagation Generally by grafting on *P. terebinthus*.
Conditions for growth In dry climates wherever the olive tree (**211**) grows. The pistachio is hardy into Zone 7 but can be counted on to fruit only in Zone 9.

213 PRUNUS AMYGDALUS
Almond

Family Rosaceae. **Deciduous**
Etymology The ancient Latin name of the species.
Habitat Native to China, introduced into Europe in the 6th and 5th centuries B.C.
Description A tree up to 10 m (33 ft) high, the trunk often twisted and the bark very dark and cracked into small scales. The lanceolate leaves (1), up to 12 cm (5 in) long, have a great many rounded teeth at the margins and grow on long stalks. The flowers (2), which appear a long time before the leaves in young specimens and just before them on adult trees, are white, slightly tinged with pink; they may be as much as 5 cm (2 in) across, with a reddish calyx, and are borne singly or in pairs on short stalks. The yellowish-green fruits are downy oval drupes, slightly furrowed along one side. The shell contains 1–2 edible seeds surrounded by a thin, cinnamon-colored skin containing prussic acid, which gives them their characteristic flavor. The many varieties of almond can be divided into two groups by the taste of their seeds: sweet or bitter. The wood, reddish and compact, takes a beautiful polish.
Propagation By seed directly on the site where the tree is to stand, or by grafting.
Conditions for growth Dislikes frosts, especially late frosts, and high winds. Very tolerant of poor soil but does best in well-drained, humusy soil.

---

214 PRUNUS ARMENIACA
Apricot

Family Rosaceae. **Deciduous**
Etymology Apparently introduced into Europe from Armenia but actually of Chinese origin.
Habitat Native to southern China and widely known in Europe since the time of Classical Greece.
Description A tree that hardly ever grows more than 6–8 m (20–26 ft), with a stout trunk and reddish-brown bark; the rather untidy branches form a rounded crown. The leaves (1) are deciduous, ovate or rounded, sharply pointed at the tip, simple, leathery, double toothed and alternate. The flowers (2), which appear before the leaves, solitary or in pairs, have white or pinkish obovate petals. The edible fruit, a velvety globose or oblong drupe, slightly flattened and divided by a central groove, is orange-yellow, often tinged with red. There are many freestone cultivated varieties. An oil is extracted from the seed and used in the manufacture of perfumes and soap.
Propagation By seed or by grafting on the wild form or on peach (**219**).
Conditions for growth Likes temperate climates, dislikes frost. In more northern climates it is sometimes espaliered against a wall. Ideally, the apricot should be planted on a north slope or the north side of a building to escape the sun's warmth in early spring. But it needs sun and a well-drained soil for good fruit production.

215 PRUNUS AVIUM
Sweet Cherry

Family Rosaceae.   **Deciduous**
Etymology The specific name comes from the Latin *avis*, birds, and in fact birds are greatly attracted by the fruit which incidentally helps in its dissemination.
Habitat Native to western Asia, from which it was introduced into western Europe by cultivation in very ancient times; it now grows wild in central Europe.
Description A tree as much as 20 m (65 ft) tall, with stout rising branches which form a broad, pyramidal crown; the red-brown bark peels off in horizontal strips with age. The alternate leaves (1), lanceolate and acuminate, double toothed at the margin, are glabrous and a little rough on top, rather hairy below, growing on a long stalk with stipules. The white, scented flowers (2) grow in umbels with a long stalk. The fruit is a round drupe, slightly heart-shaped, 1 cm (0.5 in) across, dark red with sweet flesh that adheres to the stone. Many cultivated forms, including some with red and yellow fruit, have been developed from this species and improved for fruit production.
Propagation By seed, if wild; by grafting, if cultivated.
Conditions for growth Likes temperate climates and bright positions. Can be grown in Zones 2–5 in protected locations.

---

216 PRUNUS CERASUS
Sour Cherry, Dwarf Wild Cherry

Family Rosaceae.   **Deciduous**
Etymology The Latin word used as specific name means cherries generally.
Description A little tree that reaches a height of 6 m (20 ft) less than half as tall as *Prunus avium* (**216**) —with many branches. The leaves, ovate-elliptical with a double-toothed margin, are smooth and glabrous on both sides, smaller and shorter stalked than those of the Sweet Cherry. The hermaphrodite flowers, white and stalked, grow in umbels and open in April–May. The fruit is a round, rather dark-red drupe, very juicy and sour, with skin that comes away from the flesh and a round, smooth stone. The fruits are edible, but are used mostly for jams and syrups and for the production of maraschino liqueur, of which Dalmatia is the best producer both for quality and quantity. The pinkish-white wood, with brown, half-hard heartwood, is used for small lathe-turned goods, whittled objects and walking sticks.
Propagation By seed; or by grafting onto mahaleb or mazzard stock for the various cultivated varieties; mazzard is more difficult but produces superior results. It is also possible to get new specimens from suckers.
Conditions for growth The tree adapts to all kinds of soil. Being more resistant to frost than the Sweet Cherry, it will grow at altitudes of up to 1800 m (6000 ft).

217 PRUNUS PERSICA
Peach

Family Rosaceae.   **Deciduous**
Etymology The specific name refers to the fact that the peach reached ancient Greece and Rome from Persia and was thus for a long time supposed to have originated there.
Habitat Originally from China, whence it spread all over the world as a result of cultivation in the remote past. First mentioned in a Chinese ritual of the 5th century B.C. and portrayed in Pompeii at the time of Pliny (A.D. 23–79).
Description A tree 8 m (25 ft) tall, with lanceolate leaves (1) with sawtoothed margins, and axillary flowers of a lovely soft pink, which may vary between different varieties. The fruit (2), a round drupe with velvety skin and juicy, sweet, scented flesh, has a big, woody stone pointed at one end and marked by an elaborate pattern of ridges and hollows. The flesh is usually yellow, sometimes white. Peaches can be eaten raw, preserved in syrup, as jam or jelly, or dried.
Propagation By grafting or seed.
Conditions for growth Prefers a light, deep, sandy-humusy soil that is very slightly acid. Should not be planted in the same ground in which old peach trees have been grown unless it is first fumigated. Protect from late spring frost.

---

218 PSIDIUM GUAJAVA
Guava

Family Myrtaceae.   **Evergreen**
Etymology From the Greek *psidion*, pomegranate, from a fancied resemblance between the two fruits.
Habitat Native to Central America.
Description An arboreal evergreen which reaches a height of 8 m (26 ft), with a rather slender trunk covered with darkish-brown, scaly bark. The leaves (1) are oval-oblong and leathery, light green, downy on the underside; the very conspicuous veins are depressed and raised on the underside; the stalks are short, set in opposite pairs on the two sides of the branches. The flowers (2) appear at the axils, solitary or in twos and threes, with a very short, bracted stalk; the persistent calyx is ovate and tubular, opening into 2–4 irregular whitish lobes; the petals are white and oval, generally in fives, with emergent stamens. The fruit (3) is a berry, round or pear shaped, with the calyx lobes persisting at the end. There are a number of kidney-shaped or flat seeds within an edible flesh which may be white, yellow or pink and has a strong scent. The best varieties can be eaten fresh; others are preserved.
Propagation By softwood cuttings, air-layering or grafting.
Conditions for growth Needs only average soil, but it must be moisture-retentive and well drained.

219 PUNICA GRANATUM
Pomegranate

Family Punicaceae.   **Deciduous**
Etymology The name comes from the Latin *punicus,* Carthaginian; Pliny called the fruit *malum punicum,* presumably being mistaken about its origin.
Habitat Native to western Asia, but growing wild in the Mediterranean region.
Description This plant, often of shrubby habit, grows as a small tree up to 6 m (20 ft) in warmer regions. The leaves (1) are oblong, glossy green and entire. The flowers (2) have a red, persistent calyx, leathery and bell shaped, and the red petals soon fall; the flowers are bisexual and the ovary, fused with the calyx, develops into a very unusual fruit, a bright red or purple-red berry that looks like a pome. Under the tough peel the inside is divided into a number of loculi, each containing many seeds closely appressed and faceted and enclosed in a red, juicy aril. The seeds are edible, and syrups are also made from them.
Propagation By seed, suckers or layering.
Conditions for growth Flourishes wherever olives and citrus plants will grow. Prefers heavy, humusy loam soil. Needs regular watering. There are several varieties, with white, patterned, double flowers which are sterile, and there is a variety *nana* (dwarf) which may be grown as a pot plant.

220 PYRUS COMMUNIS
Pear

Family Rosaceae.   **Deciduous**
Etymology The generic name preserves its Latin form.
Habitat Originally from central Eastern Europe and Asia Minor.
Description A tree up to 15 m (50 ft) high with a chestnut or blackish bark, cracked into tiny square scales, sometimes with spiny branchlets. The leaves (1) are ovate, up to 8 cm (3 in) long, toothed at the margins and pointed at the tip, shiny dark green on top and lighter below; they are carried on a stalk up to 5 cm (2 in) long with deciduous stipules. The flowers (2), white with violet-red anthers, grow in corymbs of 7–10 flowers and appear in April, before the leaves. The fruit, a long cone, thinner and not hollowed at the base, has deliquescent flesh when ripe, surrounding a number of hard granules called sclereids. There are conflicting views about the relationship between the wild pear and the cultivated varieties; some say that the varieties are derived from the species *piraster,* while others think they are descended exclusively from the Asian species. The wood has a fine, firm grain.
Propagation By grafting on the wild species.
Conditions for growth Very hardy; adapts to all kinds of soil but likes to stand in the sun. Trees that make very vigorous growth are very susceptible to fire blight, so they should not be fertilized too much.

221 SPOTA ACHRAS
Sapodilla

Family Sapotaceae.   **Evergreen**
Etymology The generic name comes from the name used in South America; the tree is also known by the synonym *Achras zapota*, from the Greek name of the wild pear, transferred to this genus by Linnaeus.
Habitat Tropical America.
Description An evergreen about 20 m (65 ft) tall, with horizontal or weeping branches and dark red wood with a fine grain. The glossy, light green leaves (1) are lanceolate-acuminate, growing from the ends of the shoots. The inconspicuous flowers (2) are axillary and solitary and have downy stalks, a calyx with six hairy sepals and a white, tubular, lobed corolla. The fruits (3) are large berries, round or oval, with a rust-coloured skin which may be smooth or rough; the flesh is yellowish-brown, sweet and juicy. The fruit is edible, though disagreeable if not fully ripe. The plants contain a latex which is tapped by cutting the trunk—also sometimes by expressing the unripe fruit—which is the 'chicle' from which chewing-gum is made. The wood is very resistant, and beams made from it have actually been found in Maya ruins in Yucatan. The seeds are hard, black and shiny.
Propagation By seed, or by grafting if the tree is grown for fruit.
Conditions for growth Tropical and sub-tropical climates.

222 SORBUS DOMESTICA
Service tree

Family Rosaceae.   **Deciduous**
Etymology The name is derived from the Latin 'sorbum', the word the Romans used for the fruit of this tree.
Habitat This species belongs to southern Europe, from Spain to the Crimea, as far as Asia Minor; but it is also grown for its fruit outside this area.
Description A tree up to 15 m (50 ft) high, with alternate imparipinnate leaves (1) as much as 20 cm (8 in) long, with 6–10 pairs of ovate, lanceolate leaflets, sessile and rounded at the base; those in the lower third of the leaf have a sharp point and entire margin, the others are sharply toothed, green and glabrous above, glaucescent and downy below. The flowers (2) have a calyx with five triangular sepals, a white corolla, 20 stamens and 5 styles fused with the pistil. The fruits (3) are little roundish pomes 2–4 cm (1–1½ in) across, bright reddish-yellow turning to brown when they are ripe, which may be at various times between August and February. Sorbs, or sorb-apples, are harvested unripe and left to ripen by bacterial action.
Propagation By seeds, which may take 2 years to germinate, or by grafting on to *Sorbus aucuparia* or *Crataegis oxyacantha*.
Conditions for growth Not very demanding about soils; dislikes heat.

223 ACACIA BAILEYANA
Cootamundra Wattle, Bailey's Mimosa

Family Leguminosae. **Evergreen**
Etymology From the Greek name *akakia,* used for *Acacia arabica* and derived from *akis,* a thorn.
Habitat New South Wales, Australia.
Description In its natural surroundings this tree can grow 10 m (33 ft) tall, but in cultivation it remains much shorter; the branches are often pendulous, but whippy. The leaves (1), set spirally on the branchlets, which they almost conceal, are bipinnate, each pinna having about 20 pairs of glaucescent leaflets, sometimes almost silvery, giving a generally feathery effect. The leaves are persistent. The flowers (2), distinctively globose, with reduced perianth and a great number of stamens which give them the appearance of a plume of feathers, are small, with a stalk of about 1 cm (0.5 in), clustered on big racemes, each with 15 or more flowers; they are bright yellow, and scented. The fruit is a pod with veined margins.
Propagation By seed, or by grafting onto *A. retinoides,* the only species that tolerates lime in the soil.
Conditions for growth Fast grower, needs good soil. Also needs plenty of pruning, but that can be made to coincide with the cutting of branches in flower at the end of winter or beginning of spring, according to the climate.

224 ACACIA DECURRENS var. DEALBATA
Silver Wattle

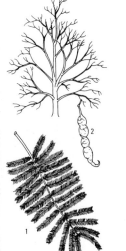

Family Leguminosae. **Evergreen**
Etymology The species name comes from the Latin *decurro,* flow, from the overlapping leaflets of one of its forms.
Habitat An Australian species, growing wild in Queensland, Tasmania and New South Wales.
Description In the wild this tree grows more than 15 m (50 ft) high, but it generally remains smaller in cultivation. The bark is smooth and the shoots slightly pubescent. The color of the leaves (1) varies from light green to a silvery blue-green; they are bipinnate, each of the 20 or so pairs of pinnae having 30–40 pairs of leaflets, giving the tree a light, feathery look. The flowers grow in fairly large compound axillary racemes, as many as 30 on the same inflorescence. Individual flowers have a distinctive appearance due to a great number of stamens that grow in a spherical shape; they have a stalk about 0.5 cm (0.2 in) long, and are bright yellow. The tree flowers in winter, and the flowers are followed by long, smooth, brown pods with the seeds set longitudinally (2).
Propagation Approach grafting.
Conditions for growth Probably the hardiest member of the genus; even so, it withstands only sporadic cold spells. Needs good soil. Grows rapidly but like all acacias is short-lived.

225 AESCULUS X CARNEA
Red Horse Chestnut

Family Hippocastanaceae. **Deciduous**
Etymology The name corresponds to the Latin *aesculus,* which the Romans used for an oak with edible acorns and which Linnaeus used for this genus.
Habitat This tree is a hybrid from the crossing of *A. hippocastanum* x *A. pavia.*
Description This hybrid has inherited its shape from one parent and the color of its flowers from the other. Actually *A. pavia* is little more than a shrub, rarely growing taller than 3 m (10 ft), but it has beautiful red or purple flowers, while *A. hippocastanum* (**226**) grows as much as 30 m (100 ft) tall. The cross generally has a trunk of not more than 6–12 m (20–40 ft), though its dense crown can make it look bigger. The compound digitate leaves (1) are deciduous, with five almost sessile leaflets, cuneate and obovate with crenate margins. The flowers have a short calyx and club-shaped, fringed petals; they grow in dense panicles of various shades of pink, from pale to deep. The fruit (2) is a spiny, dehiscent capsule with big, shiny, inedible seeds which children collect for good-luck pieces ("buckeyes").
Propagation By seed, or by grafting on a stock from the seed of *A. hippocastanum* to maintain the full color.
Conditions for growth Hardy, and tolerates some drought.

226 AESCULUS HIPPOCASTANUM
Common Horse Chestnut

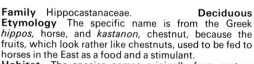

Family Hippocastanaceae. **Deciduous**
Etymology The specific name is from the Greek *hippos,* horse, and *kastanon,* chestnut, because the fruits, which look rather like chestnuts, used to be fed to horses in the East as a food and a stimulant.
Habitat The species comes originally from eastern Europe, the Caucasus and the Balkans; it was introduced into Vienna in the 16th century.
Description A tree up to 30 m (100 ft) tall, of splendid shape but not very long-lived, with a dense, rounded crown. The bark is brown and smooth and scales off with age. The digitate compound leaves (1) with 5–7 lanceolate leaflets have long stalks, the symmetrically shaped flowers (2) are white, growing in rich panicles, and appear in April–May. The fruits (3), large, round, greenish, spiny capsules split open to release three big shiny-brown seeds. The wood is of poor quality. Formerly, the bark was used as a febrifuge.
Propagation By seed, which must be planted before they are quite ripe, because they quickly lose germinability.
Conditions for growth This tree is widespread as a shade tree in gardens. In the past it was often used to line streets, but that is no longer thought advisable both because the trees lose their leaves and because there is some danger from the fall of the spiny fruits.

227 ALBIZIA JULIBRISSIN
Silk Tree, Pink Siris, Mimosa

Family Leguminosae.   **Deciduous**
Etymology The name commemorates the Florentine nobleman Filippo degli Albizzi, who introduced the plant into cultivation in the middle of the 18th century.
Habitat Asian, from Iran to Japan.
Description This tree, up to 10 m (33 ft) high, has spreading branches growing horizontally, which often produce pendulous branchlets. The leaves (1) are deciduous, pinnate and very light colored; there are up to 24 oblong leaflets, sometimes curved, less than 1 cm (0.5 in) long, giving a feathery look. The midrib has a little gland at the base. The flowers, growing in racemes, are little inflorescences in themselves, formed by short-stalked capitula with greatly reduced parts of the perianth and very many stamens, prominent, feathery and pinkish white. The flowers are distinguished from *Acacia* (**223, 224**) by a tube, fused at the base, of varying length; they appear at the beginning of summer. The fruit (2) is a pod.
Propagation By seed, in autumn or spring.
Conditions for growth Fairly hardy, will withstand cold and frost as long as they are not too long and intense. Prefers a sunny position and tolerates drought and pollution. There is a variety *rosea* with deeper-colored flowers, smaller and more cold resistant.

228 AMHERSTIA NOBILIS
Pride of Burma

Family Leguminosae.   **Evergreen**
Etymology The name was given in honor of Sarah, Countess of Amherst, wife of the governor of Burma in the first half of the 19th century.
Habitat Native to Burma, in the teak forests.
Description This tree, which may be up to 20 m (65 ft) tall, has erect, slender branches, with leaves (1) up to 1 m (3 ft) long composed of six pairs of leaflets, dark green when mature but a brownish pink, curled up and pendulous, when young. The strange, most beautiful flowers for which it is cultivated grow in pendent racemes on red stalks; they are bracted and have the two lower petals red and deflexed, while the three above them are large and uneven, white with red dots at the base, with a large yellow patch at the edge. A long red pistil and five stamens, also red, project in a curve. The fruit (2) is a yellow-green berry veined in red which turns brown when ripe and containing three big, flat seeds (often sterile).
Propagation By seed, though rarely with success. More easily with softwood cuttings.
Conditions for growth Outside its native Burma the tree grows in Japan and parts of the East Indies, also in Trinidad and Jamaica. It can grow in the greenhouse, but flowering is so rare it is still remembered that it occurred in England in 1849.

229　BAUHINIA ACUMINATA

Family　Leguminosae.　　　　　　　**Evergreen**
Etymology　The name commemorates the brothers Johann and Caspar Bauhin, botanists, who lived between 1500 and 1600.
Habitat　Native to Asia, India and Malaysia, as far as China.
Description　A little tree no more than 2–4 m (6–13 ft) high, with rather spreading branches which, especially in young trees, have a rather odd zig-zag look. The leaves (1) are stalked; the leaf blade is divided for more than two-thirds of its length into two oblique, oblong lobes each with four longitudinal veins; the base of the stalk has two spiny stipules and the midrib dividing the two lobed ends in a soft thorn. The flowers are white, with five widely spread petals, lanceolate, long and narrowing at the base, growing in cymes with not very many flowers; they soon wither, but the tree goes on producing new flowers for the whole summer. The plant flowers from its first year, before it is 1 m (3 ft) tall. It readily produces radical suckers, sometimes quite far from the trunk. The fruits (2) are flat and bean shaped.
Propagation　By seed or by radical suckers. Plants grown from suckers may flower the same year.
Conditions for growth　Does not tolerate frost unless it is quite sporadic, especially in the juvenile stage.

230　BAUHINIA VARIEGATA
Orchid Tree

Family　Leguminosae.　　　　　　　**Deciduous**
Etymology　The specific name refers to the variegation of the flowers.
Habitat　Native to India, but nowadays grown throughout the tropics.
Description　A tree with an erect trunk which can grow to 10 m (33 ft) in its native surroundings. The leaves (1), as in the whole genus, have the curious shape that accounts for the name; the leaf blade is entire up to a certain point, then divided into two lobes either side of the midrib, each with many veins. The flowers, in short racemes, have five pink, club-shaped petals, one of which is larger than the others and highly variegated in yellow and white. The fruit (2) is a pod up to 50 cm (20 in) long, with several seeds. Despite the various practical uses to which the trees are put in India, where the leaves and buds are eaten, cultivation elsewhere is mainly for ornament. The gray bark is fissured vertically. Its brown-red wood is very heavy and hard but is not much used for woodwork because the trunks are so thin. Of more use is the bark, which is a source of tannin.
Propagation　By seed; flowers in about three years.
Conditions for growth　Tropical; small specimens can be grown in the hothouse and may even flower.

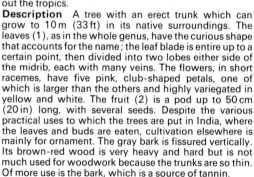

231 BOMBAX ELLIPTICUM
Silk-cotton Tree

Family Bombaceae.   **Deciduous**
Etymology The name comes from the Greek *bombyx,*
silk, referring to the silky hairs filling the seed capsule. In
Haiti they call it the *fromagier,* though this common
name is generally reserved for the Asian species.
Habitat Mexico. The tree is cultivated almost exclusively in Central America.
Description A soft-wooded deciduous tree with a
greenish trunk; the leaves are large, digitate, with five
leaflets, dark red in the juvenile stage and green when
adult. The flowers appear before the leaves and are
extremely showy; they consist of five purple petals, fused
together at first but later separating into five distinct
parts, curling backwards and forming as it were a
background to the feathery cluster of silky, pale-pink
stamens, about 10 cm (4 in) long and ending in a
golden-yellow anther. The fruit is a capsule. The tree is
cultivated mainly for its flowers, but like other species of
the genus its fruits contain a vegetable fiber rather like
kapok, almost completely surrounding the seeds, which
is used commercially.
Propagation By seed.
Conditions for growth Prefers light, open soils.
Thrives under tropical conditions.

---

232 CALLISTEMON SPECIOSUS
Bottle-brush Tree

Family Myrtaceae.   **Evergreen**
Etymology Derived from the Greek *kallos,* beauty,
and *stemon,* stamen; the true beauty of the flowers does
indeed lie in the stamens.
Habitat Native to Australia.
Description This little evergreen tree of shrubby habit
has a height of about 3 m (10 ft). The alternate leaves are
lanceolate-acuminate and rather narrow, with a very
prominent central vein and entire margin. The flowers are
borne in dense cylindrical terminal spikes, but (as in
many other plants of the same family) growth continues
at the tip of the inflorescence, which finally forms a sort
of sleeve on the upper part of the young branch. The
calyx has five small sepals, and there are also five petals,
but these are deciduous; the stamens are free, long and
very numerous, red with yellow anthers. The little anthers
are woody capsules, which persist on the plant for a long
time, clinging to the branches even while growth
continues.
Propagation By seed, at the end of winter and spring;
by softwood cuttings under glass.
Conditions for growth The trees do not tolerate
very severe and prolonged cold; they are particularly
suited to mild climates.

233　CAMELLIA JAPONICA
Camellia

Family　Theaceae.　　　　　　　　　　　　**Evergreen**
Etymology　The name was given by Linnaeus in honor of the Jesuit Camellus in his capacity as a student of botany.
Habitat　As the specific name tells us, the plant comes from Japan.
Description　This tree can reach a height of 12 m (40 ft) but it is more often grown as a shrub. The leathery leaves (1), with oval, pointed blade and crenate margin, are glossy dark green on the upper side and dull light green below. The flowers (2), with five green, leathery sepals surrounded by bracts and five petals in colors ranging from white to dark red, have numerous stamens. The fruit is a tough woody capsule with three divisions each containing one seed. There are many horticultural varieties of this species, differing in the larger or double flowers, in the perfume and in the play of color. These plants will prove long-lived in suitable conditions; they flower from earliest youth and, growing slowly, reach full maturity only after some 20 years.
Propagation　Grafting on two-year-old rootstock by layering or by cuttings.
Conditions for growth　Grows in light, humus-rich, slightly acid soils. Likes high humidity. Prefers full sun but does well in light shade.

234　CASSIA JAVANICA

Family　Leguminosae.　　　　　　　　　　**Evergreen**
Etymology　The name is derived from the Greek *kasia* for plants with therapeutic properties; it was applied by Linnaeus to this genus, and particularly to *C. fistula,* the source of the senna used in pharmacy.
Habitat　Native to the Malay Archipelago.
Description　A deciduous tree of medium height, 6–8 m (20–26 ft), though it may grow higher in its native surroundings. The trunk is rather thin, with spreading branches. The pinnate leaves (1), about 30 cm (12 in) long, are composed of 6–15 pairs of elliptical-oblong leaflets, bright green on the upper side, pale and slightly downy below. The flowers (2) are borne in large, dense, lateral axillary racemes, each flower growing on a reddish stalk with silky bracts at the base; the corolla is composed of five oblong petals rounded at the tip, pale pink or white streaked with darker pink or red to give a marbled effect. There are ten stamens, three of them longer than the others, forming a little cluster at the center; the pistil is set straight in the calyx, which is red or purple. The fruit (3) is a brown pod.
Propagation　By seed or by softwood cuttings.
Conditions for growth　Tropical climates, hot and humid.

235 CATALPA BIGNONIOIDES
Indian Bean Tree, Southern Catalpa

Family Bignoniaceae.   **Deciduous**
Etymology The name comes from *kutuhlpa,* a Creek Indian word.
Habitat Southern United States: Florida, Georgia, Mississippi.
Description An ornamental flowering tree which can grow to a height of 20 m (65 ft), with a wide spreading crown. The leaves (1), generally deciduous, are simple and long stalked, cordato-ovate and acuminate at the tip, sometimes having two lateral lobes, up to 20 cm (8 in) long and downy on the underside. They very often grow in whorls on the branches, and give off an unpleasant smell if they are crushed. The flowers (2), growing in large erect terminal panicles, have a tubular, bell-like corolla opening in five unequal lobes, two small ones above and three larger ones below; they are white with yellow streaks and purple dots on the inside of the corolla, as far as the opening. The flowers are followed by very long, thin, cylindrical pods (3) which may measure as much as 50 cm (20 in) and contain numerous small oblong seeds with white hairs at each end.
Propagation By seed or by hardwood cuttings.
Conditions for growth An undemanding tree.

236 CERCIS SILIQUASTRUM
Judas Tree, Redbud

Family Leguminosae.   **Deciduous**
Etymology The name comes from the Greek *kerkis,* used for a tree not clearly identified, probably a poplar.
Habitat Native to the Mediterranean area. Confusion between Judas and Judaea has led to the belief that this was the tree on which Judas hanged himself.
Description A small deciduous ornamental tree with blackish bark, which grows up to 10–15 m (33–50 ft) in height. The numerous flowers (1) appear before the foliage, growing in clusters directly on the branches at the same point as the previous year's flowers, and sometimes directly on the trunk. They have a papilionaceous corolla of purplish-red and are followed by long reddish-brown pods (2) which contain the seeds and which persist after the fall of the leaves (3). These are rounded, cordate, with palmate veins, smooth and dark green on the upper side, glaucous below. The twigs have a zigzag growth.
Propagation By seed or by root suckers; the plants can begin to flower when they are 5–6 years old.
Conditions for growth Grows in limy soil in full sunlight, and tolerates polluted city air, but cannot withstand severe or prolonged frosts. Needs pruning and tends to produce suckers at its foot.

237 CHIMONANTHUS PRAECOX
Wintersweet, Japanese Allspice

Family Calycanthaceae. **Deciduous**
Etymology The name is derived from the Greek *cheima,* winter, and *anthos,* flower, referring to the winter flowering of the species *praecox.*
Habitat Native to China and Japan.
Description A little tree only 2–3 m (6–10 ft) high, with deciduous leaves (1), simple, entire, opposite. From December to February it is covered with solitary, starry flowers (2), yellowish outside, reddish inside, and strongly perfumed, which appear before the leaves. This is a difficult family to classify systematically, and the various elements of the flower are not easy to separate into calyx and corolla; the number of stamens and pistils can be very high, and the multiple fruits are enclosed in a receptacle. The synonyms of this species are *C. fragrans, Marantia fragrans,* and *Calicanthus praecox.* There is a variety *grandiflorus* with flowers larger and less scented than in the type species.
Propagation By sowing in the spring or by layering in autumn.
Conditions for growth The plant is fairly hardy, especially if grown in a good position under the shelter of a wall. Very desirable as an ornamental, particularly for its winter flowering.

238 CORNUS CAPITATA
Evergreen Dogwood, Bentham's Cornel

Family Cornaceae. **Evergreen**
Etymology The generic name is the same as the Latin name, probably referring to the horny hardness of the wood.
Habitat Himalayas and western China.
Description This is the best representative of the Far Eastern species introduced into Europe for ornamental purposes. Six to ten meters (20–33 ft) high, it has a shrubby habit with long, whippy branches. The leaves (1), evergreen in the country of origin and subpersistent when the tree is grown in colder countries, are cuneate, leathery, oval or elliptical, acuminate, opposite and ternate, dark green on the upper side and whitish and downy on the underside, and up to 10 cm (4 in) long. In autumn they turn purple and gold, while the young branches are still reddish. The ovate, pointed bracts below the clustered flowers (2) display colors from creamy white to sulfur yellow. When the bracts fall the fruits, small, distinctively shaped, drupes, look like large, bright-red strawberries. *Benthamia fragifera* is a synonym of *C. capitata.* It makes a very good garden tree.
Propagation By seed. If it is desired to retain the character of the parent tree, by layering or cuttings.
Conditions for growth Temperate to warm climate; adapts to any kind of soil.

239 CORNUS FLORIDA
Flowering Dogwood

Family Cornaceae.   **Deciduous**
Etymology The specific name clearly refers to its free-flowering habit.
Habitat Native to the eastern and central United States.
Description Trees 8–11 m (25–40 ft) high with a low, wide crown due to the spreading branches. The opposite leaves (1), ovate and pointed, often wavy and curled at the edges, are green and glabrous on top, glaucous and downy along the veins on the underside; unlike *C. capitata,* the leaves are deciduous, but before they fall they turn deep red. The flowers (2), appearing in midspring, almost completely conceal the foliage in some years. They are 13.5–19.5 cm (3.5–5 in) across, sometimes more, and are actually four spatulate oblong bracts, sometimes cordate at the end, arranged in a cross. In the species they are a brilliant white, but there are numerous named varieties ranging from pale pink to a warm red. The oblong fruits (3) ripen in October and are bright scarlet.
Propagation By seed and by cuttings, layering or grafting. It self-seeds widely.
Conditions for growth A very hardy plant; likes temperate climates, not too hot, and adapts well to any kind of soil. It grows in sun or partial shade.

240 CRINODENDRON HOOKERIANUM
Lantern Tree

Family Elaeocarpaceae.   **Evergreen**
Etymology The name is derived from the Greek *krinon,* lily, and *dendron,* tree, referring to the shape of the corolla of one species, *C. patagua,* which is rather like a lily.
Habitat Chile, but has spread to many tropical countries.
Description A tree up to 10 m (33 ft) high. The simple, entire, lanceolate leaves, up to 10 cm (4 in) long, are dark green on the upper side and paler underneath, where the veins are very prominent; the stalks have stipules. The characteristic red flowers, deeply perfumed, have pendulous corollas that look like little lanterns; there is also a variety *album* with white corollas. The buds form in autumn but do not open until the end of the following spring. The bark of *C. patagua,* also a Chilean tree, is used in tanning.
Propagation It is possible to get new plants from seed planted to germinate in the spring or by softwood cuttings, about 10 cm (4 in), put to root under glass.
Conditions for growth Likes acid soils and humid conditions. Cannot tolerate temperatures below −10 °C (26 °F) and likes a shady position protected from the wind.

241 DAVIDIA INVOLUCRATA
Dove Tree, Pocket-handkerchief Tree, Ghost Tree

Family Davidiaceae.   **Deciduous**
Etymology The name was given in honor of Armand David (1826–1900), a French missionary and naturalist in China, who was the first to describe the tree.
Habitat Native to western China.
Description This remarkable deciduous tree has a broadly pyramidal form and can reach a height of 20 m (65 ft). The leaves are cordate and acuminate, with toothed margins, green, glabrous on top and downy below. But the extraordinary thing about the tree is its flowers. They grow in globose inflorescences formed by a number of male flowers and one bisexual, and have two big bracts at the base, one some four times as long as the other, creamy white, ovate and pendulous; these are what gives the tree its common name. The fruits follow the flowers after the fall of the leaves; they are fairly large drupes with a woody, crested seed, globose in form, green on the outside and covered with a lavender-red bloom which turns brownish. Var. *vilmoriniana* has glossy and glaucescent leaves.
Propagation By seed in spring, or by softwood cuttings in summer.
Conditions for growth Fairly slow growing and cannot be counted on to flower. Prefers sun but takes some shade.

242 DELONIX REGIA
Flamboyant, Royal Poinciana

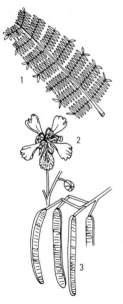

Family Leguminosae.   **Deciduous**
Etymology The generic name is derived from the Greek *delos,* visible, and *onyx*, claw, referring to the shape of the petals. The popular name of the tree in all tropical countries is Flamboyant.
Habitat Originally from Madagascar.
Description A deciduous tree that can grow to a height of 12 m (40 ft), with a stout, knotty trunk and thick grayish-brown bark. The branches are wide spreading, and the bipinnate leaves (1) are composed of a number of little leaflets, giving the whole tree a feathery look. The extremely snowy flowers (2), for which the tree is cultivated, grow in big racemes in colors ranging from carmine to orange; they have five wide sepals, red inside and green outside, and five petals, four of which are red and club-shaped with a wavy edge. Each flower has about ten stamens with long red filaments and yellow anthers, with a red patch at the top. The pollen is orange. The fruits (3) are long red-brown pods containing oblong seeds, yellowish marbled with brown.
Propagation By seed or cuttings.
Conditions for growth Once exclusively tropical, now more widely grown. Used to line streets and also grown in gardens even though it takes considerable space. Grows fast in almost any soil.

243 ERYTHRINA CAFFRA
Kaffir Broom, Coral Tree

Family Leguminosae.   **Deciduous**
Etymology The name comes from the Greek *erythros,* red, from the color of the flowers.
Habitat The tree is native to the Cape of Good Hope and other parts of South Africa.
Description A deciduous tree with wide spreading branches, which can grow to 20 m (65 ft) or even more; the trunk and branches are covered with thorns. The compound, trifoliate leaves, with rhomboid, acuminate leaflets, have very long stalks. The flowers, growing in verticillate spikes, appear on erect axillar stalks and open one after another, becoming deflexed; they are tubular, scarlet, turning purple with age, and have prominent stamens that give them a feathery look. The fruit is a pod containing ovoid seeds.
Propagation By seed, which must be fresh, since it soon loses germinability; or by softwood cuttings under glass.
Conditions for growth Semitropical; small specimens can be kept under glass but cannot be relied on to flower.

244 ERYTHRINA CRISTA-GALLI
Cockspur, Coral Tree

Family Leguminosae.   **Deciduous**
Etymology The species name refers to the red, upright standard, like a cock's comb, for which *crista galli* is the Latin.
Habitat Originally from Brazil.
Description A small tree that may grow to 3 m (10 ft) or more, with a thick, blackish, rugged trunk, often twisted or knotty; the branches are spreading and rather sparse, bearing thorns, and new shoots often appear at the base. The plant is deciduous and has brilliant green leaves, large and trifoliate, with ovate-acuminate leaflets; the stalk is long, with little spines. The flowers, for which the tree is grown, are joined in big, showy racemes which appear on the previous year's wood; the individual flower is 5 cm (2 in) long and papilionaceous, with a bright-red standard. The fruit is a hard, leathery pod, blackish when ripe, containing several kidney-shaped seeds, brown with darker patches and with a black eye. There are varieties that flower in different shades, from coral to carmine, and one, *compacta,* which is shorter and of more compact habit.
Propagation By seed, soaked in water for 48 hours before planting.
Conditions for growth Intolerant of severe frosts; can be grown in the open only in mild climates.

245 JACARANDA MIMOSIFOLIA (J. ACUTIFOLIA)

Family Bignoniaceae.   **Deciduous**
Etymology The name is a Latinized form of an aboriginal name used in Brazil.
Habitat Native of Brazil.
Description There are 50 species in the genus, and the total distribution extends from southern Mexico to Argentina; they are all very similar and the synonyms are often confused. This species, which often grows more than 10 m (33 ft) high in its native conditions, remains lower in cultivation. It is also known as *J. ovalifolia;* the leaves (1) are opposite and bipinnate, with about 16 pairs of pinnae each bearing 14–24 pairs of oval leaflets, giving the tree a light, feathery look. The flowers (2) grow in drooping pyramidal panicles formed of more than 50 flowers, with a small calyx and tubular corolla, distended and turned out from the bilabiate margin, with three bigger lobes and two slightly smaller, all bluish lavender. The fruit is an oblong, dehiscent capsule. The timber obtained from the tree is valuable; used for furniture and cabinetmaking, it is known as "false rosewood."
Propagation By softwood cuttings, or by seed.
Conditions for growth Needs mild climates where there is no frost and any possible drops in temperature will only be sporadic.

246 KOELREUTERIA PANICULATA
Golden Rain Tree, Pride of India

Family Sapindaceae.   **Deciduous**
Etymology After Joseph G. Koelreuter (1733–1806), pioneer in the study of hybridization.
Habitat Originally from China and Japan.
Description A tree with deciduous foliage, 10–15 m (33–50 ft) high with spreading branches that often begin at the base, forming a rounded crown. The leaves (1) are imparipinnate, 30–35 cm (12–14 in) long, composed of 7–15 ovate, acuminate, toothed leaflets, sometimes slightly lobed at the edges toward the base, smooth on the upper side, downy along the veins on the underside. The small yellow flowers (2) grow in long, showy terminal panicles which can reach a length of 50 cm (20 in); the flowers appear in the summer and autumn, followed by fruits that persist for the whole winter. They consist of triangular vescicular capsules, brownish yellow to violet, with a depressed venation at the center of each of the three heart-shaped sides. There is generally one round, black seed to each division of the capsule.
Propagation By seed or by cuttings; also by radical cuttings. The tree is not very long-lived.
Conditions for growth Hardy, but will not withstand intense frost; likes a sunny position and tolerates drought well. Grows in most soils.

247 LABURNUM ANAGYROIDES
Common Laburnum, Goldenchain

Family Leguminosae.   **Deciduous**
Etymology The name is derived from the Latin name.
Habitat Southern Europe.
Description A small, deciduous tree 4–6 m (13–20 ft) or more in height, often shrubby, with spreading branches and pendulous, downy, gray-green twigs. The leaves (1) are alternate and trifoliate, with glaucous leaflets, elliptical and almost always obtuse, stalked but without stipules. The golden-yellow flowers (2), with a papilionate corolla, grow in long pendulous racemes which may be up to 25 cm (10 in) long and appear at the end of the spring. The fruits (3) are straight, downy, dehiscent pods containing several black seeds; they are extremely poisonous, especially when unripe, and indeed the whole plant is toxic. There are several varieties, including *aureum,* which has yellowish leaves; particularly widespread is the hybrid *waterii,* obtained by crossing *L. anagyroides* with *L. alpinum;* its variety Vossii has racemes as much as 50 cm (20 in) long, but it is generally sterile, or at any rate produces very few seeds.
Propagation By seed or by suckers; the varieties must be grafted on stock from seed of one of the type species.
Conditions for growth Completely hardy; likes lime in the soil.

248 LAGERSTROEMIA SPECIOSA

Family Lythraceae.   **Deciduous**
Etymology The name was given by Linnaeus to commemorate his friend Magnuš von Lagerström (1691–1759), of Göteborg.
Habitat A native of India, where it is also grown as a foliage tree under the name of 'jarool'. It is cultivated throughout the tropics nowadays for its flowers.
Description A big tree, growing to a height of 15 m (50 ft) or more, with a thick trunk of strong wood used in shipbuilding and sometimes preferred to maghogany for other uses, since it is easy to polish. The spreading branches grow very high and have opposite leaves (1), entire, leathery, oblong-acuminate, which they lose for a short time in periods of drought. The very showy flowers (2) grow in apical panicles and change colour during the day: pink in the morning, turning purple in the evening. They have five club-shaped petals, greatly narrowed at the base, spreading, wavy and fringed at the edges. Each inflorescence may be as much as 40 cm (16 in) long, with flowers 5–6 cm (2 in) in diameter. A more common, hardy species, *L. indica,* grown in all temperate climates, is even smaller, and despite its name is native to China.
Propagation By seed or by softwood cuttings.
Conditions for growth *L. speciosa* in tropical climates, hot and humid. *L. indica,* deciduous, fears only severe frosts.

249 LIRIODENDRON TULIPIFERA
Tulip Tree, Yellow Poplar

Family Magnoliaceae.   **Deciduous**
Etymology The name comes from the Greek *leirion*, lily, and *dendron*, tree, referring to the showy flowers.
Habitat Native to the eastern United States.
Description An ornamental and timber tree which commonly grows as high as 46 m (150 ft) and is often taller. It is the tallest deciduous tree in the U.S. The leaves (1) are deciduous, alternate, long stalked, of a very distinctive shape, with two very prominent lobes at the basal part and the tip cut off square. Their color is glaucous green but they turn bright yellow before they fall. The bisexual summer flowers, appearing long after the leaves, are greenish yellow, large and solitary, with three spreading sepals and six erect petals tinged with orange at the base; they do not appear until the plant is at least 15 years old. The fruit (2) is a samara. The wood is light yellow, of fine grain, used for furniture and boats; all other parts of the tree contain pharmaceuticals.
Propagation By seed, not often fertile; the tree is characterized by rapid growth and its annual rings are as much as 1 cm (nearly 0.5 in) wide.
Conditions for growth These hardy trees need sunny positions with humid atmosphere and cool, deep soil, because the roots are delicate and fleshy and one is a taproot. They are not subject to disease and are rarely attacked by parasites.

250 MAGNOLIA GRANDIFLORA
Southern Magnolia

Family Magnoliaceae.   **Evergreen**
Etymology The name commemorates Pierre Magnol (1638–1715).
Habitat Originally southeastern United States.
Description This tree grows as much as 25 m (80 ft) tall, with a wide conical crown 5–8 m (16–26 ft) across. The trunk with its smooth blackish-gray bark can be up to 1.5 m (5 ft) in circumference; the reddish young branches are covered with hair and the conical buds, brownish green, are also reddish and downy at the tips. The persistent leaves (1) are ovate-oblong and leathery, entire but sometimes wavy at the edge, 8–16 cm (3–6 in) long and 5–9 cm (2–3.5 in) wide, shiny green on top and with rusty down on the underside; even the conspicuous stalk is thickly covered with hair. The flowers (2) are scented; their fleshy petals are light yellow when they open and form white cup-shaped corollas as much as 25 cm (10 in) across. The trees flower for the whole summer. The autumn fruits (3) are pods which split open to reveal brilliant red seeds. The bark is the source of a tonic used against worms and rheumatism.
Propagation By seed, cuttings, layering and grafting.
Conditions for growth Temperate climates and neutral or acid soil. Needs ample room for full development. Does best in sunlight but may form forests.

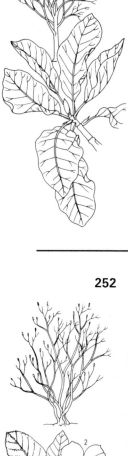

251 MAGNOLIA OBOVATA
Whiteleaf Japanese Magnolia

Family Magnoliaceae.   **Deciduous**
Etymology The specific name refers to the shape of the petals, though some authorities say it refers to the leaves.
Habitat Grows wild in China and Japan.
Description This is a tree up to 20 m (65 ft) high, with very large deciduous leaves, as much as 40 cm (16 in) long and sharply narrowed at the base, glaucescent and early in their development, downy on the underside, where the venation is slightly raised. The scented flowers, with fleshy petals, are enfolded in conical buds, opening at the beginning of the summer into corollas that may be as much as 20 cm (8 in) across, creamy yellow with red stamens. The fruits, as in all magnolias, grow on a stout axis more than 12 cm (4.5 in) long and sometimes slightly curved. They have brown scales which contain the smooth, shiny, bright-red seeds; somewhat like oval pinecones, they remind us that this family has some very primitive features: of all the flowering plants in the world today, it seems to have changed least from its fossil ancestors. Indeed, it appeared on the surface of the earth very early compared with many other plants.
Propagation By seed; also by cuttings and layering.
Conditions for growth Acid soils and a sheltered position.

252 MAGNOLIA SIEBOLDII
Oyama Magnolia

Family Magnoliaceae.   **Deciduous**
Etymology The specific name is dedicated to Philipp Franz von Siebold (1796–1866), a German doctor who joined the Dutch army and was sent to Japan, where he spent several long periods and from which he sent many plants of the local flora to Europe.
Habitat Native to Japan and Korea.
Description This is a small tree, scarcely 5–6 m (16–20 ft) high. Its young branches, leafstalks, fruit-stalks, buds and young leaves are all downy; the leaves (1), entire, elliptical and obovate-oblong and as much as 15 cm (6 in) long, are green on top and glaucescent on the underside. The flowers (2), which open in summer, have long stalks and may be pendulous; they are cup shaped with white petals, pink sepals and carmine stamens. The tree produces few seeds because it has few carpels.
Propagation By seed planted in autumn, but it is possible to get new specimens by layering or by softwood cuttings 10 cm (4 in) long, taken in July and put to root in humid conditions. Grafting is also used.
Conditions for growth This is one of the least hardy magnolias and the most sensitive to the cold; it prefers light, acid soils.

253 MAGNOLIA X SOULANGIANA
Saucer Magnolia

Family Magnoliaceae. **Deciduous**
Etymology In honor of Etienne Soulange-Bodin (1774–1846), French horticulturist.
Description A tree branched from the base, which can grow up to 6–7 m (20–23 ft) tall, and remarkably hardy; it is a hybrid obtained by crossing *M. denudata* (syn. *M. conspicua*) —a tree as much as 10 m (33 ft) tall which grows wild in China, with big white flowers that can be 15 cm (6 in) across—with *M. liliflora*, a spreading tree growing no more than 4 m (13 ft) with erect, bell-shaped flowers, purple on the outside and white inside, which grows wild in Japan. Since one of the parents has white flowers while the other has deep red coloring, this hybrid has numerous clones with flowers ranging from white to almost purple; but they are most commonly white, suffused with pink or red. When fully open, they measure 12–25 cm (5–10 in) across. The tree is greatly prized for the beauty of its flowers (2), which open before the leaves appear (1), ovate or oblong-ovate, while the branches are still bare; many varieties have been cultivated from it.
Propagation Like all hybrids, it needs to be reproduced by vegetative methods if the characteristics are to be maintained.
Conditions for growth Full sun, average soil. Flowers at an early age and grows quite rapidly.

254 MELIA AZENDARACH
Chinaberry, Bead Tree

Family Meliaceae. **Deciduous**
Etymology The name comes from the Greek *melia*, ash tree, referring to the similarity of their leaves.
Habitat Native to Asia, particularly the Himalayan region, but naturalized in all tropical and subtropical zones.
Description A deciduous tree with a spreading crown, which reaches a height of 10–15 m (35–50 ft). The branches are fragile, easily broken by the wind. The leaves (1) are pinnate, with several pairs of ovate-acuminate leaves toothed at the margin. The flowers (2), which appear at the beginning of summer, are lilac, with five petals and a central dark-violet staminal tube; small and scented, they grow in big panicles and are followed by 1.3 cm (0.5 in) round drupes (3) with yellow flesh and a bony, molded, perforated seed. (It is in fact from the seeds, which are used to make necklaces and rosaries, that the tree gets its popular name.) The fleshy part of the fruit has an unpleasant smell, especially when ripe. Its red-brown wood has little commercial importance, though it is used for small objects.
Propagation By seeds, which germinate readily; also by cuttings, in spring. The tree grows very quickly and often disseminates itself.
Conditions for growth Withstands all but severe frosts. Grows in average soil with little water, short-lived.

255 NERIUM OLEANDER
Oleander

Family Apocynaceae.   **Evergreen**
Etymology The name comes from the Greek 'neron', water, because the plant grows most luxuriantly on river-banks.
Habitat Grows wild in all Mediterranean climates.
Description A small polycormic tree with a maximum height of 5–6 m (16–20 ft); it has smooth, greyish bark and is of erect, spreading habit. The dark green, persistent leaves (1) are whorled, generally three to a verticil, lanceolate-acuminate, very tough and with strong central venation. The flowers (2) have a small gamosepalous calyx with five lobes and a tubular corolla opening into five showy segments, pointed at the mouth and flattened at the tip, often crenate or ragged at the edge; they grow in terminal cymes, and their colour can vary from white to yellow, pink or red. The fruit (3) consists of two follicles with numerous downy seeds. Every part of the plant is highly poisonous, since the sao contains several toxic elements, which affect the heart. Forms with double flowers, often sterile but persistent on the branch after flowering, have been bred in cultivation; there are also cultivars with variegated flowers.
Propagation Cuttings and layering in summer.
Conditions for growth Mild climates; tolerates drought.

---

256 PAULOWNIA IMPERIALIS
Empress Tree

Family Scrophulariaceae.   **Deciduous**
Etymology The name commemorates Anna Pavlovna (1795–1865), daughter of Paul I of Russia, to whom this plant was dedicated in 1835; the species is often known as *P. tomentosa*.
Habitat Native to central China, mainly cultivated in Japan.
Description These are ornamental deciduous trees that reach a height of 20 m (65 ft). The wood is soft, the general form erect, with spreading branches and a globose crown; the bark is blackish. The long-stalked leaves (1) are generally entire, cordate-ovate, sometimes trilobate, downy on the upper side, tomentose on the underside. The buds form in autumn and the fragrant violet flowers open in spring before the leaves, growing in erect panicles. The calyx is tomentose, rusty colored, the corolla long and gamopetalous with five short lobes. The fruit (2) is a dehiscent capsule containing many little winged seeds.
Propagation Possible from cuttings but generally by seed. Of rapid growth in the early stages, the tree is fully developed in about 25 years.
Conditions for growth Fairly hardy, but frost may make the buds drop. Withstands drastic pruning down to the foot and puts out strong new suckers.

257 PLUMERIA ALBA
Frangipani

Family Apocynaceae. **Deciduous**
Etymology The name commemorates the French botanist Charles Plumier (1646–1704).
Habitat Native to the East Indies, but nowadays found in all tropical countries.
Description A small tree that can reach a height of 8 m (25 ft), but which sometimes remains in the shrubby stage; it has a latex which runs profusely at every cut. The branches are smooth and fleshy, and at the ends of them are the alternate, obovate, leathery leaves, slightly tomentose on the underside; the plant is deciduous during the dry season and only keeps its foliage in very hot, humid climates. The highly scented flowers, in terminal cymes, are waxy and gamopetalous, with a narrow corolla tube and five big open lobes, partly overlapping; the color is creamy white suffused with yellow toward the base. The common name was suggested by the perfume, which is similar to the very famous perfume invented by Muzio Frangipane in 1500.
Propagation By hardwood cuttings, letting the latex dry as it flows, in sand that is only just wet.
Conditions for growth Cannot be grown outdoors where the temperature goes below −4 °C (25 °F) for more than a few hours. Grows rapidly in sun and good soil.

258 PLUMERIA RUBRA
Red Frangipani

Family Apocynaceae. **Deciduous**
Etymology The name was given in honor of the French botanist Charles Plumier (1646–1704).
Habitat Native to central South America, from Mexico to Ecuador, but, like the species *alba* (**258**), now cultivated widely, especially in tropical Asia. Both species are used in Hawaii to make leis.
Description A little tree that hardly reaches 6 m (20 ft), with elliptical, leathery leaves 20–30 cm (8–12 in) long. The flowers, similar in shape to those of *P. alba,* may vary from red to pink, with a patch of yellow at the mouth. This species too exudes a thick latex from any part that is damaged, and sheds its leaves in the dry season, though it will partly retain them in very humid climates. The perfume is so strong that a few flowers will be enough to scent a whole house; in Java particularly it is a common custom to use them to welcome honored guests.
Propagation By cuttings of woody shoots after the latex had dried, in sand with very little moisture, since the plant is subject to rot.
Conditions for growth Cannot be grown outdoors where the temperature goes below −4 °C (25 °F) for more than a few hours. Grows rapidly in sun and good soil.

259 RHODODENDRON ARBOREUM

Family Ericaceae.   **Evergreen**
Etymology The name comes from the Greek *rhodon*, rose, and *dendron*, tree, hence rose-tree, referring to the color of the flowers of some species.
Habitat Himalayas, Assam and Ceylon.
Description This tree, not very big, can reach a height of 12 m (40 ft) in its native surroundings. It has persistent, rough, leathery leaves (1), simple, entire and pointed; the underside may sometimes be covered with a whitish or rusty tomentum. The bell-shaped flowers (2), growing in globose inflorescences at the ends of the branches, are often deep pink but can vary from white to bright red; the corolla is often lighter with darker dots, which makes the flowers look very attractive. Flowering lasts from March to May. The ovary is tomentose and the fruit is a capsule with 7–9 loculi. This rhododendron is the progenitor of many cultivated varieties.
Propagation By seed, planted in a mixture of sand and turf in the hothouse. Can also be reproduced by layering, grafting or by cuttings, which it is advisable to soak in a hormone solution to help them to root.
Conditions for growth Likes acid soils and rather humid conditions.

260 ROBINIA HISPIDA
Pink acacia

Family Leguminosae.   **Deciduous**
Etymology The name was given by Linnaeus in honour of Jean Robin (1550–1629), herbalist to Henry IV of France, in whose garden the first specimen in Europe grew. The pre-Linnaean French botanist Cornut described the species as *Acacia americana robinii*.
Habitat From the south-eastern United States.
Description A little tree of shrubby habit whose trunk, twigs and flower buds are covered with bristly hair, though not spiny. The leaves (1) are compound, imparipinnate, with 7–13 glabrous leaflets, oval and flattened, 2–4 cm (1–1½ in) long. The flowers (2) grow on short, sparse racemes, on which between 3 and 7 flowers grow; the corolla is papilionate, fairly bright pink. The pod is bristly, with few seeds, and only becomes fully ripe with difficulty; the plant puts out many basal suckers and is most commonly propagated by that means.
Propagation By basal suckers; but if less shrubby, monocormic specimens are wanted the plant can be grafted on stock from the seed of *Robinia pseudoacacia*.
Conditions for growth Fairly hardy, but where the cold may be intense and prolonged needs a position sheltered from cold winds.

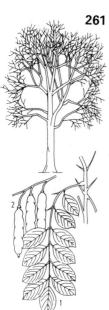

261 ROBINA PSEUDOACACIA
Black Locust

Family Leguminosae. **Deciduous**
Etymology The species name is derived from Greek *pseudes,* false, and *Acacia.* The tree looks like an acacia, though it is not one.
Habitat Native to the eastern part of the United States, its distribution extends westward as far as Oklahoma.
Description A deciduous tree which reaches a height of 25 m (80 ft), with erect, often bifurcated, trunk with scaly, furrowed bark that becomes gray-brown on maturity. The branches are spiny, with smooth bark, and spread so as to make a rounded shape; the red-brown twigs are downy and bear pale-green leaves (1) growing alternately, pinnate, composed of 7–20 leaflets; they have two strong thorns, which are transformed stipules, at the base of the stalk. The flowers, in pendulous racemes, are white and scented, and appear in May—July; the calyx is green and bell-shaped, the corolla papilionaceous. The fruits (2) are pendulous, leathery pods, red-brown when ripe, containing 4–10 kidney-shaped seeds. The decay-resistant wood is used for fence posts.
Propagation By seed or by radical suckers; growth is very rapid and the tree can become a pest.
Conditions for growth Grows in almost any soil. The root system is so strong that in the shrubby stage the plants are used to contain embankments and hillsides.

262 SESBANIA GRANDIFLORA

Family Leguminosae. **Deciduous**
Etymology The name is derived from an Arab word for one of the species, *S. sesban (S. aegypta).*
Habitat The tree has a vast distribution, taking in the island of Mauritius, India and Australia.
Description Not a very long-lived tree, 8–10 m (25–33 ft) in height. The bipinnate leaves, up to 30 cm (12 in) long, consist of 20–30 pairs of thin, oblong leaflets, pale green and slightly glaucescent. The flowers appear in the leaf axils, growing short, sparse racemes; they are papilionate, with an oblong standard; their color can be bright pink, white or dark red, almost rust-colored. The fruit is a curved pod of about 30 cm (12 in) in length. The tree flowers in summer. The soft wood has no commercial value, and the tree is grown only for ornament.
Propagation By seed or by softwood cuttings in the hothouse.
Conditions for growth Tropical and semitropical; small specimens can be kept under glass, but it is difficult to make them flower. The tree can probably grow in the open in milder climates, but must always have shelter in the winter, since it will not tolerate cold.

263 SPATHODEA CAMPANULATA
African Tulip Tree, Flame of the Forest

Family Bignoniaceae.   **Evergreen**
Etymology The name comes from the Greek *spathe,* blade, from the shape of the corolla.
Habitat Native to equatorial Africa, but widespread nowadays throughout the tropics.
Description An evergreen tree that reaches 25 m (80 ft) or more. Its rugged bark is green-gray, the leaves are pinnate with 7–19 oval, glossy leaflets. The flowers appear in apical inflorescences and open one after another, from the outside to the inside; the calyx is leathery, the corolla bell shaped and asymmetrical, convex on one side, and scarlet with fringed edges. The fruit is a long capsule containing hundreds of compressed flat, whitish, winged seeds. The soft wood is of no practical use, though some African tribes make drums from it, and it is still connected with the practice of magic in Africa. When freshly cut it has a strong smell of garlic. It is one of the most beautiful trees in the world.
Propagation By seed or softwood cuttings.
Conditions for growth Exclusively tropical; hardly ever flowers under glass because flowers only appear on adult specimens, which need more room than a greenhouse offers.

264 STENOCARPUS SINUATUS
Firewheel Tree

Family Proteaceae.   **Evergreen**
Etymology The name comes from the Greek *stenos,* narrow, and *karpos,* fruit, referring to the flat, thin fruits.
Habitat Native to Australia, where it grows in Queensland and New South Wales.
Description A tree some 10–20 m (35–65 ft) high with stalked green and glossy leaves which may either be entire and oblong-lanceolate, 20 cm (8 in) long, or else deeply incised with 1–4 pairs of oblong lobes, reaching a length of 30 cm (12 in); they have a strong central venation, are pale with a reddish underside. The trees are cultivated for their extraordinary brilliant flowers, really umbellate inflorescences in which the individual hermaphrodite flowers have an irregular perianth formed by a corolla tube open at the base while its lip is turned in so that it looks as if it were fused, giving a globular effect. All the flower stalks grow from the same central point; their bright red color and radial arrangement have earned the plant its common name. The fruit is a follicle, long and thin.
Propagation By seed or by layering; difficult by cuttings.
Conditions for growth This tree can be cultivated where the minimum temperature is about 8 °C (46 °F), as long as it has shelter in the winter.

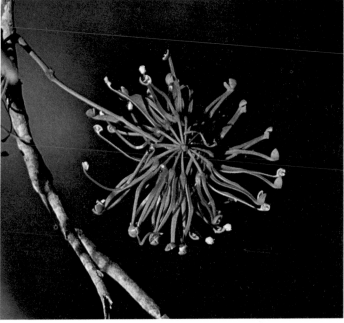

265 TABEBUIA SERRATIFOLIA

Family Bignoniaceae.   **Deciduous**
Etymology The name comes from the local name used in Brazil. In the West Indies the tree is called the *poui.* Many other local names are also applied to it.
Habitat Native to Central America, spreading to the northern border of South America.
Description Explorers' accounts from the middle of the 19th century speak of this gigantic tree, 60–70 m (200–230 ft) high, towering on hilltops in the Amazon region; there may well be such specimens living, given the weight of the wood and the difficulties of transporting it, but wherever there is intensive industrial exploitation the trees are all younger and smaller. The trunk, whose grayish bark is smooth when young, becoming fissured later, is some 3 m (10 ft) in circumference. The crown has digitate leaves (1) with 4–5 leaflets serrated at the tip. The yellow flowers (2), with a tubular, curved corolla and wavy, fringed margins, grow in open inflorescences so thick that they hide the branches at the time of the leaf change. The fruit (3) is a capsule with many winged seeds. The wood, known as Surinam wood, is one of the strongest and hardest woods in the world.
Propagation By cuttings and by layering.
Conditions for growth Tropical climates, humid and hot.

266 YUCCA ELEPHANTIPES

Family Agavaceae.   **Deciduous**
Etymology The name is derived from that used in the West Indies for a plant of the *Euphorbia* family, wrongly applied to this genus, which is often assigned to the genus *Liliaceae*, from which it was removed by A. Engler.
Habitat Comes from south-east Mexico.
Description This is one of the relatively few examples of an arborescent xerophyte; it can grow up to 8–10 m (25–30 ft); the stem is enlarged at the base and has a fissured, reddish-brown bark and many branches from the base up. The majority of the arboreal *Yuccas* are very similar in form and it is often very hard to tell one from another. Yucca elephantipes has the typical cluster of broad leaves (1) at the tips of the branches, with linear, glaucescent leaf-blades, erect at the centre and out-turned all around, but they are not pointed. The bell-shaped flowers (2), in big terminal panicles, are white shaded in cream. The fruits are fleshy and yellow, and consist of pendulous berries; in some other species they are capsules. Pollination is very rare; in the tree's homeland it is effected by a little butterfly, *Pronuba yuccasella*, but it can be performed artificially.
Propagation By seed, cuttings or suckers.
Conditions for growth Mild climates; does not tolerate extreme cold.

TREES OF ECONOMIC IMPORTANCE

267 ACER SACCHARUM
Sugar Maple

Family Aceraceae. **Deciduous**

Etymology Ancient Latin name of the maple, which also means hard, in reference to the wood, which was used for making spears.

Habitat The distribution covers eastern Canada and the United States.

Description A tree that grows to 30–35 m (100–115 ft), with gray bark with very distinct vertical flutes and fragile glabrous twigs; the buds are pointed and never turn red, which distinguishes the tree from *A. rubrum* (**77**), which it somewhat resembles. It differs also in the palmate leaves (1) with five, sometimes three, lobes set at obtuse angles; the stalk, never red, lacks the white sticky juice. The greenish-yellow flowers (2) are joined in subsexual corymbs, and the samaras (3) have slightly divergent wings. The tree assumes fantastic yellow and red colors in autumn. In the North, where cold nights and warm days alternate in late winter, the Sugar Maple is tapped for a sap that contains 1–4% sucrose, the source of maple syrup and sugar.

Propagation By sowing in a seedbed, where the young trees must remain for several years.

Conditions for growth Prefers light fertile soil, but does well in poorer soil. As a sapling the tree tolerates considerable shade but needs ample sun for full growth.

268 ANACARDIUM OCCIDENTALE
Cashew

Family Anacardiaceae. **Evergreen**

Etymology The name was given by Linnaeus and refers to the vaguely heart-shaped look of its false fruit.

Habitat Native to the tropical zones of South America.

Description This is a tree 10–12 m (33–40 ft) high, with a spreading, persistent crown and simple, oval, leathery leaves (1) set alternately. The flowers (2), growing in inflorescences at the tips of the young branches, are pinkish white, small and scented. The true fruit (3), dry and kidney shaped, is enclosed within the flower stalk, which swells up to form a fleshy, sweet, edible mass the size of a fist and white, yellow or scarlet when ripe. It is sold commercially as cashew apple, while the true fruit goes under the name of cashew nut. This last, when the juice has been extracted to get rid of the caustic quality of the essential oil, is roasted and eaten. The liquid contained in the husk is used as an insulating medium in aviation, since it can stand extreme variations of temperature; however, it has poisonous properties, and staff who work with it may sometimes exhibit symptoms of poisoning.

Propagation By seed.

Conditions for growth Tropical conditions, hot and humid.

269 BIXA ORELLANA

Family Bixaceae.   **Deciduous**
Etymology Derived from a local South American name.
Habitat Tropical America, but naturalized in many countries where climate permits as a result of widespread cultivation.
Description A little tree with alternate, simple leaves (1) resembling those of the lime, with stipules and a long stalk. The inflorescence, formed by hermaphrodite flowers (2) with a deciduous calyx, is a long, low panicle of a beautiful flesh pink. The fruit, which is what the tree is planted for, is a capsule with soft red skin and red juice. The dyestuff obtained from it, known in the trade as annatto or arnotto, is used to dye fabrics orange-red (apt to fade). An oily solution of the yellow coloring agent contained in annatto is the only method permitted by law of coloring butter and cheese. In some Caribbean countries the people dissolve it in castor oil and use it to paint their bodies, and for protection against insect stings.
Propagation By seed, or by hardwood cuttings.
Conditions for growth Tropical, hot and humid.

---

270 CAMELLIA SINENSIS
Tea Tree

Family Theaceae.   **Evergreen**
Etymology The specific name denotes that the tree comes from the Far East, and reminds us that tea growing was a Chinese monopoly until 1840, when Robert Fortune succeeded in exporting plants and bringing experienced planters from China to India.
Habitat China, Assam and India, with smaller cultivation in other countries.
Description These are small trees. In the wild state they will grow as much as 12–15 m (40–50 ft), but on plantations they are kept down by continual pruning to a height of 1–1.5 m (3–5 ft). They have leathery elliptical-lanceolate leaves (1) with finely toothed edges, a shiny dark green, with a short stalk. The little flowers (2), white and scented with numerous yellow stamens, are solitary or in cymes of 2–5; the fruits (3) are capsules containing 1–4 seeds. The plant is pruned for two purposes: to make picking easier and to encourage the production of young leaves, which are picked every three weeks from the third year on. There is a difference between green teas, prepared by simply cutting the leaves, and black teas, which are obtained by fermenting the leaves.
Propagation By cuttings and by layering, in order to maintain the varieties propagated.
Conditions for growth This species prefers mountainous tropical zones with a warm, temperate climate.

271 CEIBA PENTANDRA
Kapok Tree

Family Bombacaceae. **Deciduous**
Etymology The generic name comes from a local South American word.
Habitat Native to the tropics in both the Old and New Worlds.
Description A tall tree, as much as 30–40 m (100–130 ft) high, with a stout, spiny trunk with big buttress formations at the foot; the branches, thick and strong, are wide spreading and almost horizontal, arranged in layers. The compound leaves (1) are digitate, with 5–7 entire leaflets. The flowers (2) are white and large, growing in little clusters, with a gamosepalous calyx and oblong petals from which the staminal column protrudes. The fruit (3) is an oblong, leathery capsule, about 10 cm (4 in) long, which opens in five sections to release a great number of brown, ovoid seeds contained in masses of a thick fiber rather like cotton; this is the kapok that is used for stuffing pillows, etc. Although the soft, light wood also has its uses, the tree is chiefly cultivated for the kapok (the name comes from a Malay word). In regions where there is a dry season the tree is deciduous, and the leaves fall before the fruits appear.
Propagation By seed; the tree grows quickly.
Conditions for growth Exclusively tropical.

---

272 CINCHONA CALISAYA
Quinine Tree

Family Rubiaceae. **Evergreen**
Etymology The name commemorates the Countess of Chinchon, wife of the Viceroy of Peru, who was cured of fever by the bark of a Peruvian tree in 1638.
Habitat Native to the Andes, from Peru to Bolivia, but now almost wholly concentrated in Java.
Description An evergreen tree up to 30 m (100 ft) high with erect trunk and yellowish bark. The leaves (1) are opposite, oblong and leathery, with reddish stalk and veins. The flowers (2), pink and scented, grow in panicles and the fruits (3) are small ovoid capsules. The bark of the tree is rich in alkaloids, the most important being quinine, which is effective in the treatment of malaria. In the East Indies planters have succeeded in increasing the amount of quinine produced in proportion to secondary alkaloids, by selection of suitable varieties and perfecting the most effective of the several methods of removing the bark. The common name of the tree comes from a local word, *quinaquina;* the drug used to be known as "the countess's powder" and also as "Jesuits' powder" because Jesuits returning from South America had helped to make it known. The importance of the tree is considerably reduced now that quinine can be prepared synthetically.
Propagation By seed.
Conditions for growth Tropical.

273 CINNAMOMUM CAMPHORA
Camphor Tree

Family Lauraceae.   **Evergreen**
Etymology Derived from the ancient Greek name *kinnamomon,* used for the species known at that time.
Habitat China, Japan, Taiwan.
Description An evergreen tree that reaches a height of 15 m (50 ft). Its leaves (1) are pale green, glaucous underneath, alternate, ovate-acuminate and leathery, with three distinct veins; in the juvenile stage they are rosy. The little whitish-yellow flowers (2) grow in axillary panicles, and the fruits (3) that follow them are small ovoid drupes, dark purplish-red when ripe. Camphor occurs in the essential oil contained in all the tissues of the tree—if the leaves are rubbed they smell of camphor—but mostly in the wood, both that of the aerial parts and of the roots, where it accumulates particularly in hollows. It used to be extracted by felling the trees, but nowadays the leaves and young branches are also used and the trees are not cut down until they are 50 years old. The product, widely used in the manufacture of celluloid and as a preventive against parasites but also useful in medicine, is nowadays also obtained synthetically, since the natural substance has become so costly.
Propagation By seed or softwood cuttings.
Conditions for growth Tropical and subtropical.

274 CINNAMOMUM ZEYLANICUM
Cinnamon

Family Lauraceae.   **Evergreen**
Etymology The species name refers to the place of origin, the island of Ceylon (Sri Lanka).
Habitat India and Sri Lanka, but grown throughout the tropics.
Description An evergreen tree up to 6–10 m (20–33 ft) tall, with erect trunk and pale brown bark; young branches are almost rectangular in section. The leaves (1), about 15 cm (6 in) long, are leathery and stiff, opposite, lanceolate-ovate, bright green on the upper side, pale or glaucescent below, and furrowed by three strong veins. The flowers (2) are small and yellowish white, with a tubular corolla and six wide lobes, velvety at the edges; they are clustered in axillary and terminal panicles. The fruit is a berry with a single seed, which remains within the persistent calyx and turns black when ripe. To obtain the spice in plantations, the bark is removed and dried. A yellowish-brown oil is prepared from it which is used as a flavoring and in medicine.
Propagation By seed.
Conditions for growth Tropical and subtropical.

275 CITRUS AURANTIUM var. AMARA (CITRUS BIGARDIA)
Bitter Orange, Seville Orange

Family Rutaceae. **Evergreen**

Etymology The specific name refers to the color of the fruit, while the varietal name (Latin, bitter) emphasizes that the fruit is not sweet.

Habitat Probably native to Southeast Asia. Cultivated in Arabia since the end of the 9th century and in Sicily since the year 1002.

Description A tree that may grow to a height of 15 m (50 ft) with a diameter of 50 cm (20 in). It differs from the Sweet Orange (**196**) in the long thorn at the axil of the lower leaves (1), the darker, more aromatic foliage, the more broadly winged stalk, the rougher and more brightly colored peel on the fruit, and in the sour, bitter flesh. The peel is used to make orange bitters, used in cocktails, and sweet liqueurs such as Curaçao. The strongly scented flowers (2) are gathered by shaking the trees so that they fall into cloths placed below the branches. (3) fruit. They are distilled to make an essential oil known as neroli oil; very valuable in perfumery. Another essential oil, petitgrain, is obtained by distilling the leaves and twigs.

Propagation By seed; it may also be used as a stock in grafts.

Conditions for growth Temperate climates, warm and dry.

276 CITRUS BERGAMIA
Bergamot

Family Rutaceae. **Evergreen**

Etymology From the Turkish *beg-armodi.*

Habitat Of unknown origin, probably a hybrid. Cultivated in Italy since the 18th century.

Description This is a small tree, growing to 3 m (10 ft), with pendulous branches and rather pimply leaves (1) with slightly winged stalks. The flowers (2), with five green sepals, five white petals and ten stamens, are scented. The fruit (3), a hesperidium, is spherical, a little larger than the oranges, with a thin lemon-yellow skin; it contains 10–15 segments and has sour, inedible flesh. It is grown exclusively for the essential oil pressed from the skin. This essence is used in the manufacture of liqueurs and perfumes, including Eau de Cologne. This perfume was invented in 1670 by a travelling merchant, Giampaolo Feminis of Crana (Novara), who passed the recipe on to Giovanni Maria Farina of Santa Maria Maggiore; he founded a business in Cologne dealing in a variety of goods, including a monopoly of this *aqua amabilis,* which only became known as Eau de Cologne in 1748.

Propagation By seed. There are wild specimens from which the desired species may be obtained by grafting; also by layering.

Conditions for growth Needs minimum temperatures not lower than 2 °C (35 °F).

277 COFFEA ARABICA
Coffee Tree

Family Rubiaceae. **Evergreen**
Etymology The name is derived from the Arabic word used for the drink, which may have come from the town of Caffa in Ethiopia.
Habitat Grows wild in Ethiopia, Mozambique and Angola, and was imported into Arabia and from there, at the end of the 15th century, into Europe. Later cultivated in South America, which is now the largest producer.
Description A small evergreen tree 2–3 m (6–10 ft) in height, with spreading, flexible branches; the opposite leaves (1) are shiny green, oblong-acuminate, with a short stalk and very marked veins. The white, scented flowers (2), with a tubular corolla, appear in clusters at the leaf axils and are followed by the fruit (3), drupes with two seeds and a fleshy covering, green at first, red when ripe. Each of the two seeds is convex on the outside and flat, crossed by a furrow on the inside; these are the so-called coffee beans which are roasted.
Propagation By seed, in sandy soil; in the hothouse.
Conditions for growth Tropical or semitropical, hot and humid. The tree can be grown in southern Europe if taken into the hothouse in winter—it does not tolerate temperatures below 16 °C (61 °F)—and may even fruit in such conditions.

---

278 COLA ACUMINATA

Family Sterculiaceae. **Evergreen**
Etymology Derived from a native African name.
Habitat Native to tropical Africa.
Description This tree, about 20 m (65 ft) tall, has persistent stalked leaves (1), alternate, with a leathery lanceolate-acuminate blade with prominent veins on the underside; in the juvenile stage they may be deeply incised toward the base. The flowers (2), unisexual or polygamous, grow in dense axillary or terminal panicles and have no corolla at all; the five yellow, showy segments, with purple stripes at the base, are only the opened lobes of the thin, tubular, greenish calyx. The fruits, about 15 cm (6 in) long, are green, oblong and leathery, made of 4–6 sections which are the so-called cola nuts, appearing while unripe as tubercles within the outer covering. They are formed by the cotyledons and are irregular in shape; when fresh they vary from white to yellow or pink, when dried they are reddish. They contain some 2% caffeine and a little theobromine and other drugs. The local peoples use them as stimulants, and large quantities are exported as ingredients of carbonated soft drinks.
Propagation By seed or by hardwood cuttings.
Conditions for growth Exclusively tropical.

279 CRESCENTIA CUJETE
Calabash

Family Bignoniaceae. **Evergreen**
Etymology The name commemorates Pietro de' Crescenzi (1230–1321), a scientific agriculturist of Bologna.
Habitat Tropical and subtropical America.
Description The brown trunk of this tree, with slightly cracked and fissured bark, grows up to 6–10 m (20–33 ft). The short-stalked, lanceolate leaves are dark green and set alternately, though there are varieties with acuminate leaves growing from the nodes, native to the West Indies and Guyana. The flowers are big, solitary or paired, with a bipartite calyx and a tubular corolla, distended at the center and opening up into five yellowish flaps veined with a darker color; they have an unpleasant smell. The tree is grown for its fruit, which is globose or ovoid; the size varies, sometimes reaching a length of 50 cm (20 in). It has a single loculus, filled with flesh; local tribes make a variety of domestic utensils from it, gathering the fruit before it is ripe and afterwards hollowing out the woody shells. The flesh is used in pharmacy and the hard, white wood is used in carpentry.
Propagation By seed.
Conditions for growth Exclusively tropical.

280 DRACAENA DRACO
Dragon Tree

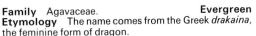

Family Agavaceae. **Evergreen**
Etymology The name comes from the Greek *drakaina*, the feminine form of dragon.
Habitat Endemic to the Canary Islands.
Description This slow-growing, strangely shaped tree belongs (like the palms) to the monocotyledons, though, having a woody stem, it is often included in the Liliaceae. The thick trunk, which becomes branching, has apical clusters of swordlike leaves (1) arranged in rosettes, and can grow 20 m (65 ft) high and over 4 m (13 ft) in diameter. It is an exceptionally long-lived tree; two specimens in the island of Tenerife are believed to be among the oldest trees in the world. The flowers (2), growing in big panicles, are bell-shaped, yellowish-white; they appear at the ends of the branches inside the leaf rosettes and are followed by orange berries. The resinous reddish liquid that oozes from the trunk is one of several resins called dragon's blood which used to be of great commercial importance as the base of fine dyes and paints and in photoengraving until the invention of synthetic colors. The tree does not branch or flower until it is about 30 years old.
Propagation By seed, or by cuttings of shoots or of a part of the stem.
Conditions for growth Mild climates where there is no frost.

281 ERYTHROXYLON COCA
Coca

Family Erythroxylaceae. **Evergreen**
Etymology From the Greek *erythros,* red, and *xylon,* wood, from its reddish bark.
Habitat Native to Bolivia, Peru and Colombia, but also cultivated in tropical Asia.
Description A small tree that reaches a height of 3 m (10 ft) and begins to branch in the juvenile stage, though it has rather slender trunk and branches. The little, short-stalked elliptical leaves (1) are alternate and entire, brilliant light green and more or less acuminate according to the variety. The small flowers (2) have a green calyx and five white petals; they grow on stalks at the leaf axils, solitary or in twos or threes, and are followed by the fruits (3), small drupes with a brilliant red aril. There are generally reckoned to be four varieties: *genuina truxillo* from Peru, *boliviana* from Bolivia, *spruceana* cultivated in the East Indies and the commonest variety, *novogranatense* (often regarded as a separate species) from Colombia, but also grown in Indonesia. The alkaloid from which cocaine is prepared is extracted from the leaves on an industrial scale.
Propagation By seed.
Conditions for growth Tropical; under glass in temperate climates.

282 FICUS ELASTICA
Rubber Tree

Family Moraceae. **Evergreen**
Etymology The name comes from that of the edible fig, *F. carica* (**203**).
Habitat Native to tropical Asia.
Description Very young specimens of this tree are often seen as house plants, but in its natural surroundings it is a tall tree that may grow as high as 30 m (100 ft), with spreading branches that give it a round crown. The leaves, 30 cm (12 in) or more long, have short stalks; they are leathery and shiny, entire, oblong or elliptical, with a strong central vein and secondary veins joining it almost at right angles and running parallel up to the margin. The fruits, covered at first by an involucre, grow from the axils of the fallen leaves and are greenish yellow when ripe; they measure a little over 1 cm (0.5 in). As in nearly all the species, the trunk and other parts of the tree exude a thick, white latex when cut; in the case of this species it is used to produce rubber. An incision is made in the trunk and the latex collected in receptacles; but production from this tree is less than that from *Hevea brasiliensis* (**284**) because the trees can only be tapped every three years for fear of damaging them.
Propagation By cuttings from shoots or buds.
Conditions for growth Warm and humid; young specimens in pots.

283 HAEMATOXYLON CAMPECHIANUM
Campeachy Tree, Logwood Tree

Family Leguminosae.   **Deciduous**
Etymology The name comes from the Greek *haima*, blood, and *xylon*, wood.
Habitat Tropical America and West Indies.
Description A tree 6–9 m (20–30 ft) high with spiny branches and compound, pinnate leaves (1) consisting of 2–4 pairs of wedge-shaped leaflets deeply incised at the edges. The flowers (2) are small, yellowish and scented. The fruits (3) are oblong pods. The wood has a heavy, hard heartwood, red-brown to violet, from which an active principal called haematoxylin is extracted—a colorless substance which is transformed on oxidation into a red dye, haematin, which can react with metallic hydrates to produce colored lacquers. Fragments of the wood treated with steam under pressure give campeachy extract, a mixture of haematoxylin and haematin used for varnishes and inks and to make a dye for silk, wool and cotton. Haematoxylin is used as a coloring agent for microscopy. The common name, campeachy, is derived from the Spanish *campeche*, from the Mexican State of Campeche.
Propagation By seed.
Conditions for growth Likes hot, subtropical climates.

---

284 HEVEA BRASILIENSIS

Family Euphorbiaceae.   **Deciduous**
Etymology The name is derived from a local word, *heve,* meaning rubber.
Habitat Native of the Amazon River basin of Brazil.
Description A tropical tree that reaches a height of 18 m (60 ft) and is the principal source of rubber, which is obtained by treatment of its coagulated latex. The leaves (1) are alternate, with long stalks, composed of three lanceolate-acuminate leaflets. The plants are monoecious, with small flowers, pubescent and lacking petals, clustered in panicles. The fruit (2) is a capsule. The latex is collected by making an incision in the bark (see photograph), which is light gray.
Propagation May be propagated by cuttings, but is generally reproduced from seed, which must be fresh since it quickly loses its germinability. The tree is of rapid growth; it produces good quantities of latex by the time it is six years old and reaches full maturity at eight.
Conditions for growth The tree can only develop in warm, humid tropical conditions, like those of the rain forest. The English agriculturist Sir Henry Wickham succeeded in exporting seeds from Brazil in 1876, and large plantations soon grew up in Malaysia, Indonesia and Sri Lanka (Ceylon).

285 ILEX PARAGUARIENSIS
Maté

Family Aquifoliaceae. **Evergreen**
Etymology The generic name is derived from that given by the Romans to the Holm Oak, *Quercus ilex* (**153**), from the similarity of the leaves of some species.
Habitat Native to Paraguay and southern Brazil, but now grown throughout tropical South America.
Description A small evergreen tree that reaches a height of 6 m (20 ft). The leaves (1) are leathery, lanceolate or oblong with a narrow base, a flattened tip and rounded teeth at the edges. The small, white flowers (2) grow in clusters at the leaf axils. The fruits (3) are red, globoid berries with four seeds. The plant is grown for its leaves, from which a drink is made that is famous all over South America; it is sometimes called "Jesuits' tea" because when they returned from their missions the Jesuits were the first to make the drink known in Europe. The dried leaves are roasted and pulverized; hot water is poured on the dry powder to make a drink that is stimulating but less so than coffee and tea. The local people drink it through straws perforated at the tip, after preparing it in specially shaped wooden gourds, known as maté gourds.
Propagation By seed or cuttings.
Conditions for growth Tropical.

286 LIQUIDAMBAR STYRACIFLUA
Sweet Gum

Family Hamamelidaceae. **Deciduous**
Etymology From the Latin *liquidus*, liquid, and the Arabic *ambar*, amber, from its secretion of an aromatic fluid.
Habitat Native to the Atlantic areas of North America, it was introduced into Europe in 1681.
Description A deciduous tree which in its native conditions reaches a height of 40 m (130 ft), with a tall, narrow crown; the bark is deeply fissured even on young branches. The alternate leaves (1) are stalked and palmate, with 5–7 acuminate lobes, smooth and glossy on the upper side, downy along the veins on the underside. Their bright green changes to vivid scarlet before they fall. The flowers (2, 3) are unisexual, growing on the same plant, insignificant and apetalous, borne on round inflorescences. The fruits are really round infructescences, made up of a number of dihiscent capsules each with 1–2 winged seeds and prominent spines formed from the persistent styles. Both wood and leaves are aromatic. When the bark is stripped, boiled and pressed it yields a resinous oil called storax which is used as a fixative in perfumes and in therapeutic preparations.
Propagation By seed or by layering.
Conditions for growth Not very particular about soil but needs sun and plenty of room to achieve maximum size and beauty.

287 MANIHOT ESCULENTA
Manioc, Cassava

Family Euphorbiaceae.   **Evergreen**
Etymology The generic name comes from the Brazilian word, *manioc*.
Habitat Native to tropical America but also widely grown in Africa and Asia.
Description This is a little tree that grows no more than 3 m (10 ft) high and sometimes has a shrubby form. The leaves (1) are palmate, with 3–7 lobes; the flowers (2), growing in racemes both axillary and terminal, are unisexual and apetalous, but may have petaloid sepals. The fruits (3) are winged capsules. The large rootstocks are poisonous when fresh because they contain hydrocyanic acid (prussic acid), but when pounded and cooked they lose their toxicity. Treated in this way they are the source of the starch known as manioc or cassava, an important local foodstuff that is also exported to make tapioca. A closely related species, *M. dulcis* (called in Brazil *macaxeiro* or *aipi*), is less productive but its roots contain much less prussic acid. There is a variety *variegata* whose leaves have pale-yellow veins.
Propagation By cuttings under glass.
Conditions for growth Tropical; small specimens under glass.

---

288 MONODORA MYRISTICA

Family Annnaceae.   **Evergreen**
Etymology The name comes from the Greek *monos*, one, and *dorea*, gift, a reference to the solitary flowers.
Habitat Native to the forests of equatorial Africa.
Description This tree, which in the wild reaches a height of as much as 20 m (65 ft), generally remains much lower in cultivation. The big leaves are glabrous, obovate, with wedge-shaped base and short stalk; the leaf blade has 10–20 lateral veins, prominent on the underside. The solitary flowers, hanging down on long stalks, recall those of certain orchids; they have three sepals and six petals joined at the base, the three outer ones lanceolate and wrinkled, yellow patterned with violet, and the inside ones shorter, ovate and hairy at the base. The fairly large, globose fruits, of a woody consistency, have a resinous flesh containing a great number of seeds. They are used for flavoring foods and also have certain medicinal properties. These qualities often lead to their being confused with the fruits of *Myristica fragrans*, source of the common nutmeg.
Propagation Normally by cuttings of mature wood under glass.
Conditions for growth Although very young specimens can be kept in the hothouse, cultivation is really only possible in the tropics.

289 MORINGA OLEIFERA
Horseradish Tree

Family Moringaceae. **Deciduous**
Etymology The name comes from the Sinhalese *morunga*.
Habitat Native to India and today growing wild in parts of Indonesia.
Description A small tree that grows up to some 8 m (25 ft), with a trunk of soft wood and corky bark; young shoots are pubescent. The leaves (1) are tripinnate, with no stipules, as much as 50 cm (20 in) long, with stalked leaflets. The flowers (2), growing in panicles, have a gamosepalous calyx with five deflexed lobes and a corolla with five petals, four deflexed and one erect with the anthers joined to it, while the stamens have long, straight filaments. Individual flowers are whitish, pedunculate and perfumed, followed by fruits (3) that are capsules up to 30 cm (12 in) long, with nine big triangular seeds with three wings. An oil is extracted from these which never goes rancid; it is used for delicate precision machinery and is known as watchmaker's oil, or sometimes behen oil. The roots, too, which have a piquant taste, are sometimes used as spices and condiments.
Propagation By seed.
Conditions for growth Tropical and subtropical.

---

290 MYRISTICA FRAGRANS
Nutmeg

Family Myristicaceae. **Evergreen**
Etymology From the Greek *myristikos,* perfumed.
Habitat From the Moluccas, in the Malay Archipelago, but also grown in the West Indies and elsewhere.
Description An evergreen tree 10–20 m (33–65 ft) high, with alternate leaves (1), oval with a short stalk, dark green on the upper side, lighter on the underside, and aromatic. The plants are dioecious, so that it is necessary to grow at least one tree with male flowers near several with female flowers. The inflorescences are axillary, the flowers, small, yellowish or greenish; the males (2) have a number of stamens joined in a little column, the females (3) have a single carpel, and both are scented. The fruit (4) that follows fertilization is a fleshy, pear-shaped berry, which opens on ripening to release the big seed, surrounded by a fibrous aril which changes from reddish to yellowish when dried. Marketed under the name of mace, it is used in cooking and perfumery. The bare seed, generally treated with lime, is the nutmeg used to flavor food and drinks.
Propagation By seed; by cuttings (rather difficult).
Conditions for growth Tropical, hot and humid.

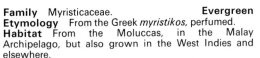

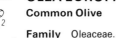

291 OLEA EUROPAEA
Common Olive

Family Oleaceae.   **Evergreen**
Etymology *Oliva* is the classical Latin name.
Habitat Hottest parts of the Mediterranean region.
Description Growing to 8 m (25 ft), it develops a large, twisted trunk covered with smooth gray bark which cracks into scales with age. The crown is about as wide as the tree is high. In good soils it is generally open and asymmetrical; in poor soils it is dense and rounded. The leaves (1) are lanceolate or oblong, 2.5–7.5 cm (1–3 in) long. They are leathery, gray-green above, silvery beneath. Small yellow-white, fragrant flowers (2) are borne in short racemes on the previous season's growth. These are followed by the familiar fruits, which are actually fleshy, oily drupes (3). The olive tree is also an extremely handsome ornamental.
Propagation Normally by cuttings, shoots or suckers. Germination of large seeded varieties is slow and erratic; and the seedlings should then be grafted.
Conditions for growth Requires full sun. Protection against frost is essential, but only occasional deep watering is required. Although the trees are self-fruitful, best results are obtained by planting two or more different varieties together.

292 PIMENTA DIOICA
Allspice, Pimento

Family Myrtaceae.   **Evergreen**
Etymology The name is derived from the Spanish *pimento,* not to be confused with *pimiento,* which is a species of piquant pepper of the genus *Capsicum.*
Habitat Native to Central America, from Mexico to Jamaica.
Description A little tree that in the countries of origin may reach a height of 10 m (33 ft) but which remains lower when grown under glass. It has a flexible trunk with silver-gray bark and many thin branches, with leathery, opposite leaves (1), oblong-acuminate, with strong veins. The little, whitish flowers (2) grow in cymes, generally apical, sometimes axillary, and have 4–5 petals; the calyx has four lobes, which distinguishes this from other species. The globose fruits (3) are very small, only about 3–4 mm (0.12–0.16 in). It is for this spice that the plant is cultivated. It is used as a flavoring for foodstuffs and the scent of it seems to combine several aromas, so that it has acquired the name of allspice. Another species, very similar but smaller and so easier to cultivate under glass, is *P. acris,* the Wild Clove or Bayberry of the West Indies.
Propagation By seed; by cuttings (more difficult).
Conditions for growth Tropical; young specimens under glass.

293 QUERCUS SUBER
Cork Oak

Family Fagaceae.   **Evergreen**
Etymology The old Latin name survives.
Habitat Grows wild round the central-western Mediterranean and on the Atlantic coasts of Africa.
Description This tree, with its twisted trunk, does not exceed 15–20 m (50–65 ft) in height. It has a thick, deeply cracked bark, whitish outside and red inside. The irregular branches form a broad, not very symmetrical crown, of leathery evergreen leaves (1), lanceolate with slightly toothed margins, of a beautiful dark glossy green on the upper side and white and downy below from the presence of stellate hairs. The flowers, which appear in April–May, are of separate sexes; the males in long, pendulous catkins (2), the females in erect spikes with 2–5 flowers. The fruit is a typical acorn (3), the cup made of gray, downy scales. The basic importance of this plant is due to the exploitation of its thick, corky bark, which is stripped every 9–10 years as required, leaving the distinctively rusty-colored trunk bare.
Propagation Best sown where it is to grow, or else in a pot, transplanting later complete with soil ball.
Conditions for growth This plant likes hot, dry places in the climates where the olive grows. It needs a sunny position and will thrive in poor, acid and sandy soils.

---

294 RHUS VERNICIFLUA
Varnish Tree

Family Anacardiaceae.   **Deciduous**
Etymology The specific name denotes that this tree exudes a sap used for varnishes.
Habitat The distribution covers China and Japan.
Description A tree up to 25 m (80 ft) high, the tallest of its genus, with big, imparipinnate leaves carried on a short stalk and formed from 11–15 ovate-oblong or oblong-lanceolate leaflets 12 cm (5 in) in length, entire, rounded or pointed at the base and downy on the underside. The fruit is a drupe thicker than it is long, and yellowish. The sap is a poisonous, sticky juice which oxidizes on contact with the air. For use as a vitrifying lacquer it must be applied with the brush before it hardens, which for no known reason happens better in humid conditions. When set the lacquer (known as Japanese lacquer) becomes extremely hard, so that it can be polished to a high level of brilliance. The extraction of this sap has been practiced in China since prehistoric times, and it was already subject to official regulations under the Chou Dynasty (1122–256 B.C.). The making of lacquered objects reached its highest degree of perfection under the Ming Dynasty (A.D. 1368–1644), which was when they became known in Europe.
Propagation By seed or by root suckers.
Conditions for growth Subtropical climates.

295 STRYCHNOS NUX-VOMICA
Nux Vomica

Family Loganiaceae. **Evergreen**
Etymology The name is derived from the Greek name for certain poisonous plants, probably species of Solanaceae; it was applied by Linnaeus to this genus on account of the poison.
Habitat Native to India (Malabar) and Sri Lanka.
Description A tree that grows to a height of 12–14 m (40–45 ft), with grayish bark and many branches. The leaves (1) are opposite, short stalked, oval and acuminate, with five strong veins prominent on the underside, which is dark green. The flowers (2) are small and white, growing in apical corymbs and followed by fruits (3) that are large, globose berries, green at first, turning a reddish yellow when ripe. The flesh is white, sticky and bitter, with 5–8 round seeds containing extremely poisonous alkaloids, a source of strychnine as well as of nux vomica. Even the bark contains active principles; a tonic is extracted from it in India. Valerio Cordo first described the seeds in 1561, followed by Jacobus Tabernaemontanus (both German botanists) in 1564.
Propagation By seed, in the hothouse.
Conditions for growth Exclusively tropical; young specimens can be kept in the hothouse.

296 SYZYGIUM AROMATICUM
Clove Tree

Family Myrtaceae. **Evergreen**
Etymology Derived from the Greek *syzygios*, paired, on account of the leaves and twigs that in several species grow at the same point; better known under the old synonym *Eugenia caryophyllata*.
Habitat From the Moluccas, but cultivated throughout the tropics.
Description A tree 10–12 m (33–40 ft) high, with a grayish trunk and erect ramification, giving it a conical or cylindrical shape. The persistent leaves (1) are ovateacuminate and leathery, with conspicuous stalk and veins. The flowers (2) are arranged in terminal corymblike cymes, three to each branch of the inflorescence; they have a yellowish-red gamosepalous calyx, long and cylindrical, with five lobes, red petals and a number of projecting stamens. The flower buds are picked and dried while the petals are still closed, looking like a little light-colored ball on top of the calyx; these are the cloves used as spice and in medicine. The fruit is a fleshy red drupe.
Propagation By seed.
Conditions for growth Cultivated in tropical countries.

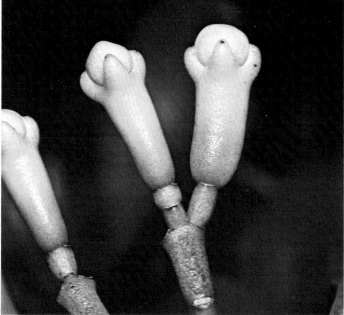

297 TAMARINDUS INDICA
Tamarind

Family Leguminosae. **Evergreen**
Etymology Derived from the Arabic *tamar*, Date Palm, and *hindi*, Indian. Though known in Europe in the Middle Ages, probably via the Arabs, it was believed that the seed was that of a species of Indian palm. The first true description dates from 1563.
Habitat Native to tropical Africa and widely cultivated in Asia; also today in America.
Description A big tree as much as 25 m (80 ft) in height, with a trunk about 7 m (23 ft) in circumference, with gray-brown bark. The pinnate leaves (1) have 10–20 pairs of leaflets; the flowers (2) grow in big racemes and have three upper petals, yellow veined in red, and two small lower petals; the staminal tube is long and down-curved. The fruit is a long, curved, indehiscent pod, slightly flattened between the fleshy seeds, which are surrounded by a thin membrane. Their flesh is rich in sugars and acids, the source of ingredients for drinks and substances used in medicine; the bark, and even the flowers, are also used for pharmaceutical purposes. The wood is strong and easy to work.
Propagation Reproduction by seed gives plants of poor quality; layering is generally preferred.
Conditions for growth Tropical, subtropical.

298 TERMINALIA CATAPPA
Myrobalan

Family Combretaceae. **Deciduous**
Etymology The name comes from the Latin *terminalis*, ending, because the leaves grow at the end of the twigs.
Habitat Native to the Andaman Islands in the Gulf of Bengal, where it grows wild in the extremely wet forests; nowadays widespread throughout the tropics.
Description A deciduous tree 20–25 m (65–80 ft) high, with the branches growing horizontally on the main axis, in whorls. The bark is brown-gray. The leaves, about 30 cm (12 in) long, are obovate and blunt at the tip, and grow at the ends of the young twigs; they have a raised venation, especially on the underside, where they are pubescent. The flowers, small and whitish, with yellow anthers, are clustered in recurved terminal spikes. The fruit is an oval, indehiscent drupe 5 cm (2 in) long, with a fleshy outside and a woody interior, rather like an almond, which contains the seed. It is regarded as edible in India, and an oil is also extracted from it, but the main value of the fruit lies in its content of up to 50% tannins, which make it much in demand for tanning skins. The fruits were once used in pharmacy.
Propagation Exclusively by seed.
Conditions for growth Tropical, hot and humid.

Family Araliaceae.   **Evergreen**
Etymology From the Greek *tetra,* four, and *Panax.* This genus has only four stamens in each flower and is closely related to the genus *Panax.* The species name refers to its use for papermaking (see below).
Habitat Native to southern China and Taiwan.
Description This is an evergreen tree which in its native surroundings reaches a height of 9 m (30 ft); in cultivation it does not normally exceed 3–6 m (10–20 ft). The leaves are big, palmate and deeply lobed; each lobe has strong veins, and the leaf blades are corrugated between the secondary veins. The juvenile parts of the trunk are covered with a white tomentum, and so are the leaves when they first appear. The white flowers are clustered in long panicles almost 1 m (3 ft) long. The white pith of the trunk and branches is extracted, cut in thin strips and pressed to make the very expensive so-called rice paper. Paper of this kind, produced in China since as long ago as 123 B.C., is also obtained from another plant, *Broussonetia papyrifera.*
Propagation By cuttings rooted in sand, or by seed.
Conditions for growth Half-hardy; tolerates short frosts.

---

300 THEOBROMA CACAO
Cacao, Cocoa Tree

Family Sterculiaceae.   **Evergreen**
Etymology The name comes from the Greek *theos,* god, and *broma,* food, and means the food of the gods.
Habitat Probably native to the Amazon basin, but it was already cultivated in other parts of South America when that continent was discovered.
Description Not a very large tree—it may grow more than 8 m (25 ft) but in cultivation it is kept lower by pruning. It is evergreen, with a dense crown of alternate, stalked leaves (1), oblong and glossy green; the flowers (2), small, white or pink, with a deeply divided calyx, grow directly on the trunk or old branches. The five petals are club shaped, the ovary is sessile and the style threadlike. The fruits obtained from the tree are big, ovoid, ribbed berries, brown-red when ripe, containing a large number of seeds arranged in five rows, which are gathered when ripe and placed in trays to ferment until they are ready for the processing by which chocolate is produced. Although one of the substances they contain, theobromine, is used in medicine, the main purpose of cultivation is the production of cocoa.
Propagation By seed; the best quality by grafting.
Conditions for growth Nowadays the tree is widespread in all tropical zones. Cultivation is only possible in those conditions.

GLOSSARY

achene dry indehiscent fruit containing only one seed.

actinomorphous having stellate or radiate form (of an organ, generally a flower).

adnate grown together with another organ.

adventitious occasional, not occurring regularly.

alate having thin outgrowths like wings.

androecium the male part of a flower, the stamens as a whole.

anther the part of a stamen that contains the pollen.

aphyllous having no leaves.

apical at the tip, or apex, of stems, branches, etc.

aril external growth round a seed, nearly always fleshy, often colored.

armed provided with organs of defence, generally spines or thorns.

attenuate growing narrower toward the base, or sometimes toward the tip.

axil the angle made by a stalk or shoot with the stem on which it is growing.

axillary growing at the axil.

bacciform berry-shaped (of fruit).

berry fleshy indehiscent fruit which may contain one or more seeds.

bifid divided in two longitudinally.

bipartite very deeply divided into two parts.

bipinnate compound leaf whose midrib is branched into secondary parts which bear the leaflets.

bract modified leaf which may be of various colors, shapes and consistencies and may appear on the foliar or floral parts.

broadleafs term used to denote all trees that have a relatively broad leaf blade, in contrast to those with needlelike leaves.

bud the germ of branches, leaves or flowers; unopened leaf or flower.

bulb underground shoot, greatly modified and swollen, with a single bud at the center.

calyx external covering of the flower bud which

protects the internal organs of the flower.

capillary   very thin, like a hair.

capsule   dry dehiscent fruit, generally with more than one loculus.

cladodes   flattened branches that take over the function of leaves.

clone   term used in biology to denote a group of individual plants derived from a single stem by agamic propagation.

collar   the junction between the root and the stem.

compound   formed of several parts; a leaf made up of a number of leaflets set on the same axis.

connate   joined, of any organ adhering to another.

cordate   heart-shaped.

corolla   part of a flower, which may be more or less developed and colored, which has the function of protection and of attracting fertilizing insects. It is composed of petals: if they are joined the corolla is called gamopetalous; if separate, dialypetalous.

corymb   an inflorescence with a flat top in which the outer flowers open first.

cotyledon   rudimentary leaf contained in the embryo, which acts as a store for reserves of nutrients.

culm   a stem that is cylindrical and hollow, or contains pith.

cultivar   a variety obtained by cross-breeding in cultivation, or the name given to the variety.

cuneate   wedge-shaped, with the narrow end at the base.

cuspidate   ending in a sharp point.

cutting   a method of propagation of plants: a shoot (herbaceous, half-ripe or woody) or a leaf is detached from the plant and planted in soil, where it takes root.

cyme   a broad, flat inflorescence in which the inner flowers are the first to open.

deciduous   having only a temporary function; used particularly of plants that lose their leaves in winter, and for leaves, bracts etc., that fall in that way.

decumbent   having prostrate or creeping stems with upturned tips.

decussate   intersecting at right angles, as with two opposite leaves which form a cross with the preceding and following pairs.

deflexed turning outward and downward.

dehiscent opening spontaneously to release the seed (of fruit).

deltoid triangular.

dichotomic continuously bifurcated into divergent axes.

dicotyledon a plant whose embryo has two cotyledons.

digitate having appendices which all originate from the same point but then diverge, like the spread fingers of a hand.

dioecious bearing male and female flowers on separate plants.

disamara a winged fruit having two wings.

distichous term used of organs, particularly leaves or shoots, arranged alternately on opposite sides of the same axis.

drupe fleshy indehiscent fruit with the seed contained in a woody stone.

emarginate notched at the apex.

embryo those parts of a fertilized seed that form the essential germ of the future plant: cotyledons, plumule and radicle.

endemic peculiar to a limited, defined environment.

epiphyte a plant that grows on another without being parasitic on it.

fastigiate growing erect, columnar (of a tree).

flabellate fan-shaped.

frond term used for the leaves of ferns and palm trees.

frutex plant with woody stem, branched from the base.

germinability capacity of a seed to germinate.

glabrous hairless and smooth.

glaucous bluish green, covered with a bloom.

glomerule inflorescence with sessile flowers growing in a spherical head.

gynaecium the female part of a flower, comprising the pistil.

habitat place or region in which a plant grows wild, determined by climatic or environmental factors.

heartwood the wood nearer the center of a trunk, which no longer carries sap (see Sapwood).

herbaceous lit., having the consistency of grass; not woody.

heterophyllous having leaves of different shapes on the same plant.

hybrid individual derived from seed obtained from natural or artificial fertilization between plants belonging to different forms, species or genera.

hygroscopic capable of absorbing and retaining moisture.

indehiscent (of fruit) not opening spontaneously to release the seed but remaining with it until germination or until withering away.

inflorescence arrangement of flowers on the stem; the term includes the branch stems, flower stalks and bracts as well as the actual flowers.

infructescence similarly, the arrangement of the fruits on a plant.

integument defensive tissues forming an outer covering of various organs.

internode interval between two nodes on a branch or stem.

kernel commonly used to denote the edible part of a nut; a seed containing a large amount of reserve nutrients.

lamina the flat part of a leaf, the leaf blade.

latex milky juice, varying in thickness and color, which flows from the tissues of some plants when they are cut.

layer shoot which puts out roots at the nodes when they come in contact with the soil, naturally or artificially.

leaf outgrowth of a stem or branch, arising from the nodes, consisting generally of the stalk, which may be short or long, and the lamina or leaf blade, larger or smaller in area.

lenticels organs that replace stomata in the structure of the stem; they are often clearly visible, looking like little nodules.

micropyle small opening in the membrane surrounding the ovule, through which the pollen reaches the nucleus.

midrib central axis of compound leaf or inflorescence.

moniliform like a necklace formed by seeds; used also for pods which are swollen where they cover the seeds and depressed in between.

monocarpic flowering and fruiting only once.

monocotyledon plant whose embryo has only one cotyledon.

monoecious bearing male and female flowers on the same plant.

mucronate having a hard, sharp point.

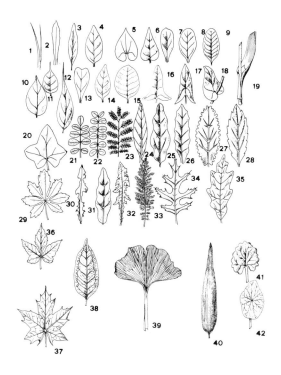

Various types of leaves, which differ from each other in the shape of the leaf blade (1–36), in the venation (37–40) and in the stalk (41, 42) : (1) agriform; (2) linear; (3) lanceolate; (4) oval; (5) cordate; (6) truncate; (7) cuneate; (8) obovate; (9) elliptical; (10) acute; (11) mucronate; (12) acuminate; (13) emarginate; (14) obtuse; (15) rounded; (16) hastate; (17) sagittate; (18) amplexicaul (clasping the stem); (19) sheathing; (20) palmato-lobate; (21) imparipinnate; (22) paripinnate; (23) bipinnate; (24) entire; (25) sinuate; (26) sinuate-dentate; (27) dentate; (28) serrate; (29) palmately divided; (30) septate; (31) crenate; (32) runcinate; (33) bipinnatisect; (34) divided; (35) lobate; (36) palmate; (37) palminervate; (38) reticulated; (39) fan-shaped with dichotomous venation; (40) parallel-nerved; (41) petiolate; (42) peltate.

muricate covered with sharp protuberances or stiff spines (derived from the shell of a mollusc, *Murex*).

node the point at which buds and leaves arise from a stem or branch.

obovate in the shape of an inverted egg, point downward.

ostiole generally, an opening; specifically, the apical opening in the inflorescence of the genus *Ficus,* or syconium (q.v.).

CYMOSE (OR DEFINITE) INFLORESCENCES, OR CYMES

*Each secondary axis
bears a flower*

monochasium

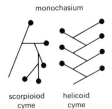

scorpioiod
cyme

helicoid
cyme

*Two daughter-axes
grow*

below the apex

dichasium

*More apices
grow*

below the apex

pliochasium

Simple

catkin

corymb

capitulum
or head

raceme

umbel

spike

pappus small tuft of hair that appears in the Compositae by a modification of the calyx and helps with anemophilous (wind-assisted) dissemination.

pedicel, peduncle the stalk that joins the flower to the point where it is attached.

perianth the petals and sepals as a whole.

perigone the tepals (q.v.) as a whole, i.e. the perianth of flowers that do not have distinct petals and sepals.

petals the parts of a flower making up the corolla.

petiole the stalk that joins the lamina of a leaf to the stem on which it is growing.

phyllode leafstalk flattened so that it resembles a leaf blade.

pistil the female part of a flower, which constitutes the gynaecium.

plumule the undeveloped stem in the embryo.

pod dry dehiscent fruit containing several seeds, characteristic of the Leguminosae.

pollen granules formed in the anthers and producing the male gametes.

pollination the carriage of pollen to the stigma from the anther.

polycormic having several stems rather than a single main axis.

pruinose covered with a powdery substance or bloom (of a leaf or fruit).

pubescent covered with short, soft hairs; downy.

radicle the first root formed in an embryo.

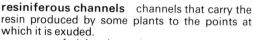

Compound

compound
umbel

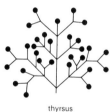

thyrsus
or panicle

compound
spike

resiniferous channels channels that carry the resin produced by some plants to the points at which it is exuded.

samara a fruit bearing a single wing.

sapwood the outer part of the wood of a trunk, in which the sap flows.

sessile (of a leaf, flower or fruit) attached directly by the base, with no stalk.

sheathing (of a leaf) having a base rolled around the stem.

stamens the organs composing the androecium, which carry the anthers containing the pollen, generally at the tip of a filament.

staminodes stamens without anthers.

stem the principal axis of a plant, carrying all the accessory parts such as the branches, leaves and flowers.

stigma the enlarged section at the tip of a pistil which will receive the grains of pollen.

stipule bract at the base of a leafstalk.

stoma opening between two special cells in the epidermis of a leaf which provides communication between the aeriferous chambers and the surrounding air and controls the leaf's exchanges with the atmosphere.

stomatic adjective used to indicate the lines on the underside of certain leaves, especially the needles of conifers, along which the stomata are arranged.

strobiles, cones the inflorescences of gymnosperms, with unisexual flowers, composed of scales bearing the pollen sacs or of carpellary leaves which carry the ovules and, later, the seeds.

sucker lateral underground shoot which leaves the roots or rhizome and roots itself, forming an independent individual plant.

suffrutex plant whose stem is woody for a short distance and herbaceous above.

syconium inflorescence typical of the genus *Ficus*, formed by a fleshy receptacle, generally pear-shaped, which contains the unisexual flowers and houses the infructescence, composed of little achenelike fruits.

syncarp compound fruit formed by the fusion of the carpels so as to form a fleshy axis; characteristic of some tropical plants, including *Annona* and *Ananas*.

taproot main root, leaving the collar in the

opposite direction to the stem and growing more powerfully than the other, secondary, roots.

tepals   name given to the sepals and petals as a whole when these are not distinguished by size, color or consistency.

tissue   fabric in a plant composed of cells which all perform the same function.

tomentose   covered with short, thick, soft hairs (tomentum).

topiary   a gardener's art, trimming the heads of trees or shrubs into special shapes for ornamental purposes.

trifid   divided into three parts or lobes.

tuber   a greatly swollen underground shoot, generally irregular in shape, which acts as a store of nutrients and contains a number of buds.

tubercles   excrescences which may be of various shapes or consistency.

umbilicate   having a round depression, like a navel.

umbonate   (of cone scales) having an umbo, a prominent outgrowth such as was found in the center of Roman shields.

unisexual   (of flowers) having organs that are only either male or female, i.e. only stamens or only pistils.

urceolate   shaped like a pitcher, with a rounded body and narrow opening.

verticil, whorl   point of attachment of two or more leaves or branches at the same node.

xerophilous   able to withstand drought.

INDEX OF SPECIES

Photograph credits